MAKERS OF THE ENGLISH BIBLE

Makers of the English Bible

Edwin Robertson

The Lutterworth Press
Cambridge

In memory of F. F. Bruce

The Lutterworth Press
P.O. Box 60
Cambridge
CB1 2NT

British Library Cataloguing in Publication Data
Robertson, E.H. (Edwin Hanton, *1912-*)
Makers of the English Bible.
  1. Bible. English versions. Translation & publishing history
  I. Title
  220.5'201

ISBN 0-7188-2774-0

Copyright ©Edwin Robertson 1990

First published in 1990 by The Lutterworth Press

All rights reserved. No part of this publication may be
reproduced, stored in a retrieval system, or transmitted
in any form or by any means, electronic, mechanical,
photocopying, recording or otherwise, without the
prior permission in writing of the publisher.

Printed and bound in Great Britain by
The Guernsey Press Co. Ltd., Guernsey, Channel Islands.

Contents

Introduction	7
1. Jerome: A Bible for the People	11
2. Wycliffe: A Liberation from Priestdom	29
3. Tyndale: A Martyr for Truth	46
4. Miles Coverdale and the Great Bible	67
5. Whittingham and the Geneva Bible	81
6. Lancelot Andrewes and the men of the Authorised Version	97
7. An Acceptable Catholic Version	112
8. Revising a Classic	125
9. A New Language	155
10. Catholic Modern Translations	171
11. C H Dodd and J B Phillips	193
Epilogue	214
Bibliography	216
Index	217

Introduction

The heroic story of the translation of the English Bible has been told so many times and with every shade of prejudice that it seems scarcely credible that one more is needed! It is a great story and it is a temptation to retell it as new evidence appears and new assessments are made and new translations are published. But this book is not about the *translations*, it is about the *translators*.

The classic work of F F Bruce, *History of the Bible in English*, now in its third edition, a quarter of a century after its first appearance as *The English Bible*, provides us with all we need to know about the translations which followed the development of the English language itself and helped to shape it. From Alfred the Great, laying down principles for translation to the revised edition of J B Phillips, *The New Testament in Modern English*; the growth of the English Bible is traced with care and scholarship which is not likely to be replaced. It will have to be brought up to date as new translations appear and they too will need the kind of assessment that F F Bruce gave to those he treated.

Behind the translations, there are individuals who had a burning passion to make the Scriptures intelligible to ordinary people and to be faithful to the original texts. These translators were more than instruments for the provision of access to the Scriptures. They all lived lives within the church and participated in its struggles and controversies. They had rounded lives.

In the past 40 years, I have known many of these translators. I have helped some of them to broadcast and even brought them together to discuss their different approaches. What has impressed me is their strong character, they have spent many lonely hours wrestling with the text and living within the Bible world, emerging to let those ancient texts speak in words that we can understand and relate to. In every case, the nature of their work has fascinated me.

Even more outstanding than their devotion is the impression of the men themselves: Ronald Knox, J B Phillips, E V Rieu, Hugh Schonfield, William Barclay and so many others. They are by definition pioneers whose first priority is communication.

When I worked on a little book to celebrate the 600th anniversary of the death of John Wycliffe, I felt the same fascination with the man who for the first time supervised a translation of the whole Bible from Latin into English. He was so different from those modern translators I had known and yet at the same time he was so similar: isolated in his work, sure of his faith, angry with those who used their superior knowledge to confuse the simple, a pioneer who was prepared to risk everything for what he believed, a master of communication. What of the others? Brave William Tyndale who died for his faith, Coverdale, Matthews, the men behind the King James Version, the Revisers on both sides of the Atlantic, Weymouth, Moffatt, Goodspeed and C H Dodd, who more than any man carried through the New English Bible.

This book is about these men: what kind of men they were, and why they sacrificed so much to put the Bible into a language understood by all people; that 'the boy who drives a plough' may know more than the careless priest of the Word of God.

I have taken the story a little further back to the pioneer of translation from the Hebrew and Greek into Latin of the day for the vulgar people, Jerome and his Vulgate. Recently, wandering through his spacious cave in Bethlehem, so much more interesting than the silver star marking the place where Christ might have been born, I realised how he could live in caves with so vast a library. For all these men were readers, acquainted with the original language of the Scriptures - Hebrew, Aramaic and Greek - and also at home in the best vernacular of their day. They had all to face those who accused them of 'vulgarising' the sacred text. Translation is usually a thankless task, because it is easier to criticise than to do; but the translation of the Bible is fraught with dangers of offence. Even accuracy cannot be used as a defence if the evocative power of language has been destroyed.

It is not only the original texts which have special claims to plead. It is also the older translations which have borne the weight of religious experience, comfort in sorrow, revelation of God and conviction of sin. The translator himself may also love the well-known translation. When J B Phillips was ill and depressed, he confessed that he drew little comfort from his own translation, but went back constantly to the Authorised Version. Wycliffe found his assurance in the Latin Version with which he had been brought up. There is more in Bible translation than accuracy. When Jerome undertook to revise the Latin texts at the request of the Pope he was howled down as blasphemous when he changed a familiar line. This is not mere obscurantism, although there is always some of that in the protests, it is the recognition that the Bible says more than its plain meaning would convey. People relate to it with their whole being and not only with their minds.

Aware of the danger of disturbing the rich experience of a remembered version, the translator must choose carefully. However much he tries he can never produce a completely new version. For him as for his readers the cadence of the older and well known version will be heard through the changes. Some translators, like C H Dodd, were so familiar with the original that they thought they had forgotten the old translations. But when it came to it the memories of childhood could not be shrugged off easily. This may be why he insisted that the New English Bible was not intended to replace the Authorised Version, but should be used side by side with it.

The Effect of Bible Translation

Time and again we have seen Bible translators changed by their own work, because of the texts with which they were dealing. When J B Phillips finished his translation of the Acts he saw the church differently and made his most powerful criticism of it in the introduction to *The Young Church in Action*. When he was translating the 'Gospels', he described his feelings as 'like rewiring a house with the mains switched on'. When E V Rieu was translating the Gospels, his son made the shrewd comment: 'I shall be interested to see what father does with the Gospels, but I shall be even more interested to see what the Gospels do to father'. And he was right. No one can work through these texts, understanding them and rethinking them in another language without feeling their powerful effect.

It was his work upon the translation of part of the New Testament that led John Wycliffe to risk the loss of all his influential support by condemning Transubstantiation. Part of the story of this book will be to show the effect of the translators' work upon themselves. What kind of men were they? They range over many centuries and I have been able to select only a few. But these few should illustrate the type of men who in this lonely occupation of translating the Bible had the courage to maintain their integrity and let their generation know what the Bible really says, or perhaps better, what God is saying to that generation through the Bible.

They believed in the Bible

Although it is often very difficult to pinpoint the theory of inspiration which any one of the great translators held, they all maintained an unshakable confidence in the Bible. If you were to put Jerome, Martin Luther and J B Phillips together and ask them to discuss fundamentalism or modernism, verbal inspiration or liberal scholarship, you would find all three very impatient with you for introducing trivial issues. They would all want to talk about how the Word of God can be mediated to men. Each would have different theories of inspiration appropriate to the age in which they lived. But all would agree upon the authority of the Bible.

Jerome could deal critically with some texts; Martin Luther would give short shrift to the Epistle of James; J B Phillips was doubtful about the Old Testament at times and certainly opposed any naive fundamentalist approach to it. But for all three, the burning passion was that people should hear the Word of God.

Jerome's endless commentaries, which preceded his translation of the Bible were addressed to those who wanted to understand the Bible and he could dictate as much as 25 pages a day to get them ready in time. He hated a false understanding of the Christian faith and believed that it could only be corrected by a proper knowledge of what the Bible says.

Luther's lectures on the Epistle to the Galatians were a passionate argument for putting into practice the words of St Paul. He saw these words misunderstood and misused and his one over-riding purpose in giving those lectures or publishing them as a commentary was to let them speak to his generation.

When J B Phillips emerged from his deep depression to enter the conflict that arose after the publication of John Robinson's *Honest to God*, he strengthened the faith of many in the midst of doubt with his little book *Ring of Truth*. In that book he said that he had spent years with these documents that constitute the New Testament and he could assure his readers that they had the ring of truth about them.

In the above examples there is no clear-cut theory of inspiration, but for all of them there was a confidence that in the deepest sense the Bible is true. Common to them all was a threefold cord: the books that made up the Bible were written by men (and perhaps some women) who were raised up by God to write them; the single message of all the varied books of the Bible is concerned with God's relationship with humanity and the human search for God; the Bible has no rival in all literature as a means whereby God mediates his will to men and women.

1. Jerome - A Bible for the People

The central battle of the Reformation for the Bible in a language all could understand masked the original purpose of the Latin Bible itself. It was called the *Vulgate*, because it was intended 'for the people'.

The Bible was written to be read and understood. The Old Testament was in Hebrew and later parts of it, Daniel and Ezra, in the related language of Aramaic. These were languages the people could understand at the time. When Jews forgot their Hebrew in such places as Alexandria, the Bible was translated into Greek and the opportunity was taken to add a few more books or, in the case of Daniel, to add a few more stories. The Old Testament was swollen with these additional writings, usually referred to as the Apocrypha. But all was in the Greek of the first century BC, which most of the known world was gradually learning to understand. So, the books of the New Testament appeared in the most widely understood language of the Roman Empire - in Greek. But like the Jews who forgot their Hebrew, the Christians forgot their Greek as the western Roman Empire under a Christian Emperor spoke Latin.

Various attempts were made to put the Bible, or portions of it, for worship into Latin - the Psalms and the New Testament mostly. They were often poor translations, just giving enough of the sense for people to get an idea of the general meaning of the original; or in the Old Testament, of the Greek translation which was known as the Septuagint. There was no effort made to put the whole of the Bible into the language of the people until Jerome. At a time when the Church was growing because it was fashionable and profitable to be a Christian under a Christian Emperor, Jerome wanted a vital Christianity with a living use of the Bible. That meant a translation into Latin and thus he set the pace for that long line of translators who age after age put the Bible into the language of the people. If he was not the first maker of the English Bible, he was the patron saint of its translators and therefore we begin with him.

Jerome did not translate the whole of the Bible and some of his translations were not accepted. There was much opposition to his revision of the old Latin texts. Augustine reports that in 403 there was a riot in Tripoli at the reading of his version of Job and the bishop nearly lost his flock! But by the time of his death, the controversies had waned and Augustine himself used Jerome's version of the Gospels, although he preferred the older versions for the Acts. The new version was completed by an unknown monk who followed Jerome closely. By the eighth century Jerome's Vulgate was the Bible of the Church and remained so, much as later the Authorised Version would for the English-speaking people or Martin Luther's for the German.

For 14 years, 391-405, Jerome worked on the translation of the Old Testament. But he would have nothing to do with the additional material of the Septuagint. He refused to regard the books of the Apocrypha as of equal authority with those of the Hebrew canon. Under pressure, he was persuaded to translate the books of Judith and Tobit (both from the Apocrypha), but he made it plain that it went against the grain to translate books which lacked the authority of the Hebrew Bible.

His version including additions from later hands, eventually gave the medieval Church its authoritative Bible. And this Vulgate was sufficiently trusted by the Anglo-Saxon and early English translators even up to the great John Wycliffe, who used it as the basis for his Bible for the people.

So let us begin this English story with a man who never spoke English.

Born in a Christian Empire

Jerome was born in Dalmatia, almost certainly in 346. It had been a time of revolution within the Roman Empire which deeply affected the Christian Church. The worst appeared to be over: the barbarian invasions, civil war, economic breakdown, which had marked the middle years of the previous century were dying down. A totalitarian state had been created and controlled every part of life. At the apex of this state was an Emperor who in 312 became a Christian. From 324, Constantine the Great had become sole Emperor of east and west after a long power struggle and he began to push through policies which were increasingly favorable to Christianity. The shock to a Church which within the living memory had been threatened with extinction can be imagined. As the Emperor was Christian, it became expedient to become a Christian if you wanted promotion in any sphere of public life. This brought into the Church thousands of time-servers who lived uneasily with the sons of martyrs. In 330, Constantine had solemnly consecrated the new Rome on the Bosphorus with the name of Constantinople, which, furnished with many lovely churches, was to become the chief administrative centre of the eastern part of the Roman Empire. When he died in 337, Constantine the Great was succeeded by his two younger sons, both keen Christians. Briefly Julian, his nephew, succeeded to the control of the Empire (361-363) and tried to put the clock back to the old classical religions; but Julian the Apostate was an irrelevant incident. After his death the Emperors, both of east and west were always Christian.

The full implication of a Christian Empire did not emerge until the end of the century, but already in the reign of Constantine the Great, two immensely important facts were evident: the fashionable joined the Church and the Emperor was expected to take a leading role in its internal affairs. The first of these was the most evident; but the second had more lasting consequences. In 325 Constantine called the first Ecumenical Council at Nicaea. This council was intended to settle once and for all the divine status of Christ and his relation to the Father. It issued the Nicene definition, which after much adaptation became the Nicene Creed and an authoritative document. A new authority was born in the Church, no longer merely a spiritual one but with all the force of a secular power. The Cross of Constantine weighed heavily on the Church. Its triumph had been bought at a price. The Emperor was now the natural leader of the Church, which was rapidly dividing into two parts - the minority of deeply committed believers, and the great majority of new converts who followed the Emperor. Into such a world Jerome was born.

The Young Jerome

His father was called Eusebius, which suggests that he came from a Greek speaking area, especially as his son was called also by a Greek name, Hieronymus (Jerome). Many Greek-speaking people from the eastern Mediterranean had migrated to Dalmatia, but by the time Jerome was born it was thoroughly Latinised. He appears to have been born in a small town called Stridon in Dalmatia, not too far from the Pannonian border. His family could be described as wealthy. His parents were Christians, and as was common in the fourth century he was not baptised as a baby, but simply enrolled as a catechumen. 'As a baby', he tells us, 'he had been nourished on Catholic milk'. Although his parents were Christian and not among the time-servers that came in with the Emperor, they were not particularly zealous. At the age of twelve, Jerome was sent to Rome to study. There, with the help of some very good teachers including Donatus the grammarian, he fell under the spell of classical literature. His natural eagerness to learn all he could was further stimulated by the music of the language. The rhythm of the poets and the harmonious cadences of the prose writers charmed him. All his life he was under that charm and he began to feel it a temptation. In 374 or 375, he had a famous dream in which he appeared before the judgment seat of God and was told, 'You are a Ciceronian, not a Christian'. He vowed never again to read secular writers, but years later he was still having them copied and presumably reading them as he moved his vast library from cave to cave. All that lay in the future. For the moment he was thoroughly enjoying himself. The study of grammar was followed by the study of rhetoric and he listened to the foremost orators of the day, advocating their client's case or attacking the case of another with little regard as to who was right. Jerome later described their performances: 'in feigned wrath tearing one another to pieces'. He learnt his lessons well and they added violence to the language of his later controversies.

The final stage of these studies was philosophy, which he completed at the age of 20. He collected a library while in Rome and as he grew from boyhood to manhood enjoyed the pleasures of the city. But he also developed a personal Christian commitment and a sense of duty to God. He visited the catacombs with his friends and it was while at Rome that he was baptised. When he left Rome it was to go to Treves, where the Emperor often held his court.

The Appeal of the Monastic Life

His parents must have thought that the visit to Treves was to advance his career, but what really attracted him was the flourishing monastic life that Athanasius had inspired during his first exile there. This attraction is confirmed by the fact that when he went on from Treves to return home he at once visited friends who were living a monastic life at nearby Aquileia. It was obvious to any sensitive young man that the compromises made by those who had embraced Christianity for the sake of the Emperor and their careers were not to be admired. He soon spoke out strongly for a pure Christianity and saw it as reflected in the monastic movement. Men and women were beginning to devote themselves to God, living in extreme poverty to follow the poverty of Christ. This appealed so strongly to him that he set out for the east, undertaking a long and exhausting journey through Thrace, Pontus, Bithynia, Galatia, Cappadocia and Cicilia. He arrived eventually at Antioch, a very sick man. His friend Evagrius cared for him and it was probably about this time that he had his dream and vowed never again to read secular literature.

When he had sufficiently recovered he fulfilled his ambition of retiring to the desert of Chalcis to lead a monastic life. This gave him the peace and quiet that he had lacked in Rome. He learned Hebrew, attended lectures in Greek by the somewhat heretical bishop of Laodicea, Apollinarius, and journeyed to Beroea (Aleppo) where he had the Aramaic Gospel or pseudo-Matthew copied for his collection. He seems not to have picked up the heresy of Apollinarius, but he learned much from him. So, apart from his passion for the monastic life and its poverty and seclusion, the young Jerome seemed to be thoroughly enjoying his intellectual development, his freedom and his growing mastery of Greek and Hebrew.

The two main schools of Biblical exegesis were those of Alexandria and Antioch: the one allegorical and the other historical. Jerome was later to come under the spell of Origen of Alexandria when he read extensively his commentaries and regarded him as the most creative thinker of the century. Later still, he was to turn against him, because of his heretical teaching. But Antioch was the historical school and this had an earlier and deeper influence upon Jerome's reading of the Bible. This began with Apollinarius and continued as he lived under the influence of Antioch. It was there that he was ordained by Bishop Paulinus, but he stipulated that he must retain the freedom of a monk and not have pastoral care of a church.

Constantinople

The quarrelling of the monks in Chalcis and the heretical teaching he found in Antioch soon drove him in search of more orthodox teachers. He made his way to Constantinople, attracted by what he had heard of the learning and goodness of Gregory of Nazianzus, its bishop from 378. There, he continued his study of the Bible. Reading Origen had a profound effect upon him and he undertook to translate many of his biblical homilies into Latin. His own commentary on the vision of Isaiah, in Chapter 6 of that prophetic book, shows a curious blending of Antioch and Alexandria; it started with an historical analysis of Uzziah and his reign and led into a spiritual commentary on the event. There was an Ecumenical Council in Constantinople in 381 in which Jerome had no part, but he met many of the Christian leaders of the day, including Gregory of Nyssa. His interests widened greatly and he seemed intent upon putting the wisdom of the Greek speaking eastern church into the Latin of the west. One most interesting task was to translate the *Ecclesiastical History* of Eusebius, a very important Greek work containing many quotations from earlier writers. He was not content with a straight translation. He added details of Roman history which would not have been so interesting to the Greeks and continued the account of the history of the Church from 325 where Eusebius had left off, up to the death of Valens in 378.

Jerome began to tire of Constantinople, particularly after Gregory of Nazianzus had resigned his see, and was glad to be invited to accompany Paulinus of Antioch and Epiphanius of Salamis (Cyprus) when they journeyed to Rome for a Council. They were pleased to have one who was proficient in Latin and Greek, and acquainted with Rome. It was on that visit that Pope Damasus discovered him and they became close friends.

The Bible Translator

In that year, 383, the Pope asked him to revise the many and confusing Latin texts of the New Testament. There were so many translations from different parts of the Empire and such careless copying that it was impossible to talk of an accepted text. The Christians had inherited a Greek translation of the Old Testament from the Jews (the Septuagint) and there was enough Greek scholarship in the Church to render the whole Bible into the Latin which was more widely understood. Some translators had introduced colloquial forms into the Gospels, making Jesus speak a dialect of the area and even rearranging some of the pages. The Bible was a muddle and Damasus had a great respect for Jerome's scholarship. He was one of the few Christian leaders who could understand Hebrew for one thing. Later he would use this skill to translate the Old Testament into a dignified Latin; but in 383 Pope Damasus wanted only the New Testament in a good Latin for church use. Within a year Jerome had translated or rather revised the Gospels. It was a thankless task. Although he had been very conservative in his revisions, changing only that which was plainly wrong or unsuitable in style, he was branded as sacrilegious and a falsifier by those who detected an 'unfamiliar taste' in his revisions. However, he had the authority of the Pope and he alone decided which version should be accepted at Rome. Within a year his revision of the Four Gospels was presented to Pope Damasus with a typical preface setting out Jerome's difficulties and methods. By then, his eye was on a momentous task, which he alone was capable of executing: the translation of the whole Bible from its Hebrew and Greek into an acceptable Latin which any educated person could read in Rome, and gradually throughout the western Empire. He was a solitary worker and never had the joy of true collaborators. Luther complained that he denied himself the fulfillment of the promise that where two or three are gathered together in Christ's name He is in their midst. But Jerome was difficult to work with!

Jerome's appeal to the Roman women

When Jerome's revisions of the ancient Latin versions of the Gospels were attacked for their 'alterations', he did not take kindly to these criticisms and showed himself at his worst in responding. He called his critics 'little two-faced asses'. But even more unpopular was his advocacy of asceticism and especially of virginity.

He was three years in Rome and during that time he gathered around him, because of his ascetic teaching, a group of Roman ladies, both mature women and young girls of high rank and considerable wealth.

Jerome did not make friends easily and he often behaved in a very hostile way when they disagreed with him. Those who did make friends with him became very attached to him and retained their active friendship over many years. But he was uneasy with women. In Rome, something quite new happened to him when he was accepted as spiritual guide and scriptural teacher of a remarkable group of Roman aristocratic women. Almost immediately on arriving in Rome he was introduced to these women who some years before had modelled their lives on the desert fathers of Egypt and adopted an extreme form of asceticism. This made an immediate appeal to Jerome. J N D Kelly, in his book *Jerome*, puts one side of this attraction, which is undoubtedly true:

> Strongly sexed, but also because of his convictions, strongly repressed as well, his nature craved for female society, and found deep satisfaction in it when it could be had without doing violence to his principles.

If that is true, Jerome had found the ideal group. It was led by two aristocratic women, both deeply religious widows, who had now determined upon a life of virginity - Paula, whom he met first, and Marcella. Paula was of high aristocratic rank and wealth, who had been widowed 25 years. Through the study of Athanasius' *Life of St Anthony*, she had come to admire the monks, virgins and widows of the Nile Valley. She was very beautiful and had many offers of marriage. But she turned them all down and devoted herself to 'chaste widowhood, a life of simplicity, fasting and Bible reading'. Jerome describes her as the first Roman lady of rank to accept 'the monastic profession'. Her home on the Aventine, with her mother whom she had won over to the life of asceticism, became a meeting place for a whole group of upper-class women and girls inspired by the same ideals. Jerome in his many letters gives little portraits of these women which show a varied and quite large group.

Paula's household was similar to that of Marcella and included some of her daughters. The third daughter, Eustochium played a leading role and eventually accompanied her mother in travels to the east. Blesilla, the eldest was a lively young woman of 20 when Jerome first arrived and unlike her mother full of exuberant fun and ready for a society wedding. Jerome's influence changed all that and she became an avid follower of the monastic life. Her death brought a scandal from which Jerome had to flee.

In his vivid letters Jerome gives us a clear picture of what Christianity meant to those committed women living in their stately homes and seeking to imitate the desert fathers. They met for Bible study, visited the tombs of the martyrs and other holy places, they withdrew from ordinary society, fasted rigorously, wore coarse clothes, neglected their personal appearance and avoided all luxuries such as baths, and of course lived in chastity. All this was earnestly supported by Jerome who believed it to be the way Christ commanded in the Gospels.

It was Marcella who encouraged him to give classes to these women on the text of the Bible, Old and New Testament. She herself asked searching questions and even persuaded him to write down some of his answers in letters, some of which still survive, although he also made frequent visits to her house. The letters tell us as much about Jerome as about Marcella. He can complain that her questions keep him up all night. He insists that Bible study should be enjoyed, not made a burden. But she continued and he did not fail her or the earnest Bible students she had gathered around her in her 'monastery'. There was no rule that had to be kept and the communities in Rome were simply households with friends who sought to follow the way of Gospel simplicity. Paula also had a Bible reading circle at her house. It was with Paula and her daughter Eustochium that Jerome developed the closest friendship. Paula learned Hebrew under Jerome's instruction and he reports that her interest in exegesis was two-fold; care for the historical, but a love for the allegorical. This parallels Jerome's own mixture of Antioch and Alexandria (Origen). Even dearer than Paula to him was her third daughter Julia Eustochium who was to be his devoted companion until her death, only a few years before his own.

J N D Kelly had an equally illuminating few lines on Eustochium. After describing her asceticism he adds:

> Not that we should picture Eustochium either as repressedly stuffy in her piety or as overawed by her fussily exacting director (Jerome). On St Peter's Day, probably 29th June 384, she sent him some presents in honour of the feast - bracelets, doves, a basket of cherries, with an accompanying note. We get the impression of an entirely natural girl, happy in her religion and choosing with care, for a day popularly observed in Rome, charming gifts which might please him.

Jerome related very closely to Eustochium and found in her his ideal virgin. He constantly extolled the virtues of virginity. He applauds her vows and like many before him relates the 'vow of eternal chastity' to the marriage to her Lord Jesus. In frankly erotic terms he draws upon the imagery of the Song of Songs and bids her wait for the attention of her beloved. One might well wonder today why he was feeding her with such erotic fantasies of being loved by Jesus, while he urged upon her a virgin mind!

The Flight from Rome

Jerome's unpopularity grew in Rome as he made more and more wealthy friends. He was protected and favoured by the Pope and had dared to revise the sacred text of the ancient Latin versions of the Gospels. It came to a head with the death of Blesilla, Paula's eldest daughter. Her beauty of which she was very conscious caused some worry to Jerome. Although a Christian, she enjoyed the society life of Rome. She made a smart marriage and even when widowed quickly married again - an adulterous second marriage in Jerome's eyes! She paid great attention to her dress and her appearance. Jerome was deeply worried and her relatives were annoyed by the way he pestered her. Then suddenly after a sharp bout of fever from which she recovered, she was transformed. Under Jerome's guidance she undertook a course of rigorous asceticism, giving herself to prayer and penitence. She delighted Jerome also with her passion for studying the Bible and even started to learn Hebrew. The strain, both emotional and physical proved too much for her and she died within four months. Paula grieved and was inconsolable, Jerome did not try to console her, but rebuked her for grieving!

His enemies, and there were many in Rome, blamed him for Blesilla's death and voiced their complaint: 'How long will it be before the hateful breed of monks is driven from the city?'

Jerome had tired of Rome and after the death of Pope Damasus, he had no protector but his pious, wealthy ladies. The worldliness of Rome displeased him, he longed for the asceticism of the desert and the quiet calm for his studies which Rome would never allow. So in 385, a disgruntled Jerome left Rome by way of Ostia and sailed to Cyprus with the intention of settling in Bethlehem. He took a small community of monks with him who were also tired of Rome, including his young brother Paulinianus and a priest called Vincentius. He was received in Cyprus by Bishop Epiphanius and then went to Antioch where he was received by Bishop Paulinus. He spoke of St Paul who had made that journey at the beginning of his missionary enterprise in the other direction: Antioch to Cyprus, and later on to Rome. He was already planning a tour of the holy places. Somewhere, in Cyprus or in Antioch, he was joined by another party who thought it unwise to leave Rome with him: Paula and her daughter Eustochium, with some of their ladies.

Pilgrims or Tourists

Very few people go seriously to the Holy Land today without complaining at some point that the atmosphere is spoilt by coach-loads of tourists who descend upon the holy places. But this is not new. Whether you call them pilgrims or tourists, the Holy Land has been beset by crowds of visitors, steadily mounting in number from the second century onwards. In the middle of the second century, Bishop Melito of Sardis went to ascertain the exact number of books of the Old Testament; in the third century, a Bishop Alexander from Cappadocia went to 'pray and gain information about the holy places' in Jerusalem. Again in the third century, Origen made frequent trips to sacred sites to help him in his biblical studies. In his 'Contra Celsus', a polemical tract against the Jews in the form of an argument, he says that he has seen the cave where Jesus was born. By 315, Eusebius can speak of Christian believers streaming to Jerusalem from every corner of the earth. A boost was given by the Royal Tour, when Helena, the mother of Constantine, visited the sacred sites in 324. That was followed by lavish restorations. Eusebius had already written a guide book, *Onomasticon*, which was a kind of gazetteer, with the descriptions of all the places to visit. Jerome and Paula were not strictly speaking pilgrims, because they intended to settle in Bethlehem and did. The whirlwind tour of all the places associated with events in the Bible is all written up in *Letter 108*, with some supplementary information in a later polemical writing defending himself against insinuations by an old friend, Rufinus.

First, they went from Antioch to Jerusalem and Bethlehem, moving down the coast road with innumerable diversions to see every possible site. Paula would have no comforts and insisted upon travelling by donkey like the others. They then stayed in Jerusalem while they made arrangements for the building of two monastic houses at or near Bethlehem. While there, they made extensive journeys to holy places. They went south to the Dead Sea and looked upon the desolation of Sodom and Gomorrah. Paula wept when she recalled how virtuous Lot had been made drunk after escaping the disaster and in a drunken state was seduced by his daughters. She thereupon warned her virgin companions of the perils of wine. Later they stayed at Jerusalem and visited the home of Martha and Mary and many other sites including Nazareth, Cana and Capernaum. With Paula's incredible faith, the enthusiastic band pressed on to what must have been near exhaustion. Paula was excited, and so too was Jerome. Later, in the introduction to his commentary on the Greek text of *Chronicles*, he writes:

> Just as Greek history becomes more intelligible to those who have seen Athens, and the third book of Virgil to those who have sailed from Troas by Leucata and Acroceraunia to Sicily and so on to the mouth of the Tiber, so that man will get a clearer grasp of the Holy Scripture who has gazed at Judaea with his own eyes and got to know the memorials of its cities and the names, whether they remain the same or not, of the various localities.

After Palestine they visited Egypt to see the desert fathers, the innumerable monks of Nitria, and then on to Alexandria. During this Egyptian visit Jerome took time to learn from the blind scholar, Didymus, and attend his lectures. Didymus could not write or read, but he had a wonderful knowledge of the Bible which Jerome admired. After collecting some commentaries which Didymus dictated, to add to his already vast library, Jerome went with Paula to Bethlehem. The time with Didymus was important for Jerome. He had already sat at the feet of one of the foremost scholars of the school of Antioch, Apollinarius, historical and literal; now he added to his knowledge of the Alexandrian school with the allegorical interpretation he had so admired in Origen.

Bethlehem

It took three years to build the two monastic houses, one for Paula and her community and one for Jerome and his monks. Paula also built a hospice for pilgrims 'because Mary and Joseph had not found a lodging'.

Once he had settled in Bethlehem, Jerome's travels abroad were over. For the next 34 years, until he was over seventy, Jerome worked out the meaning of the monastic life in Bethlehem. He was never free from turmoil, nor did he achieve that quiet which he longed for, but he learned much about himself and the possibilities of monastic life. Rome had forced upon the scholar many distractions from study, but Bethlehem had its distractions too! He had the care of a monastery under his charge, instructions and exhortations delivered to his monks with letters to Paula almost daily, beside a vast correspondence with various countries, including lengthy exchanges with Augustine in Hippo in North Africa. There were visits from pilgrims who became his postmen and made the exchange of letters possible.

In 410, when Alaric sacked Rome, many refugees fled to Jerusalem and he cared for some in Bethlehem. He seemed also to be in constant controversy with other scholars and defended himself against heresy. His main protagonists were Joviniam, Rufinus, Vigilantius and Pelagius. In 416 one of these controversies took a violent form when there was an armed attack upon his monastery by Pelagian monks who set fire to the building. Despite all this, he carried on through a monumental amount of work, translations and commentaries. Gradually his interest concentrated entirely upon the Bible and he began to see the need for a reliable translation into Latin of Old and New Testament. This was a formidable task. The Hebrew texts were all unpointed, written without their vowels. The pronunciation of any word had to be carried in the memory long after it had been learned from some converted Jew.

At first he did not attempt a new translation, but contented himself with revising the existing Latin versions of the books of the Hebrew canon. He then, still within his first few years at Bethlehem, enhanced his reputation as a biblical scholar by compiling three aids to Bible study: an etymological dictionary of biblical proper names, a gazetteer of places mentioned in the Bible and a critical analysis of difficult passages in Genesis. All three became very useful for Jerome when he started work on his famous Bible translation.

A New Translation

It was around 390 that Jerome embarked upon an entirely fresh translation of the Old Testament. He knew the magnitude of his task and says quite frankly, 'with my eyes open I thrust my hand into the flames'. The intensive study which he had undertaken particularly over the previous decade convinced him that the only satisfactory translation of the Old Testament for a Christian was one which reproduced the Hebrew original. If the Christians were to be able to confront the Jew with the message of Christ in the Old Testament, Jerome saw that they must have an 'authentic' text, which both could agree. This, of course, meant accepting the Hebrew canon. The task once undertaken took him years and although he did many other things at the same time, this was his major work. He completed it in 405 or 406. A little over 15 years is not long. This Old Testament, together with his revision of the Gospels was to be Jerome's crowning literary achievement. It was to become accepted as the standard *Vulgate*, Latin text of the Bible. It is a pity that Jerome did not complete the New Testament, limiting his final version to the Gospels although indications of his translations of other parts do appear in his commentaries. The rest of the New Testament was revised by an unknown hand.

The lifelong labours of Jerome will bear witness to his ardent devotion to the Bible. For him, 'knowledge of the Scriptures means knowledge of Christ; ignorance of the Scriptures means ignorance of Christ'. His correspondence is full of exhortations to read, learn and inwardly digest the Scriptures. 'Make knowledge of the Scripture your love and you will not love the vices of the flesh'. He never fails to remind his reader that apart from knowledge we also need the guidance of the Spirit of God.

The Death of Paula

One of Jerome's late joys was the care of Paula's granddaughter. Her daughter, Laeta, gave birth to a girl in 401 whom she named Paula. The mother at once wrote to Jerome asking how she should be brought up as a child born to the religious life. Eventually, little Paula arrived in Bethlehem, but her grandmother was never to see her. She died in 404.

Her death greatly affected Jerome and, forgetting the stern line he had taken with Paula when she grieved over the death of her daughter Blesilla, he was inconsolable. Eustochium realised the deep effect her mother's death had had on Jerome and did her best to provide the affection and support which Jerome, who was desperately lonely, needed. Eustochium had also to bear the burden of the convent upon which her mother had exhausted her energies. She performed these tasks admirably and Jerome owed much to her in his declining years. She enabled him to emerge from his grief and work. His monastic order had been founded upon the ideas and routine of St Pachomius, the reputed founder of the communal form of monasticism in Egypt around 120. Jerome worked out his own order and did not slavishly imitate Pachomius, but he admired him. At the moment of his grief in 404, the disciples of Pachomius came to him and asked if he would translate into Latin the fundamental writings of their saintly founder. This included the rule of Pachomius and as Jerome translated it he realised that there were certain elements missing in his own monastic system. He began the revision of the order of monastic life in his own monastery and that which Paula had led, now Eustochium. This translation and his own comments upon it made some significant contribution to the Rule of St Benedict.

The Fall of Rome

In distant Bethlehem, Jerome was kept informed about the tragedy that

Rome was facing and at one point his monastery was beset with refugees. The fifth century opened with Rome unable to hold her borders. The young king of the Visigoths, Alaric, had threatened Constantinople and ravaged Greece. In 401 and again in 403, he invaded Italy. He was defeated on both occasions by Stilicho who was himself half-Vandal. In 405, a horde of Ostrogoths crossed the Alps under the leadership of Radagaisus and again Stilicho drove them back, inflicting a crushing defeat by enlisting provincials and slaves into the once proud Roman legions. A few months later a massed invasion of Vandals, Sueves and others swarmed over the Rhine into Gaul and sacked most of its major towns. Alaric tried different tactics, nominally serving the western government of the Empire and accepting 'protection money' from Stilicho. When Stilicho was assassinated and the anti-barbarian party took power in Rome, relations deteriorated and Alaric blockaded Rome. He was bought off twice, but at the third blockade he starved the city to surrender and sacked it for three days. Jerome watched this terrifying drama from a distance. His calls to those who wrote to him to abandon this world became even more confident. He saw the world perishing in flames like Sodom and Gomorrah and called upon Christians to flee from it. But he insisted that the world-renunciation must be voluntary, not imposed upon us by our conquerors. His political assessment of the world-shattering events was certainly naive. He did not blame the effete emperors, whom he continued to reverence as 'devoutly Christian men'. He complained as many others did, that Rome had been delivered into the hands of the enemy because her own people would not defend the empire, depending upon the help of barbarian tribes. His basic interpretation of events was that it was the vengeance of God upon a rotten society.

He was far more at home in exegesis than in politics. His commentaries on the Minor Prophets were finished in 407 and in the same year he published his long awaited commentary on Daniel. Then he plunged into Isaiah. This became an 18 volume commentary, started in 408 and, interrupted by illnesses, completed in the year of the fall of Rome, 410.

Jerome's commentary on Daniel is of special interest because it shows his acceptance of critical scholarship. In the third century, the Neoplatonist Porphyry had shown that Daniel was written not in the sixth century BC as it purports to be, but as a tract for the times written between 167 and 164 BC. Jerome was forced to admit that Porphyry was right. Although, in his Prologue he differs from Porphyry in regarding Daniel's vision in Chapter 11 concerning the Ptolemies and the Seleucids as genuine prophecy. Porphyry had treated it as 'history after the event'.

He never quite grasped that Isaiah was written by more than one prophet and this hindered his otherwise brilliant exegesis. He presented Isaiah not only as a prophet but as an evangelist also. Despite his usual preference for the Hebrew text and his poor opinion of the Septuagint, he insisted that the latter was right in Isaiah 7, 14: 'A virgin shall conceive and bear a child'.

Having completed Isaiah, he intended beginning a commentary on Ezekiel, but the terrible news of Alaric's sacking of Rome reached him with the personal tragic news that Marcella and many other Christian friends were dead. He was numb and unable to do more than grieve or try to feel their pain:

> For days and nights I could think of nothing but the universal safety; when my friends were captured, I could only imagine myself a captive too ... When the brightest light of the world was extinguished, when the very head of the Roman Empire was severed, the entire world perished in a single city.

Also in the prologue to the commentary to Ezekiel, he writes:

> Who could believe that after being raised up by victories over the whole world Rome could come crashing down, and become at once the mother and the grave of her peoples.

By 411, Eustochium had persuaded him to overcome his grief and perhaps also to stop chasing controversies. Combating heresies was not his best work! She persuaded him in that year to begin the massive commentary on Ezekiel. The work was held up by the need to deal with crowds of refugees from Rome; the biblical scholar had to turn aside and minister to their needs. He had reached the end of the third book of the commentary when an invading horde 'overran like a torrent the frontiers of Egypt, Palestine, Phoenicia and Syria'. These were probably Arabs.

Despite all these interruptions and complaining all the way, he managed to continue with Ezekiel. By 413 he was on the ninth book; he there refers to events in Africa of that year. He then had a fit of depression fearing that he did not have the ability to deal with Ezekiel's restoration of the Temple. Chapter 40-48. However he completed this masterly commentary in 414: 14 books in all. He handles most complex issues, gives grounds for his rejection of the Septuagint Text, reconciles the different periods of Ezekiel's prophecies and keeps his eyes open for relevant writing with undiminished force and clarity, and embellishing his exposition with skilfully chosen quotes from Cicero, Virgil and other classical writers. But there are vivid touches about himself also and the delays caused by his need to care for the refugees. He has to work at night and his eyesight is growing increasingly dim so that he cannot read his Hebrew text by lamplight.

Pelagius

Jerome had been in controversy all his life. The most serious was probably with his once close friend, Rufinus. His last controversy was with the British heretic Pelagius. At the time of the controversy, Pelagius had not been condemned, but was rather honoured as a most holy man and the great favourite of leading figures in the Church. He crossed swords early with Jerome by accusing him of undervaluing marriage. In fact, many of Pelagius' attitudes were also those of Jerome. He was appalled by the easy-going standards of conventional Christianity and he tried to impress upon people the nature of the authentic Christian life. Every baptised person, he was sure, was called to total commitment. Jerome agreed with all that, but they divided when Pelagius rejected as Manichean (ie hatred of the flesh) and stultifying to endeavour, the concept that human nature was corrupted by original sin transmitted from Adam. He maintained that although a habit of sinning had set in, man could shake it off. By the exercise of his will he could choose to do right or wrong. A man can, in principle, live without sin. Because sin is a voluntary act, he refused to teach that infants are tainted with sin. Oddly enough he retained the practice of infant baptism, which seems to lose its point if sin is not inherited. Men need God's grace but he defines grace not as an inner power transforming, *but* as Man's original endowment with rational will, the divine forgiveness he obtains through baptism and the illumination provided by the law of Moses and the teaching of Christ.

Both Jerome and Augustine attacked him. At first the sheer quality of his life as a Christian made it difficult, but soon what he taught was seen to be dangerous and undermining to the official teaching of the Church. This was Jerome's last controversy. The controversy was not one-sided. Pelagius accused Jerome of depending too much upon the teaching of Origen, whose errors had been exposed and condemned. He also repeated his accusation that Jerome deprecated marriage. Jerome felt that he had already dealt with both charges against him and replied fiercely. It was personal wrangling, but it represented a serious theological difference also. This theological dimension of the disagreement came into the open when Augustine of Hippo sent a Spanish priest, Paul Orosius, to Jerome with letters confessing his own difficulties and confusion on certain issues that were clearly related to the teaching of Pelagius about free-will and the possibility of living without sin. The Spanish priest proved a catalyst for further controversy which dragged Jerome into the public eye.

In 416, in a letter which Orosius carried back to Augustine, Jerome admits that he found the period of controversy 'a trying time, when it was better to keep silent than to speak, so much so that serious study had to cease and speech degenerated "in Appius" phrases into the snarling of dogs'. Jerome wrote a thesis against Pelagius and before it was completed a Synod had pronounced Pelagius orthodox. It was this controversy which led to the attack upon the monastery in 416, when some hooligans set fire to the two monasteries and assaulted the monks and nuns physically, and brutally murdered a deacon. Jerome, with Eustochium and the young Paula, escaped by fleeing to a fortified tower built as a refuge from Bedouin raids. Who was responsible is not known, but suspicion fell upon the mob supporters of Pelagius. The news was effective in raising Jerome in the popular esteem from a cantankerous old monk to a luminary of Latin Christianity. Eustochium and little Paula were likewise regarded with immense respect. All three were persuaded to leave their monasteries and live in safer surroundings. Pope Innocent supported Jerome and pressure was brought upon Pelagius to leave Palestine, which he did. Jerome, now in his seventies lived almost in obscurity for the next two or three years. He returned to his reconstructed monastery early in 419. Pelagius was eventually condemned as a heretic by the African Episcopate and on 27th January 417, Pope Innocent I added his anathema. His successor, Pope Zosimus reversed this. Finally after a winter of anguish and furious activity by Augustine the whole thing was reversed again and in the summer of 418, even Pope Zosimus changed his mind and condemned Pelagius. Jerome watched all this, well informed, but silent except for a few phrases in his letters.

Early in 419, Eustochium died. She was not much more than fifty and she died suddenly. Jerome was devastated. She had been his spiritual daughter. For more than thirty years since those distant days in Rome he had guided her and since the death of Paula had depended upon her. Now only little Paula, a mere teenager, remained of that noble house:

> 'I have been saddened beyond measure' he writes, 'by Eustochium's passing; it has virtually altered the whole tenor of my existence'.

His letters begin to show the burden of his years; 'I just cannot do many of the things I want to do, for the feebleness of old age undermines my mental energies'. But he did not forget his hatred of heresy and particularly of Pelagius. He saw Augustine as the champion of orthodoxy now, but did not go out with a whimper! 'With these heretics we should put into practice that programme laid down by David, "I spent the morning destroying all the sinners of the land". They must be cut to pieces with Christ's sword, for neither plasters nor soothing medicaments can enable them to recover sound health'. After that, silence. His last letters are lost. His great commentary on Jeremiah, interrupted by the fire at the monastery, was never finished. He died in 420, well on in his seventies.

2. Wycliffe: A Liberation from Priestdom

The opposition of the Church to the Wycliffe translation was based upon several objections. The understanding of Scripture was felt to belong to the priest by virtue of a special grace, which he received at his ordination. Lay people did not have this grace and a translation would impart only the views of the translator, not the sacred teaching of the Church through the Scriptures. Private reading of the Bible by the laity and even uneducated clergy, who were not able to read the Latin of the Vulgate, was liable to lead to heresy. Only the Vulgate, made by the holy and blessed Jerome, could be trusted and even that should be explained by a competent priest. Only a few surviving papal letters actually condemn translation and one of them was by Pope Innocent III in 1199, in reference to the Waldensian translation. It condemns the users of these, especially those who use them as a basis for preaching, for holding conventicles or for setting themselves up as more learned than the priest. It is to this letter that Wycliffe refers when he says that the teaching of Innocent is in contrast to the teaching of the Word of God. There was in England, in the fourteenth century no automatic condemnation of translating the Bible, but those who had the day to day running of a parish or diocese, tended to assume a suspicion of heresy among those who used the vernacular Scriptures.

Permission to possess

There is an English New Testament of this period in the John Hopkins Library which has a note signed by two doctors of divinity giving permission for some lay person to possess it. Anne of Bohemia, wife of Richard II, was also given such permission. Indeed, Archbishop Arundel who later so roundly condemned 'the pestilent and wretched John Wyclif' had earlier, in 1394, preached at her funeral and praised her piety, saying that he had approved for her to use an English version of the Gospels. This book was almost certainly a work of the Wycliffites. Such permission given to eminent persons was of course very different from a general permission.

The aim of the Wycliffites, however, was not only to extend the right to possess, but in the oft-quoted words to see 'that the boy who drives the plough shall know more of the Scripture' than the idle priest, (ascribed by Foxe to Tyndale.) Better documented is the reply of Wycliffe to his detractors who said that it was casting pearls before swine:

> Many nations have had the Bible in their own language. The Bible is the faith of the church. Though the Pope and all his clerks should disappear from the face of the earth, our faith would not fail, for it is founded upon Jesus alone, our Master and our God.

Wycliffe had many supporters; even in parliament, the rights of Holy Scripture found defenders. John of Gaunt's last word in defence of Wycliffe was in the Upper House in 1390, more than five years after Wycliffe's death, when a motion was being debated to seize all copies of the Bible and destroy them: 'Are we then the dregs of humanity, that we cannot possess the laws of our religion in our own tongue?'

The Anglo-Saxon Versions

In his somewhat verbose sketch of the successive versions from 1382 to 1885, H W Hoare asks rhetorically:

> How are we to explain the fact, that, although for at least a hundred years before the coming of the destroying Danes, English literature flourished so vigorously in the North, and although it revived again, in the form of prose, with King Alfred in the South, yet no English Bible appeared before Wycliffe, and no English Liturgy before Cranmer?

Part of the answer to that question is seen in the opposition which Wycliffe faced when he attempted to provide an English Bible, but part is also due to the non-literary culture of England during most of that time.

Beautiful manuscripts were produced in the monasteries, but the people did not read and a noble family would not regard it as a defect to be illiterate. The content of the Bible was communicated by carvings, wall paintings, plays, poems and songs. Our first named translator of parts of the Bible was Caedmon, an illiterate peasant of Northumbria, working as a labourer for the Abbess of Whitby. Bede tells us the story in his *History of the English Church and People*.

Although Caedmon had no experience of versifying, in fact he withdrew from the hall when his turn came to sing the Saxon songs, he was thought to have received a gift from God to turn passages from the Bible into song. He knew no Latin and could not therefore translate from the Vulgate, but the monks translated for him and he immediately sang 'sweet songs'. This is probably how the translation of much of the Bible took place in Anglo-Saxon times. Monks would read aloud spontaneous translations and the rich poetry of the Saxon tradition would versify where they could not accurately translate. But there was little regard for the canon and biblical passages were mixed with religious legends and even pagan mythology. As late as the time of Wycliffe, the friars were brightening up the Bible stories with mythical tales.

Some of Caedmon's songs were noted down and soon an English paraphrase of parts of the Bible was available. Caedmon's date is around 675, a little after the Whitby Conference separated Northumbria from Iona and Celtic Christianity to follow the rule of Canterbury and Rome.

Bede tells us that it was not only the laity who knew no Latin. As Christianity spread, more clergy were needed, yet many of them knew only Anglo-Saxon. So, there arose the need for translation, at least of the Lord's Prayer and as much of the Liturgy as it was necessary for them to understand - certainly the Creed. The ideal that was aimed at is well described in the canons of Aelfric, a tenth century Abbot of Eynsham, near Oxford:

> The mass-priest shall on Sundays and mass days tell to the people the sense of the Gospel in English, and so too of the Pater Noster and the Creed. Blind is the teacher if he know not book-learning.

The great devotional book of the period was the Psalter and many copies survive with translations or 'glosses' in Anglo-Saxon written between the lines. These Old English glosses exist also for Proverbs, part of Ecclesiastes and, most famous of all, the Gospels. The Lindisfarne Gospels have a word for word gloss which was written in the mid-tenth century.

Translation as a means of instruction

Glossing was part of Anglo-Saxon teaching. There is an account of Alcuin's schooldays in York. There Egbert taught grammar and other liberal arts as a preparation for the study of Scripture:

> Sitting on his bed from sunrise until the sixth hour of the day and often until the ninth hour, Egbert would explain the mysteries of Holy Writ to his pupils as far as they were prepared to receive them.

The Anglo-Saxons regarded Bede as the father of their way of teaching and his last letter to Egbert of York was treasured. In it he reminds the new bishop of the essential pastoral duty of instructing his people:

> Let those who can read Latin, use it to increase their faith. This is the best method. But let those priests and laymen who only know the vernacular, use the vernacular for the purpose.

For the unlettered, Bede recalls that he himself had translated the Lord's Prayer and the Creed into English for this purpose. This free attitude was soon to be regulated and the full weight of dogmatic and ecclesiastical tradition used to crush the Anglo-Saxon spontaneous love of learning. It started already with the work of Alcuin (735-804). He was charged by Charlemagne to establish a standard text of the Bible. This meant more than an agreed text for the Vulgate, but also a standard interpretation. The full truth of Scripture was already deposited by the Fathers of the Church. The Lord had no more light or truth to break forth from his Word. Alcuin initiated a scholastic attitude to Scripture which lasted for centuries. Thence forth, Scripture was not considered to be directly accessible to the intelligent reader, nor would such a reader consider himself free to draw out of it or put into it his own meaning. Each verse of the Bible acquired a cluster of meanings provided by tradition out of the Fathers.

Despite the high regard paid to tradition and particularly to the sacred text of the Vulgate, there occurred in the ninth century a remarkable extension of the use of the vernacular. Alfred, the one Englishman to be called Great, looked back in 894 and recalled that when he came to the throne there were very few clergy anywhere in England who knew or could translate Latin. By the end of his reign, there was a body of learned clergy and with their help he set up a system of education in two stages: first, he and his helpers translated into English certain books of knowledge, and then, the free-born youth who could be maintained at school were set to learn to read - English. Those who were called to the priesthood were expected to stay on and learn Latin. This was an extension of Bede's educational system.

The next figure in this twilight world of Anglo-Saxon England was Aelfric, the greatest prose writer in Old English. He did not translate the Bible but adapted it. When he was serving as a mass-priest at Cerne he compiled sermons and homilies in English and some years later, in 994, gathered them into two series of *Catholic Homilies*. These were followed by more homilies in *Lives of the Saints*. He talks of having turned Scripture into English and indeed lists his achievements, 'the Pentateuch, often dealt with the Creation story, translated Joshua for Ethelweard, treated Judges, Kings, Esther and the Maccabees'. He notices also that Judith is available in English but does not claim it as his own. These 'translations' are really conveying to the English hearer or reader the content of the Vulgate. The most extreme case of his treatment is the Four Books of Kings, which he reduces to 15 pages and includes one homily.

All this was not entirely blown away by the Norman Conquest of 1066. The West Saxon Gospels and much of Aelfric's work continued. None the less, the use of English was not encouraged by the Normans and the monasteries, which had been the centres of learning, were reorganised.

By the end of the 12th century, men knew that the old ways were passing and that the English language as a cultural medium was all but destroyed. An unknown cleric of the 12th century writes:

> Saint Bede was born here in Britain among us and learnedly he translated books by means of which the English people were instructed. Abbot Aelfric was a scholar and translated (the Pentateuch). These taught our people in English. Now is the learning lost and people forlorn. Those who teach the people are men of other tongues.

Anglo-Norman developed as a language and there was some translation. All serious work however was done in Latin. It was dangerous to handle the Scriptures in a way necessary for translation. Walter Map, archdeacon of Oxford from 1197 tells in revealing fashion how he discomforted a handful of 'Bible-reading Albigensians, who had the simplicity to believe what they read of Scripture and lived by their light of understanding'.

Canon Orm

Early in the thirteenth century, a monk of the Augustinian order, Ormin or Orm, and often referred to as Canon Orm, produced a metrical version of the Gospels and Acts, which is known as the Ormulum and is preserved at the Bodleian in Oxford. Orm assured his brother Walter, in a dedication at the outset, that he had carefully checked everything, but feared that detractors would still charge him with lack of judgment! It was not a good translation. But his intentions were good. He paraphrased the Gospel for the day and added a short exposition, taking great care to help readers pronounce the words properly. He justifies his version with a preface that I shall quote in modern English:

> If anyone wants to know why I have done this deed, I have done it so that all young Christian folk may depend upon the Gospel only, and may follow with all their might its holy teaching, in thought and word and deed.

The Ormulum was not much read and had no imitators. N J Hunter, writing on The Gothic Bible in the *Cambridge History of the Bible*, gives one reason for its lack of use: 'The verbal flabbiness of the writing is a convincing demonstration of lack of confidence in English as a literary medium'.

English was used only for summaries and metrical paraphrases, which circulated during the twelfth and thirteenth centuries. Down to the middle of the fourteenth century, there was no 'translation' into English prose of any complete book of the Bible.

John Wycliffe (1324-1384)

John Wycliffe was a Yorkshireman, born in Richmond in the 1320s, probably 1324, although the exact date of his birth is unknown. He was an academic, an illustrious son of Oxford, student at Balliol College, where he was awarded his MA in 1358. He was not a rich man and had therefore to use the means of the day to procure a living and continue his studies. He was granted two benefices and was non-resident in both. Not a very good start for one who was to become a Reformer of the Church! He was awarded his doctorate in 1372. It has been said that he was promised a lucrative post by Pope Gregory XI, but the Popes were always notorious for breaking their promises! He therefore did what any young clergyman would try to do at the time. He entered the services of the crown and Edward III gave him the living of Lutterworth, which he held until his death.

His first public duty was in 1374 when he joined a commission from the king to meet a papal representative in Bruges. The issue concerned the sovereignty of England. King John had made himself a papal vassal more than a century earlier and the curia (or papal court) was still claiming tribute as a feudal right. The commission appears to have won its case but Wycliffe was not satisfied. He began to work seriously upon the rights of church and state.

Shortly after returning to Oxford from Bruges, he started a series of lectures on 'lordship'. By this he meant the right to own property. His theory was that God was Lord of all possessions and that men had the right to own only in so far as they were 'in grace'. The logical step was to say, as he did, that the state could seize the property of a corrupt church. He put his theory into writing in 1374 and attracted a great deal of attention. This first book was called, *Determinatio*. It needed a great deal more work on it and over the next two years he was encouraged to work out his theory under two headings - on divine lordship and on civil lordship.

On Divine Lordship

Wycliffe was impeccably orthodox when he taught that God is the supreme Lord of all and that all lordship derived from him. He deduced from this that God's rights were in no way abrogated, diminished or nullified when he bestowed an infinitesimal part of his possessions upon his human creatures. Such temporary loan of lordship is neither permanent nor unlimited. The continuance is dependent upon the condition of the recipient. He writes:

> Hence, such a person is improperly called a lord, but is rather a steward of the supreme Lord. It is clear from this that every creature is a servant of the Lord, possessing whatsoever he has of pure grace that he may husband it.

On Civil Lordship

Wycliffe pressed on from this impossible stance to argue that all power, civil and ecclesiastical is held 'righteously' only as long as the possessor remains in grace. Of course, powers are held 'naturally', but only the righteous hold them rightfully, or as Wycliffe puts it, 'from dignity and merit'.

So long as Wycliffe applied these theories to civil powers, he greatly pleased the church. It gave the priest power over the lord. But when he persisted in his logical way and applied the same teaching to the property held by the churches, he found enormous opposition. However, among the civil powers and particularly with John of Gaunt he found great support. The Church had acquired more land than any other owner, largely due to legacies of frightened souls. It was hard to argue that these were held rightfully on Wycliffe's theory. The civil powers now saw a way of relieving the Church of its wealth. This was not what Wycliffe had in mind.

Certainly, the Church had too much wealth and it was not held rightfully, but if it were to be taken away, it should surely be used for the poor. The economic crises of the fourteenth century had left great poverty among ordinary people and Wycliffe had a deep concern for them. His supporters, however, had other ideas. Principal among these were John of Gaunt and Lord Percy.

The Riot in St Paul's

By 1377, John Wycliffe was known as one of the greatest scholars in the land. His arguments for the disendowment of the church appealed both to greedy dukes and over-burdened tax-payers, to John of Gaunt and the citizens of London. His opinion spread over the country and he was invited to preach 'disendowment' in the churches of the City of London. He made the most of his opportunities. He preached with conviction and soon won supporters among the citizens. Bishop Courtenay of London however persuaded the Archbishop of Canterbury to call Wycliffe to account and he was summoned to St Paul's where the Church was sitting in Convocation. On 19th February, 1377, John Wycliffe answered the call. But he came with John of Gaunt and Lord Percy as his protectors.

Two quite different issues were in the air and Wycliffe found himself caught up in them both. The citizens of London were defending their liberty against the tyranny of John of Gaunt and Lord Percy, while these two nobles were Wycliffe's strong defence against the Church. Wycliffe, though not politically involved, found his advocacy of disendowment threatened to lead to his condemnation by the Church as a heretic, while at the same time it had the support of the two warring factions of the City of London: its citizens and the two lords. When Wycliffe walked down the aisle of St Paul's flanked on either side by armed support, the crowds were howling for the blood of his supporters while ready if need be to defend him. The riot that ensued is vividly described by G W Trevelyan in his *England in the Age of Wycliffe*. The riot in the cathedral was followed by a hunt for the two lords and chaos broke out in London. The rioting had nothing to do with Wycliffe. He was never in danger and he was not condemned. Bishop Courtenay had instigated proceedings against Wycliffe without reference to the Pope. It was the year in which Gregory XI was busy moving his court from Avignon back to a ruined Rome. The Lateran Palace was in ruins and he established the Vatican where it now stands. A year later he died and three Popes contended for the throne. It was not a good year for papal efficiency! Neither was its reputation high throughout the world. But Bishop Courtenay was determined to get Wycliffe and cited him as a heretic before Pope Gregory in February 1377, within a month of his return to Rome. By May, the Pope had issued a Bull against Wycliffe addressed to Church and State. In view of his high reputation at Oxford, he had been elected Master of Balliol in 1361, and of the dependence of the Church upon Oxford, its 'second school', that Bull caused an unusual stir. The University of Oxford rallied around Wycliffe and protected him. A careful study of his teaching was undertaken and the university declared in favour of the soundness of his opinions.

The Poor Priests

Wycliffe was becoming more and more concerned about the state of the church and in particular the state of its teaching. The wealthy church cared little for the extreme poverty in the land; the friars preached in a way that put power into their hands as alone knowing the truth of the Gospel, a truth which they perverted with pagan fables. It was this that led John Wycliffe to train 'poor priests' to go out and preach the Gospel according to the Scripture.

This perversion of the Gospel by the friars and the need of his 'poor priests' to have a good English rendering of the Scripture led him to devote more time to the study of translation. He did not concern himself with the original languages, which may seem strange to us, but was content that the truths of the Bible be accurately conveyed, so that men might live by them. For him, the Bible was the Vulgate.

These 'poor priests' became known as 'Lollards', a nickname whose origin is lost. Certainly, it was not meant to be a compliment! It may come from the medieval Latin - 'Lollard' seems to mean one who mumbles hymns and prayers; or from Middle English - 'loller' means a vagabond or an idler. They learnt from Wycliffe that there was a higher authority than the Church. They recognised a ministry independent of Rome, 'every minister can administer the sacrament and attend to the care of souls as well as the Pope'. To the rich and indulgent clergy, who were a scandal in a poor land, they preached a Christian poverty; to the degenerate asceticism of the monks, they called for a spiritual and free life. Wycliffe so inspired these men that, with the help of his fellow-scholars at Oxford and later in Lutterworth, and equipped with an English translation of the Vulgate, crowds flocked to hear them. That took time to develop, but the popularity was already challenging that of the friars during Wycliffe's lifetime. A few years after his death it could be recorded that the townsfolk crowded around these humble preachers; the soldiers listened to them armed with sword and buckler to defend them. The nobility took down the images from their baronial chapels; and even the royal family was partly won over to this 'morning star of the Reformation'. The walls of St Paul's were hung with placards aimed at a corrupt priesthood and the abuses of the friars. After Wycliffe's death they gained in strength and for a while almost effected a Reformation in England. They petitioned Parliament for a general reform. Their petition of 1395 is worth quoting, although 11 years after Wycliffe's death, for it still reflects his spirit.

> The essence of the worship which comes from Rome consists in signs and ceremonies, and not in the effectual ministry of the Holy Ghost: and therefore it is not that which Christ hath ordained. Temporal things are distinct from spiritual things: a king and a bishop ought not to be one and the same person.

The things they called upon Parliament to abolish were a mixed lot, including celibacy of the clergy, transubstantiation, prayers for the dead, offerings to images, auricular confession, war, the arts unnecessary to life, the practice of blessing oil, salt, wax, incense, stones, mitres and pilgrim's staffs. 'All these', they said, 'belong to necromancy and not to theology'.

The Morning Star of the Reformation

There is a frontispiece in a Psalter published in Bohemia in 1572 which gives a symbolic representation of John Wycliffe's place among the Reformers. It shows Wycliffe striking a spark. John Hus kindling the coal, and Luther brandishing the lighted torch. Hus was a faithful disciple of Wycliffe and it was he who preserved his writings when they were all but totally destroyed in England. And it is beyond dispute now that the Hussites played a very important part in hastening and influencing the German Reformation. John Milton recognised the truth of the influence that Wycliffe had upon the Reformation when, in a somewhat nationalistic mood, he complained that had it not been for the obstinacy of our prelates against 'the divine and admirable spirit of Wycliffe', the names of Hus, Luther and Calvin might never have been known and 'the glory of reforming all our neighbours would have been completely ours'.

When Wycliffe was first charged in 1377 there was little that was theological in the charges, they were mostly political. He was standing for England against Rome, for the state against the church. The Papal Bull said that he had declared against the power of the Pope to loose and to bind and had said that excommunication, when it was unjust, had no value and no effect. It also declared that he had pronounced it the duty of the state to secularise the property of the church when it became too rich, in order to purify her. The nineteen charges of heresy were all about the administration of the church and its preservation of wealth and power. There was no serious charge of heresy in his theological teaching.

But as he trained his 'poor priests' and became more and more concerned with the proper teaching of 'Goddis law', as his followers called the Bible, a change came over the controversies surrounding him. Looking back, we may see that he was proposing a form of Presbyterianism and, in political matters, even a primitive form of Communism. He certainly seems to have anticipated Henry VIII in advocating a national church. But what he was really charged with in that 1377 Bull was a plea for reform rather than heresy.

In the following year, he was summoned to appear before the Papal Commissioners (Bishop Courtenay and the Archbishop of Canterbury, Sudbury.) The issue at stake was not whether he was a heretic, but whether the Pope had jurisdiction over the laws of England. The King's councillors had sought his advice about the payment of 'Peter's pence' and other moneys to Rome and they had constituted him their champion. But he was in danger as he moved into the jurisdiction of the Bishops. Just before the trial, Sir Lewis Clifford arrived with a message from the Queen Mother (widow of the Black Prince) forbidding the bishops to take any 'decided action against the prisoner'. Earlier, a London mob, fearing for the safety of their champion, broke up the proceedings by entering Lambeth Chapel and showing violent support for Wycliffe. Thomas Walsingham, the somewhat biased chronicler, was outraged:

> In this way slippery John Wycliffe deluded his inquisitors, mocked the bishops, and escaped them by the favour and care of the Londoners, although all his propositions are clearly heretical and depraved.

Later in the year Wycliffe became involved in the dispute of the Law of Sanctuary. He strongly opposed the teaching that a criminal could evade punishment by seeking sanctuary in the church. The law of sanctuary also involved the immunity of offending clergy. In dealing with this matter Wycliffe went further than expected and asserted that it was the proper office of the King to compel the bishops to look at the state of the clergy in their dioceses and remove notoriously immoral and inefficient pastors. The King should also have the power, acting of course through the bishops, to compel incumbents to live in their parishes, prevent the appointment of ignorant clergy and insist that all clerks should study. Wycliffe in fact proposed an English Church governed by the King, and coextensive with the State.

Transubstantiation

After two years of quiet study and teaching in Oxford a new storm blew up. Wycliffe was translating the Scripture and his closer study began to change many of his accepted and unchallenged views. At first, he simply taught in his lecture room at Oxford that the doctrine of 'Transubstantiation', namely that the bread and wine at the altar become the body and blood of Christ in the hands of the priest, was contrary to the teaching of the New Testament. In this he was attacking a central doctrine of the Catholic Church. The Church had not always taught this miracle of the changing of the bread and wine into the body and blood of Christ, a supernatural power given to the priest alone. Wycliffe found that it was not believed by the early Fathers of the Church and that it ran counter to the teaching of the New Testament. He could see how useful it was to the

Church, who thereby held the supreme sanction in an age of faith. He argued that the 'orthodox' view of the Eucharist was the cause of idolatry; the people made the host their God. He further declared that nothing was more horrible to him than the idea that every celebrating priest created the body of Christ. The Mass was, in his view, a false miracle invented for worldly reasons to give the Church power over the people. The storm arose at once and became violent when he published his views in a controversial essay, *On the Eucharist*. John of Gaunt hurried to Oxford at once and ordered him to be silent. He refused and so sacrificed the support of the most powerful man in the kingdom.

John Wycliffe was a man of prayer and devoted to the Eucharist. His attacks were upon a theory of the Mass, not upon the humble devotion of a believer before the mystery. He believed that the body of Christ was present, but the bread also. Although he did not care for many of the ceremonies of the Church, he preferred the direct access of a believer through Christ to God, he never attacked the sacraments as many of his followers did. His own attitude is best shown in a passage from that controversial essay:

> Just as when the cup (chalice) is seen we break forth into worship, so also when the consecrated host is seen we do the same, not on account of the fact that that very cup has been consecrated by the priest, but because of the excellent sacrament hidden in the vessel. Thus when we see the host we ought to believe not that it is in itself the body of Christ, but that the body of Christ is sacramentally concealed in it. And this is the meaning of the Church when it sings: "Beneath these many forms we see signs only, not reality; The wonder lies concealed"

For him the test of a ritual's value was the degree to which it increased the devotion of the people. Thus he found that intoning and elaborate singing took the mind off the meaning of prayer. He quoted from St Augustine, a quote which later became very popular with his followers, 'as oft as the song delighteth me more than what is sung, so oft I acknowledge that I trespass grievously'.

By the same standards he judged that the splendid buildings and gaudy decoration of the Churches distracted the minds of the worshippers. At a time when beautiful gothic architecture had left its early simplicity and singing had forsaken the pure beauty of the Gregorian chant for more elaborate entertainment, Wycliffe gave voice to those who desired simplicity in worship. He advocated the worship of God, rather than attendance at a performance. To Wycliffe, preaching seemed the most effective means of arousing people to a sense of responsibility and a personal relationship with God. Yet he was not an iconoclast. He respected the images in the churches and thought they could be an aid to worship. He did not attack prayers to saints, although he preferred a general respect for saintliness to attachment to any one saint. If prayer to a saint helped the worship of the believer, he had nothing against it. But the misuse to which saint worship and adoration of relics was put filled him with anger.

His treatment of the Virgin Mary was sensitive and devout. He held her up as an example to be followed. Wycliffe wrote an interesting treatise called *Ave Maria*, in which he describes her exemplary life in language full of sympathy and beauty. But he does not advise people to pray to her. He does not speak in praise or condemnation of the image of the Virgin which then looked down from every Church in the land.

Wycliffe was a man of his time and spent much of his life in the piety of his age. But he had attacked the central doctrine of the Mass and had called for far-reaching reforms of the structure of the Church. It was obvious that sooner or later the Church would get him. What is remarkable is that he continued so long to exercise his dominant influence in the University of Oxford.

The Peasants Revolt of 1381

Although John Wycliffe directed his teaching primarily to the reform of the Church, there was no mistaking the consequences of what he taught for the reform of society. There comes a time when theoretical ideas are matched by a glimpse of the possibility of change and then a spark is set off. When there is abject poverty, the people may be docile for a while, until they become conscious that they are poor and need not be. The fourteenth century was a watershed between the Middle Ages and the world of Enlightenment. Men were becoming aware of the common origin of mankind in Adam and Eve, which was not read mythologically but historically, and the common catchphrase was:

When Adam delved and Eve span,
Who was then the gentleman?

The awful experience of Black Death, the years of war with France, the oppressive governments which tried to keep wages fixed while prices rose, at last broke the endurance of the people. Often their leaders were simple parish priests who did not share the wealth of the bishops, but cared for their impoverished parishioners. From their ranks came Wycliffe's 'poor priests' and later 'Lollards'. These were the men who were most in touch with the people and whose preaching had stirred up aspirations to equality and freedom. Further, they were influenced by Wycliffe's teaching of the 'rightful' holding of property only by those who were 'in grace'. Wycliffe would never approve of the violence, but it was his teaching which gave justification to the Peasants Revolt.

Wycliffe's attitude to the Peasants Revolt is linked with his fear of the effect of the friars. He saw that many of those itinerant preachers were leading people on to extreme actions and for their own gain. In fact, it appears to be because of the damage done by the friars that he started to organise his 'poor priests'. He is quoted as saying: 'If begging friars stroll over the country... we must do for God's glory what they do to fill their wallets, and form a vast itinerant organisation to convert souls to Jesus Christ'. Friars and followers of Wycliffe had some points in common in their teaching, but their aims were different. Many of the friars courted popularity among the crowds, although of course many were sincerely concerned about the growing poverty and injustice in the land. The followers of Wycliffe cared deeply about the truth. They were concerned less to change society than to change people's hearts. It was the kingdom of Christ which concerned them more than the kingdom of England. Both friars and followers of Wycliffe were effective, whether they intended it or not, in giving new revolutionary fire to dissatisfied peasants.

Wycliffe condemned

Bishop Courtenay, a persistent and avowed enemy of Wycliffe, was appointed to the see of Canterbury after the Revolt had been suppressed. He lost no time in calling a Synod at Westminster which opened in May 1382. It was intended to condemn Wycliffe and associate him with the rebellion:

> 'Let us recognise', he said, 'the malice and iniquity of Master John Wycliffe, both by means of his pestilential doctrines as well as the preaching of his followers and adherents who invariably sowed dissension and provoked the people to rebellion'.

The most notorious of Wycliffe's followers named was John Ball, whom they claimed made confession of the influence of Wycliffe before he was executed. The Synod assembled on St Dunstan's Day (May 19) to condemn Wycliffe and all the Lollards. On that day, England experienced a violent earthquake, which put fear into the hearts of many at the Synod. Courtenay persisted, maintaining that the earthquake was sent to purge England of her errors. There were many who feared that Wycliffe's preaching would bring about another rebellion. Oxford could not save him now and he was dismissed from his beloved university and exiled to the parish of Lutterworth for the last two years of his life.

Lutterworth

Presumably his eminence as a scholar and his popularity saved Wycliffe's life and perhaps the fact that he was old and ailing led to the conclusion that he would be harmless in his country parish of Lutterworth. Nothing could have been further from the truth as subsequent generations recognised. What they failed to do to his body when he was alive, his enemies did to his bones when dead. Realising the mistake they had made, they dug up his body, burned it and scattered his ashes into the river. But they could not undo those last two years of his life at Lutterworth.

In November 1382, Courtenay visited Oxford with the express purpose of condemning Wycliffe. He gathered around him a number of bishops, doctors, priests, students and laymen, and summoned Wycliffe to appear before him. There was the usual tumult of crowds spoiling for a fight, but when Wycliffe began to speak a silence fell upon all.

Wycliffe said that it was not he who was condemned, but those he called 'the priests of Baal', who disseminated errors to sell their Masses. Wycliffe saw the hopelessness of his case and simply said at last, 'the truth shall prevail'. Then he left the court with no one daring to stop him.

He withdrew to Lutterworth to live peacefully among his books and his parishioners. But another blow fell when he was summoned to Rome by Pope Urban VI. He did not go to Rome, but although Urban would gladly have dropped the affair, Wycliffe did not. He confessed his faith to Urban VI. Thus the Pope who sought to condemn him gave him the opportunity to profess in clear language the principles for which he stood. They encapsulate Wycliffe and are a treasure to any who wish to know this strangely secret, private man:

> I believe that the Gospel of Christ is the whole body of God's law. I believe that Christ who gave it to us, is very God and very man, and by this it passes all other laws. I believe that the bishop of Rome is bound more than any other man to submit to it, for greatness among Christ's disciples did not consist in worldly dignities and honours, but in the exact following of Christ in his life and manners. No faithful man ought to follow the pope, but in such points as he followed Jesus Christ. The pope ought to leave unto the secular power all temporal dominion and rule; and thereunto effectually more and more exhort his own clergy ... if I could labour according

to my desire in mine own person, I would surely present myself before the bishop of Rome, but the Lord hath otherwise visited me to the contrary, and hath taught me rather to obey God than man.

At Lutterworth, Wycliffe continued with his Bible translation. He was left in peace with his disciples. His 'poor priests' went out from the little country town to spread the Gospel and to read the Bible. No one knows how many went, but the people of England were being prepared for their 'Reformation', which would be firmly based upon biblical teaching.

Trialogos

In his last work, Wycliffe described his last days as spent in the company of three personages - two, his particular friends, and the third his constant adversary. The book was called *Trialogos* and the three personages were: Aletheia, Phronesis, and the adversary, Pseudos. Aletheia (truth) posed questions; Phronesis (understanding) laid down sound doctrines; Pseudos (falsehood) urged objections. These three characters carried on a conversation in which great truths were boldly professed and errors sharply rebuked. 'The church has fallen', says one of the characters, 'because she has abandoned the Gospel, and preferred the laws of the popes'. These were the last flicker of the torch. Wycliffe saw that his end was near. He expected martyrdom, a dungeon in one of the seven hills of Rome or a burning pile in London. Then he recollected that there were other forms of martyrdom: 'Why do you talk of seeking the crown of martyrdom afar? Preach the Gospel of Christ to haughty prelates and martyrdom will not fail you. What! I should live and be silent. Never! Let the blow fall, I await its coming'. But he was spared the blow. He continued tranquilly to preach Jesus Christ and on 29th December 1384, as he was in his church at Lutterworth, in the midst of his flock, he was suddenly stricken with paralysis. He was carried to his home by affectionate friends and after lingering for two days, he died on the last day of the year.

John Wycliffe - England's Jerome

There is a portrait of John Wycliffe hanging in Balliol College, Oxford, where he spent the greater part of his active life. He is a bearded and apparently aged man. In his gloved left hand he holds a staff and in his right hand a book or file of papers. It is the portrait of a man who has suffered and unmistakably that of a scholar. There is a purpose burning in his eyes that suggests obstinacy. We recognise the figure whom we have been considering. For quite apart from what he did and the messages he proclaimed, he was a man whom you would hesitate to oppose and whom it would be difficult to impugn. He was upright, unafraid, persistent in the service of his Lord, a man who feared God and after that had nothing else to fear. The characteristics of this successor to Jerome, the second of the giants among the makers of the English Bible, were a total trust in the message of Holy Scripture, a conviction that his message was relevant in his day, a firm determination that every person should have direct access to this fountain of his faith, an impatience with all kinds of cant, pretence, hypocrisy and unmerited privilege, and his honesty and total integrity. He would not have wanted to be canonised, but he was the kind of saint that he was looking for.

In England every effort was made to eradicate all trace of Wycliffe's teaching and to vilify his person. There is no record of him kept except strings of abusive epithets from his enemies. His writings were destroyed in England. They were, however, preserved in Bohemia where they laid the foundations of the Reformation.

3. Tyndale: A Martyr for Truth

William Tyndale was born into an age of intellectual turmoil and, if Foxe does exaggerate a little when he writes 'William Tyndale was brought up from a child in the University of Oxford', there is no doubt that the influences of Oxford and then Cambridge were dominant in his intellectual life. He was born in 1490, which was about the time when Grocyn and Linacre returned from Italy, soaked in the atmosphere of the Italian Renaissance, and began to teach Greek at Oxford. John Colet, the Dean of St Paul's, represented the New Learning and continued the work of these two. He had himself been to Italy and it was said that he came under the influence for a while of Savonarola. But his memorable contribution was his famous lectures on the Epistles of St Paul. They were a little too early for Tyndale to have heard, but he must have read them and felt their influence in the University where they were delivered. In Cambridge he was too late for Erasmus, but he read and translated his works and felt his influence on the spirit of the University there.

In his comparatively brief life the Reformation was born, Erasmus attempted a peaceful alternative, Thomas Wolsey rose and fell, Rome was sacked by the forces of Charles V, the Church of England separated from Rome, the clergy submitted to the crown, and Thomas Cromwell dissolved the monasteries. Fisher, Colet and More joined Erasmus in trying to bring about a peaceful reform of the abuses of the Church without destroying the unity of Christendom, Calvin's *Institutes* were published, Geneva adopted the Reformation and an English New Testament translated from the original languages was issued.

In all this turmoil, it was sometimes difficult to know whose side you were on. The Middle Ages had come to an end and England was becoming more and more conscious of its identity as a country separate from Europe and yet part of it. The fires that burned in Europe scorched England and the battle lines that were drawn often put England in one camp or another without due regard to her own interest. Many groups had many purposes and often those who agreed least on most matters found themselves defending the same cause; while those who had most in common were on opposite sides.

Some were primarily concerned to deal with the abuses of the Church, others with the excessive demands of Rome, yet others were concerned with truth and closely allied to them were those who wished to assert the authority of the Bible over that of the Pope. The Enlightenment was dawning and people everywhere were awakening from their self-imposed tutelage. They were coming of age and challenging all authority including that of the Church.

In all this, William Tyndale's absorbing passion was the truth of the Bible. He found an ally in Erasmus who provided him with the text of the original New Testament, rather than the Latin Vulgate; he also found an ally in Luther who insisted upon putting the words of Scriptures into the language of the people. In summary we might say that up to about the year 1523, Tyndale remained more or less a disciple of Erasmus and John Colet. After that he came powerfully under the influence of Luther.

The Early Years

Like Wycliffe he began in Oxford, but he did not stay. That is the first mystery for any biographer. It would have made a good theory to say that he went to study under Erasmus, but he was too late. Erasmus left Cambridge in 1514. It is more likely that Tyndale was forced to leave Oxford. He was at Magdalen Hall (attached to Magdalen College) and remained there some few years after he had been awarded his Master of Arts. Foxe gives us the first hint of possible trouble, 'he grew and increased as well in the knowledge of tongues and other liberal arts, as especially in the knowledge of the Scriptures, whereunto his mind was singularly addicted, in so much that *he read privily to certain students and fellows of Magdalen College some parcel of divinity instructing them in the knowledge and truth of the Scriptures*'.

There were two parties in Oxford at that time, 'the Trojans' and 'the Greeks'. The latter were those who with enthusiasm supported the new learning, 'men come of age'. But the Trojans laboured with great diligence to suppress them. There is no doubt to which party Tyndale belonged and his Bible readings were probably already getting him into trouble with the doctors of the College.

The move from Oxford to Cambridge was probably also due to the changing atmosphere at Oxford since Colet came under suspicion. His lectures had given offence to the champions of traditional scholastic 'orthodoxy'. On all sides the ecclesiastical authorities were becoming alarmed at the spread of 'heretical' doctrines, which appeared to come from the 'new learning' which Colet had championed and Tyndale followed with enthusiasm. Colet himself was in some danger, he had not only founded St Paul's School which was suspected of teaching the new learning, but he had even translated The Lord's Prayer into English. The Bishop of London, Fitz James, wanted him burned as a heretic! Without the esteem of the King, and the friendship of the Archbishop of Canterbury (Warham), who also admired Erasmus, Colet might well have met the usual fate of a heretic. Tyndale was known at Oxford as an eager follower of Colet and his private lectures made him more suspect. As Erasmus was rapidly becoming the rallying point of the new learning in Europe, it was not unreasonable to flee from a suspicious Oxford to a Cambridge, where Erasmus had recently taught. Cambridge was, in any case, the place to go, if not for safety, at least for good Greek.

William Tyndale graduated as Master of Arts in 1515 and probably left for Cambridge a few years later. Meanwhile he had become ordained. When and where he was ordained we do not know. It was probably before he left Oxford, but even that is not certain. He was well known as a preacher and even Sir Thomas More who attacks him makes one of the characters in his dialogue say: 'Tyndale was, as men say, well known before he went over the sea, for a man of right good living, studious and well learned in Scripture, and in divers places in England was very well liked and did great good with preaching'. Later in the dialogue he endorses that opinion himself: 'Tyndale was indeed, as you said at the beginning, before his going, taken for a man of sober and honest living, and looked and preached holily'. Sir Thomas More, of course goes on to say that even then he smacked somewhat of heresy. More was in touch with both universities and must have got his report from them. The double mention of preaching is interesting because at that time it was much neglected.

Various guesses have been made about the date of the move to Cambridge. J F Mozley sums up the matter with 'All things considered, it is best to fix his ordination in the Oxford years, and to bring him to Cambridge about 1519'. I am inclined to agree with Mozley.

It was a good period to be in Cambridge. The influence of Erasmus had led to an understanding of Luther's complaints against the Church, even though it is not the way that Erasmus himself would have wanted his influence to go!

In the year 1517, Luther nailed his theses to the door of Wittenberg but something similar happened in Cambridge. Both events are concerned with Indulgences whose abuse so troubled Martin Luther and many others. In that same year, a notice of Indulgences was posted on the gates of the common schools at Cambridge. A young Norman student, Peter de Valence, wrote on the notice in Latin, 'Blessed is the man whose hope is in the name of the Lord, and pays no attention to the vanity and insanity of these false things'. When Tyndale arrived in Cambridge these things were still being talked about, because Bishop Fisher who had posted the notice was not prepared to regard it as merely a student protest. He summoned an assembly and, after explaining and defending the purpose and nature of Indulgences, named a day on or before which, 'the sacrilegious writer was required to reveal himself and confess his crime and avow his penitence under pain of excommunication'.

William Tyndale was now moving into the orbit of Luther's influence. Thus, he had progressed without too much change of direction from Colet's sermons with their emphasis upon the truth of Scripture and his attack upon the abuses of the clergy; to Erasmus' scholarship and Greek text of the New Testament, as well as his vicious wit ridiculing the ignorance of the clergy; and then to Luther's attack upon Indulgences. There were many at Cambridge who would encourage him, in the way he was already travelling. But it was not those who were to become famous in England's history who influenced him most.

Cranmer, he knew only as a hard-working student; Gardiner was a clever college tutor; Latimer was a grave and upright man, a great admirer of the schoolmen and a determined opponent of Greek and of the study of the Holy Scripture which Erasmus had encouraged. These had little influence upon him. Far more influential was a group of younger men who had been touched by the 'new fire'. Among them was Thomas Bilney, who had been converted by the reading of Erasmus' Greek New Testament when it appeared in 1516. He was a gentle and timid man, affectionately called 'little Bilney' by Latimer, whom he persuaded to adopt the protestant cause. Bilney was the centre of this little group who adopted the evangelical truths as their way of life. There was Robert Barnes, Prior of the Augustinian monastery, and Coverdale, a member of the same house; John Lambert, or Nicholson, who later became chaplain to the English merchants at Antwerp. These three men retained contact with Tyndale when he later crossed over to the continent and helped him at great cost. Another may have been at Cambridge who became his most devoted disciple, John Frith or Fryth. If they met at Cambridge they could only have overlapped by a few months, but that was long enough to inspire John to give his life for the cause. He heard the Gospel from the lips of William Tyndale.

Little Sodbury

Tyndale was in his thirties and a brilliant scholar, with the experience of Oxford and Cambridge behind him. He was ordained and might have been expected to accept a living somewhere in the country or a teaching post at the university. Instead he went to a country house to be a tutor to the family of Sir John Walsh. The oldest child was about 6 and it did not seem much of a post for so accomplished a man. The explanation is not easy. He was growing more and more disillusioned with the Church as he knew it and did not relish the prospects of going through the old, meaningless routine of an unreformed Church. Neither did he expect to find much companionship with the ignorant clergy of his day. He liked teaching and would gladly have taught Greek. But no post was vacant and he had to live. His brother suggested to Sir John Walsh that perhaps he should have a learned man on his staff now that he was rising in the county and recommended William. It does not appear that he was appointed chaplain to the household, but he was treated as more than a servant. Sir John liked him and often had him at table when there were guests. All very pleasant, but why did William accept so modest a post when all his study seemed to point to something much grander? The only answer seems to be that he did not know what to do. He had not yet discovered his life's work. Little Sodbury in Gloucestershire seemed to be a good retreat where he could study, for the tutoring of a six-year-old boy is hardly a full-time job.

The family liked him and he soon talked on easy terms with the dignitaries who came to grace his master's table. Abbots, Deans and Bishops came and soon found this young man a worthy opponent in their arguments. In fact, he displeased them by his ability to counter all their attacks on Luther, Erasmus or whoever happened to be their pet enemy at the time. The effect was that they no longer dined at the table of Sir John Walsh, but rather indicted this young man as a heretic. Sir John stood by him. Lady Walsh spoke critically to him about his opposition to the ecclesiastical dignitaries and, although he acted humbly towards her, he quietly translated a book by Erasmus which attacked the abuses and ignorance of the clergy and gave it to her. The family was convinced, but not the clergy! After much thought he came to two conclusions. The first was that he should not remain in the house of Sir John Walsh, whose rising in the community might be endangered by his support of his house tutor; the second was that he had discovered his life's task - to translate the Scriptures into the English tongue. After speaking with Sir John about the matter he had permission to leave and sought out the man who could help him: Bishop Tonstall of London, whom Erasmus had praised.

London

In July 1523, William Tyndale said goodbye to Sir John Walsh, whose kindness had made his first job so pleasant and who had generously provided opportunities for study. Sir John gave him a letter of introduction to Sir Henry Guildford, who might be able to smooth his way. Armed with this letter and a translation of a speech by Isocrates into English to show his ability, he set forth with great hopes. He fondly imagined that away from the superstitions of the countryside and aided by a bishop of whom Erasmus thought so highly, he might settle to some service which left him time to study and translate the New Testament into English. He was no rebel, but prepared to be a willing servant.

The bishop was much involved in other things when Tyndale arrived, Wolsey had been trying to persuade one of his rare Parliaments to grant an exorbitant sum from taxation to assist Papal interests and to prepare the way for his king to be declared Emperor. Sir Thomas More supported Wolsey and he was partially successful. The bishops were much involved in this machination and Tonstall was not available until September.

Sir Henry Guildford had done his part. He liked Tyndale and as a scholar himself appreciated the quality of his translation. Tyndale went through the proper channels. Tonstall was about 49 at the time, an educated man with a good knowledge of Greek and some Hebrew. He belonged to that circle of humanists which included Erasmus, More and Warham. Thomas More praised him in his *Utopia* and Erasmus was unduly flattering: 'Our age does not possess a more learned, a better or a kinder man. I seem to not be alive now that he is taken from me'. But there was another side to this bishop. He had a rather smooth and accommodating nature, and was not the man to take up an unpopular cause, or to renounce the world for the sake of his conscience. In recent years he had been drawn more and more into the service of the crown and he was an ambitious man. As keeper of the privy seal, he had recently delivered the king's speech before a splendid company. Caution and worldly wisdom were his more common guide than enthusiasm. However he granted an interview and Tyndale did not make the best of it. He knew that he was not fitted to ask favours of the great. Ten years later, he could still describe himself to his friend Frith as 'evil favoured in this world, and without grace in the sight of men, speechless and rude, dull and slow witted'. He might well have used those words after he had failed to impress Bishop Tonstall. Tyndale was bitterly disappointed. There was no place for him in Tonstall's household and without such support he could not accomplish his work, but Tonstall had assured him that he would not fail to find work in London. That was true, but such work would mean giving up his cherished project. He found a friend in Humphrey Monmouth, a wealthy cloth merchant, living in Barking. Monmouth was a kindly and generous man and his mind was already turning towards reform. As Latimer says of him he 'became a Bible man and began to smell the Gospel'. He met Tyndale when he heard him preach in St Dunstan-in-the-West.

For a year Tyndale preached in various churches in London, but never wavered in his decision to devote his life to the translation of the New Testament. The meeting between Monmouth and Tyndale was important to both men. To Tyndale it meant help when he sorely needed it; to Monmouth it meant suspicion, loss of fortune and even imprisonment. Four and a half years after their meeting, Humphrey Monmouth was arrested on the charge of Lutheranism and examined by Sir Thomas More. On 19th May 1528, in the presence of Bishop Tonstall, Monmouth signed a petition to Wolsey defending himself against the charge of heresy. The charge against him came to an accusation that he had given succour to William Tyndale. In the course of his explanation, he gives us a good account of the way that Tyndale lived in London:

> I took him into my house half a year; and there he lived like a good priest as me thought. He studied most part of the day and of the night at his books, and he would eat but sodden meat by his good will, nor drink but small beer. I never saw him wear linen about him in the space he was with me (ie but only woollen.) I did promise him £10 sterling to pray for the souls of my father and mother and all Christian souls; I did pay it to him when he made his exchange to Hamburg.

Monmouth was released from the Tower, but had to abjure his opinions. He became an alderman of London in 1537. When he died, instead of leaving money for the thirty masses for his soul, which was customary at the time, he left money for thirty sermons to be preached at his Parish Church by the four reformers, Latimer, Barnes, Crome and Taylor. But meanwhile Tyndale had discovered that there was no place in London for him to translate his New Testament. He had heard at Humphrey Monmouth's table much that interested him about Luther and the freedom of the Word of God in Germany. In 1524 he left London for Hamburg.

Germany: 1524-1526

Tyndale appears to have stayed only a few days with the van Emmerson family in Hamburg before travelling south to Wittenberg. He had to learn German and travel was none too easy. He travelled either by horse or up the Elbe by boat. When he reached Wittenberg, the Mecca of all reformers he stayed there nine or ten months. He returned to Hamburg in April 1525 and sent to England for his £10! By this time his New Testament must have been completed. When Tyndale wrote to Monmouth asking for his £10 he also sent to him 'a little treatise'. Monmouth burnt it eighteen months later together with his 'Lutheran books'. There has been much speculation about this 'little treatise'. Mozley thinks it was Bugenhagen's *Letter to the English*, the first greeting of the German reformers to England. No wonder Monmouth burnt it, for it would be incriminating evidence. It was a little treatise, only eight pages, beginning:

> We could not but rejoice, dear brethren, when we heard that in England also the gospel of the glory of God has a good report. But we were also informed that many were turned away from it because of the slanderous stories against us and our way of living. Know therefore, that whatsoever ye may have heard, and however simple minds may be puzzled and confused by the flood of controversy, we have only one doctrine: Christ is our righteousness.

William Tyndale could only say, Amen, to that. This independent young man was attracted to Luther, although he resolutely denied that he was in 'confederacy' with him. Tyndale was not a Lutheran, although he, like so many young men of his time, hurried to the freedom of Wittenberg where men could speak openly of the Gospel and could denounce the abuses of the Church that had so long kept this Gospel from the people. He shared the sense of freedom but did not accept all the teaching of Luther, nor did he find himself constrained to do so.

Much as he enjoyed Wittenberg, and helpful as he found the libraries there, his task was not sightseeing, even of Luther, but to print an English New Testament. Wittenberg was too far inland for easy transport to England and he therefore sought printers in Cologne. From there, his Bible would easily travel down the Rhine and across the Channel to England, probably London. Tyndale travelled with William Roye to Cologne and found a printer to undertake the work. The disturbances of the peasants' wars had subsided and the printing was able to proceed apace, until John Dobneck (often called Cochlaeus) put a stop to it.

John Dobneck was a shallow and conceited man, whose life ambition seems to have been to root out Lutheran heresy. He was a prolific writer of pamphlets and the same printer as printed Tyndale printed his flood of abuse. He had been Dean of St Mary's Church in Frankfurt and was driven from there and subsequently from Mainz by popular risings. Many years later, in his most abusive *History of Luther*, he tells at length how he stopped the publication of Tyndale's New Testament:

Two English apostates, who had been some time at Wittenberg, not only sought to ruin their own merchants, who were secretly encouraging and supporting them in their exile, but even hoped that, whether the king would or not, all the people of England should shortly become Lutherans, by means of Luther's New Testament, which they had translated into the English tongue.

He tells us that these two apostates (Tyndale and Roye) had asked the printer for an edition of six thousand. The printer was cautious about so large a quantity and issued only three thousand. Cochlaeus learned of this by loosening the tongue of the Cologne printers with wine. He reported to Sir Hermann Rinck a senator at Cologne, who had the work prohibited. "The two English apostates, seizing the printed sheets, fled up the Rhine to Worms".

William Tyndale and William Roye were men of very different stamp. Tyndale had been careful not to make enemies or to talk over much of his delicate enterprise. Roye boasted, and no doubt it was he who gave so much information to the printers. Only a single fragment remains of the Cologne edition. That fragment contains an introduction by Tyndale which quotes Luther at length, but has much original Tyndale in it. The sentence which horrified his opponents was, 'If I live chaste, I do it not that I look for a higher room in heaven than they shall have that live in wedlock, or than a whore of stews (if she repent); for that were the pride of Lucifer; but truly to wait on the evangelion, and to serve my brother withal'.

Tyndale's admiration for Luther comes out most clearly in the glosses on the text and it is not surprising that his enemies accused him of being Luther's stooge, but they were wrong. Spalatin, a friend of Luther, and secretary to the Elector of Saxony, gives a better picture when in his diary he describes a dinner party at which Hermann von dem Busche tells of his visit to Worms: "Busche told us that at Worms six thousand copies of the New Testament had been printed in English. The work has been translated by an Englishman, staying there with two other Britons, who is so skilled in seven tongues, Hebrew, Greek, Latin, Italian, Spanish, English, French, that whichever he speaks you would think it his native tongue".

The English bought whatever they could lay their hands on of Tyndale's New Testament. The price seems to have been about four shillings. The Worms edition differs considerably from the Cologne fragment. The glosses are gone and instead of the long introduction so dependent upon the Luther quote, there is a simple epistle to the reader and the plain text. Mozley thought it worthwhile to quote the short epistle in full and I can see why. It is beautiful and shows us much of the mind of Tyndale at that time. We know practically nothing about his life in Worms and I will therefore quote from the epistle:

> Give diligence, dear reader, I exhort thee, that thou come with a pure mind, and as the scripture saith, with a single eye, unto the word of health and of eternal life: by the which, if we repent and believe them we are born anew, created afresh, and enjoy the fruits of the blood of Christ. Them that are learned Christianly I beseech - forasmuch as I am sure, and my conscience beareth me record, that of a pure intent, singly and faithfully I have interpreted it, as far forth as God gave me the gift of knowledge and understanding - that the rudeness of the work now at the first time offend them not; but that they consider how that I had no man to counterfeit (imitate) neither was help with English of any that had interpreted the same or such like things in the scripture beforetime ... Count it as a thing not having his full shape, but, as it were born afore his time, even as a thing begun rather than finished.

In that epistle he asks for help and understanding, not boasting of any achievement, but appealing to 'them that are learned and able, to remember their duty, and to help thereunto, and to bestow unto the edifying of Christ's body .. those gifts which they have received of God'.

The simplicity and modesty of his appeal did not help him. His enemies were soon after him like a pack of hounds.

After the publication of the *New Testament* in 1526, Tyndale remained in Worms for about a year. He separated from William Roye. There was obviously a clash of temperaments. The careful Tyndale, who had no desire to be branded as a heretic or to fight a battle for Lutheranism, did not want his delicate work of translation put in jeopardy by the belligerent Roye. The one visitor Tyndale had in Worms that we know about was a certain Jerome and Tyndale warned him against Roye's 'boldness'.

For Tyndale, Worms was a safe place of refuge. There he supervised the revision of his translation and the publishing of all the books of the New Testament. He paid careful attention to distribution and sale. How they were shipped to England we do not know. It would have been a risky business to send them down the Rhine via Cologne which was hostile to the Reformation. He might have sent them overland to Antwerp. Tyndale the gentle scholar became a shrewd businessman. The first copies of his New Testament reached England by March 1526, about a month after the burning of four 'Lutheran' merchants at St Paul's Cross. Wolsey sat in splendour with thirty-six bishops, abbots and priors, while Fisher preached the sermon. Sir Thomas More was the detective who ransacked the Steelyard for offending literature. In this atmosphere, the New Testament sold. The buyers knew nothing of the translator, because his name appeared nowhere on the book. The antagonism to Tyndale was greatly increased when Roye and Jerome, working from Frankfurt, began to publish poems, lampooning the leaders of Church and State. In the summer of 1528, Wolsey stung by the lampoons against him, attempted to have Tyndale and Roye seized and brought to England for punishment.

In April 1527, Tyndale visited Marburg, but he did not stay there. Where he went was not clear and it was dangerous to reveal his residence until he knew himself to be safe from Wolsey's spies. But his German period was over, apart from some correspondence with Hamburg, and Antwerp was to become his refuge.

Tyndale's Protestant Writings

Tyndale's major task was translation, but he now had a cause to fight for. He wanted the people of England to have access to the Bible and the pure teaching of the Gospel. He had to argue for this and in doing so attack the abuses of the Church. The first of his writings to carry his name was, *The Parable of the Wicked Mammon*, dated 8th May 1528, but obviously written before he had news of the fierce persecution started in February.

In it, he excuses himself for writing his own words instead of the pure words of the New Testament. He attacks Roye and Jerome for their lampooning. He then turns to his main enemy - Antichrist, whom he says is no outward thing as our fathers supposed, but a spiritual thing. He is ever present, in the Old Testament and in the New. He is here now, and he will endure to the world's end. He recognises Antichrist in the leaders of the Church who are seeking to turn the king away from Christ. As in his translation he asks for corrections, but the gentle tone has gone, the battle is joined:

> They would divide you from Christ and his holy testament, and join you with the Pope, to believe in his testament and promises.

The treatise itself starts from the parable of the unjust steward and develops into the doctrine of justification by faith. It is much dependent upon Luther, whose sermon on this parable was preached in 1522. Whole sections of that sermon are quoted. But Tyndale has added many practical examples and developed his doctrine that the man who denies help to his neighbour is a thief. He attacks many abuses including the hiring of professional prayers:

> If thou give me £1000 to pray for thee, I am no more bound than I was before... I am bound even to love the Turk... And what can I do more for thee if thou gavest me all the world? Where I see need, there can I not but pray, if God's spirit be in me.

The appearance of this book led Wolsey to demand from the Regent of the Netherlands the delivery of three heretics on June 18th. The three were named as Tyndale, Roye and the English merchant Richard Herman. The Regent replied that her council could not send a heretic into another land without examination. Search was made for the three, Tyndale and Roye could not be found. Herman was arrested and thrown into prison. In August Wolsey sent a friar observant of Greenwich, who knew both Roye and Jerome, to help in the search. The English authorities were obviously in the dark about Tyndale's movements.

At the very time when Richard Herman was making his first appearance before the judges in Antwerp, and when Wolsey's spies were hunting for Lutherans in the Rhineland, Tyndale was putting his most powerful piece of writing through the press at Hoochstraten. This was *The Obedience of a Christian Man*. The work is an answer to the charges brought against the Reformers, of teaching disobedience to princes and stirring up rebellion. Just as in Wycliffe's days, the Peasants Revolt of 1381 had been blamed upon him, so now the peasants war in Germany, 1524-5, was laid at Luther's door and Tyndale accused of being an accomplice to rebellion. He therefore answered the charge. In fact he showed that the Reformers were those most obedient to princes - 'The powers that be are ordained of God' was from the Word of God their command. Those who disobeyed were the leaders of the Church who usurped the King's power. In the prologue to the book he says that the prelates tell the kings:

> that we are teaching the people to rise above their princes. It would hardly be wonderful if we were ready to fight for God's Word with the sword; for we are not all perfect and we have been taught as babes to kill Turk and Jew, and to burn heretics for the Pope's cause. Nevertheless it is not so.

Tyndale turns his attack on the Pope and declares that it is the Pope's followers who have caused disobedience, disaffection and rebellion. The Reformers on the other hand teach, what Christ taught, to obey civil powers, and to leave all to the vengeance of God.

In the course of the book, Tyndale takes up an idea of Wycliffe that the king should be the final authority in the Church, under Christ, and not the prelates. The book fell into the hands of King Henry VIII who had just quarrelled with the Pope over the dissolution of his marriage.

Tyndale also said that the prelates should not hold high office in the state, but that laymen should be appointed. Henry, whether taking his cue from this book or not, appointed Sir Thomas More as Lord Chancellor when Wolsey was deposed. Sir Thomas More was the most distinguished layman in the land.

The tone of this book is sharper than anything Tyndale had so far written. The persecution of his friends in England was having an effect upon his mind. Fiercely and with unsparing zeal he strikes at the abuses, the evils and vices of the Church. Yet he is no mere destroyer; he wishes to purge and rebuild. He loves his country and grieves for the common people, misgoverned and robbed of their rights. There is a charming story of how Anne Boleyn found her maid reading this book and brought it to the king. Mozley thinks that the reading of this book by Henry hastened the ruin of Cardinal Wolsey. Henry obviously thought it was a book for all kings to read, but he took from it what he wanted to hear and his support did not save it from being condemned. Sir Thomas More called it a 'holy book of disobedience, whereby we were taught to disobey Christ's holy Catholic Church'. The ecclesiastical authorities discovered heresies therein and it was denounced by royal proclamation.

Further Translation

Moving between Antwerp and Hamburg, partly to escape the vigilant eyes of More's spies, Tyndale continued his translation work. He had been perfecting his Hebrew and during 1529 to 1530, he continued the translation of parts of the Old Testament which he had started in Wittenberg. The evidence suggests that he started early in 1527 on part of the Pentateuch. He worked quickly despite the fact that he was so often on the run. In 1528 he had a particularly difficult year. He was in trouble over the printing of *The Parable of the Wicked Mammon* in April; in June, the Regent began to search for him in the Netherlands; in September, Rinck and West were on his track in Antwerp, Cologne and Frankfurt. In January 1529, his name was mentioned in open court as a heretic and a rebel; in February, a fresh hunt was planned.

It is about this period that Foxe, not always a reliable historian, tells a colourful story. He is writing in 1570, but the evidence shows that it was substantially correct.

After writing that Tyndale finished the fifth book of Moses in 1528, he tells of a misadventure and a meeting with Coverdale:

> Upon the coast of Holland Tyndale suffered shipwreck, by the which he lost all his books, writings and copies, and so was

compelled to begin all again anew, to his hindrance and doubling of his labours. Thus, having lost by that ship both money, his copies and time, he came in another ship to Hamburg, where at his appointment Master Coverdale tarried for him and helped him in the translating the whole five books of Moses, from Easter to December, in the house of a worshipful widow, Mistress Margaret van Emmerson, anno 1529, a great sweating sickness being the same time in the town.

Foxe tells us that he then returned to Antwerp.

From this time onwards, Antwerp became his headquarters. England was busy with other things; the king's divorce, the fall of Wolsey, parliament was once more assembled. He felt safe and once again printed at Hoochstraten. At Antwerp he was in easy touch with England; he could transport his books, welcome refugees, follow the course of the conflict. The other English Reformers sought the safer places in Germany, waiting until the tide turned. Tyndale remained at his post, knowing that the slightest change of wind could make him vulnerable. By 1530, about midsummer, the five books of Moses were freely circulating in England together with Tyndale's New Testament. The Bishop of Norwich wrote in panic to Henry, who summoned to the palace at Westminster an assembly of thirty bishops and divines to discuss the whole question of 'Lutheran Books'. The list included Warham, Tonstall, Gardiner, More, Latimer (both Hugh and William), John Bell (Tyndale's old opponent), Crome, and Sampson. Sir Thomas More took the lead in these discussions and a public instrument was issued on 24th May 1530. It condemned the circulation of Old and New Testaments in English (although some, probably including Hugh Latimer, were in favour of an English Bible) and several propositions from Tyndale's books. The next day, the king entered the Star Chamber and let his will be known. He had taken the advice of his divines and issued a royal proclamation in June. In that proclamation he denounced both Tyndale's books as 'blasphemous and pestiferous English books', imported into the realm to pervert faith and stir up sedition and disobedience.

While the king denounced the present translations of the Bible and thought that it would do more harm than good to have the two Testaments in the common tongue, he promised that if the people 'forsake all perverse, erroneous and seditious opinions', he may consider arranging for an accurate translation to be made by 'great, learned and catholic persons'. There followed the various burning of the books, particularly at St Peter's Cross by Bishop Tonstall. The bishop's thorough purchase of

Bibles to burn provided much needed funds for revision of the New Testament and the Pentateuch.

On the matter of the king's divorce, Tyndale condemned it on biblical grounds. He also produced a most untypical book called, *The Practice of Prelates*, a savage book which can only be excused by the treatment he had received. Most of his friends could have wished that Tyndale spent his time in translation rather than such polemic. However, although the king condemned it at once, he unexpectedly withdrew his displeasure a little later. Thomas Cromwell, who had succeeded Thomas More, saw in such an author a useful ally. He tried to win the author over to his side. He probably thought that every man had his price, but he had misjudged his man.

Instead, Tyndale turned to more translation. He added Jonah in May 1531 and then selected those four Old Testament passages in the liturgy which take the place of the Epistle in Advent. These latter were published in November 1534 and there is a strong tradition that he left behind a draft translation of the historical books, Joshua to II Chronicles. It is said, with no clear evidence, that his disciple Rogers included these in the so-called *Matthew's Bible* of 1537.

A Call to England

It was probably Thomas Cromwell who persuaded Henry that Tyndale would be a useful man to support his separation from Rome. The agent employed was Stephen Vaughan, a merchant adventurer of Antwerp. Like many of the merchants, he was sympathetic to reform. Thomas Cromwell promoted him and he soon became the king's factor in the Netherlands. Henry had persuaded the prelates that his divorce was legitimate and they had, albeit reluctantly, approved the marriage to Anne Boleyn. Politically, Henry had separated from Rome, but he was anxious to present himself as a good catholic and truly Defender of the Faith. This meant that heretics were still burnt and a friend of Tyndale could be in danger. It was a delicate mission to approach Tyndale, which he did in 1531. His correspondence shows that he was greatly impressed by him, but he could not persuade him. The king's guarantee of safe-conduct was not very safe, and so many of Tyndale's friends were being put to death for heresy. Vaughan pays a very high tribute to Tyndale. In one of his communications to Cromwell he writes:

> It is unlikely to get Tyndale into England, when he daily hears so many things from hence which feareth him ... The man is of a

greater knowledge than the king's highness doth take him for; which well appears by his works. Would God he were in England.

It soon became clear to Henry that he was not going to get this man as a penitent seeking the king's pardon. Yet Cromwell persisted. Eventually Stephen Vaughan met him at a secret meeting outside Antwerp. Again, Vaughan insisted upon the quality of this man. But Henry had no mind to receive him as a hero, as a great man unjustly persecuted, as more orthodox than the bishops of his realm.

In the course of this fruitless effort to get Tyndale as an ally of the king, grateful to him and therefore doing his pleasure we have a glimpse of William Tyndale which tells most eloquently of his one consuming passion. It occurs in Vaughan's last letter, when he tells of a moving appeal to Tyndale which brought tears to his eyes at the thought of returning home from exile.

> I assure you, he said, if it would stand with the king's most gracious pleasure to grant only a bare text of the scripture to be put forth among the people, like as is put forth among the subjects of the emperor in these parts, and of other Christian princes, be it of the translation of what person soever shall please his majesty, I shall immediately make faithful promise never to write more, nor abide two days in these parts after the same; but immediately to repair into his realm.

But Henry did not want terms; he wanted repentance and tore up the letter which brought him tidings of William Tyndale.

In England the persecution gathered strength. Thomas More cross-questioned every prisoner whom he held at his mercy about Tyndale. If Lutheranism was to be stamped out, the priests and bishops and Thomas More knew that they must have Tyndale burnt.

Tyndale and More

The controversy between William Tyndale and Sir Thomas More was one of the most famous literary battles of history. The initiative came from Bishop Tonstall of London. He was utterly failing to stem the flood of Lutheranism, despite his banning of the books. He therefore relied upon Sir Thomas More to enter the lists against these doctrines. He gave him permission to receive and read the forbidden books and appealed to him:

> Go forward then to this holy work; succour the church, and win for yourself an immortal name, the eternal glory in heaven; and to this end I give you licence to keep and to read books of that nature.

Tyndale is not mentioned in the letter to More, but his New Testament, carefully marked by Tonstall himself and his *Introduction to Romans* were certainly in the parcel sent to him with the request which was made as early as 7th March 1528. More had not long to wait before *Mammon* and *Obedience* arrived from Antwerp. By June 1529, Sir Thomas More had written '*A dialogue of Sir Thomas More knight* . . . wherein be treated divers matters, as of the veneration and worship of images and relics, praying to saints and going on pilgrimage, with many other things touching the pestilent sect of Luther and Tyndale, by the one begun in Saxony, and by the other labored to be brought into England'. They had long titles in those days! The defect of the *Dialogue* is its refusal to admit the moral corruption of the Church of the day. He attacks Tyndale most vehemently as having 'sucked out the most poison that he could find in all Luther's books' and 'in many things far passed his master, running forth so mad for malice, that he fareth as though he heard not his own voice'. Tyndale, he says, has wilfully mistranslated, deceived blind unlearned people; his life as evil as his teaching. He is a beast who teaches vice, a forewalker of antichrist, a devil's limb and so on.

Tyndale replied and published his reply in July 1531. There is a bitterness about Tyndale's reply which shows that he had expected something better from a man like Thomas More who had been a friend of Erasmus and a humanist, a brilliant writer and thinker, who knew better than he wrote in this pamphlet. He can only think that More is betraying his own high standards for the sake of gain. He compares him to Judas who did what he did, 'not for love of the high priest', but to obtain what he thirsted for. When he accuses More of doing it for money, he is unfair and knows it. Just as More read into Luther's marriage 'only a token of lechery and the hollowness of his religious profession', so Tyndale saw the love of money where it was not.

The style of Tyndale's *Answer* lacks the grace of More's *Dialogue*. It is plain and workmanlike, terse, direct, and vigorous. He rises to some eloquence when answering More's question, How do we know what the scripture is unless an infallible church tells us:

> Who taught the eagles to spy out their prey? Even so the children of God spy out their father; Christ's elect spy out their lord, and trace out the paths of his feet and follow; yea, though he go upon the plain and liquid water, which will receive no step, and yet there they find out his foot: his elect know him, but the world knoweth him not.

Tyndale's defence reached More in late summer 1531. Despite the pressures of high office, he began to prepare his reply at once and it was sent in the early months of 1532. It consisted of three volumes, *The Confrontation of Tyndale*. A year later six volumes were added. Tyndale took no further notice, but a lawyer named Saintgerman responded with an attack upon the clergy for their treatment of Lutherans. In reply, More published his *Apology* in 1533, which defended the clergy and continued the attacks on 'Tyndale, Frith and the rest of the brethren', as he mockingly called them. The debate between More and Saintgerman continued until the end of the year. Tyndale kept out of it except for a short work on the Lord's Supper to help Frith to answer the charges against him. It was becoming clear to Tyndale that while More began the controversy on a high level, he was degenerating in his style and temper until he did not deserve an answer. There was indeed a nobler side to More but he never showed it in his controversies with the reformers.

In the heat of the debate it is clear that More recognised the weakness of the position he was defending. Tyndale was able to remain more calm although he too could be stung into abuse. What he did do was to make certain permanent contributions which are still part of our spirituality today and honoured even by those Churches which have remained in communion with Rome. Tyndale emphasised the spiritual side of religion, attacking the medieval emphasis on bodily acts ordained by the Church. His, was an inward approach which made external ceremonies secondary. They are not abolished, but they are used in obedience to the spirit of the Christian man. As regards the authority of the Bible, Tyndale does not advocate a slavish fundamentalism, but instead of dependence on such fantasies as ceremonies passed on by word of mouth from generation to generation from the apostles, he maintains that 'nothing ought to be considered to be of the essence of the Christian religion, unless it is found in the New Testament'. Tyndale's treatment of the Bible is more liberal than More's. Tyndale's most damaging criticism was of the Church of his day, which he maintained was not the true Church, 'it had abandoned the teaching of the Gospel and disowned its Lord'.

Like Wycliffe before him Tyndale soon discovered that words could not reform the Church. There could hardly be more competent protagonists in a controversy than William Tyndale and Sir Thomas More, but the great debate settled nothing. If words could have reformed the Church Erasmus would have done it. The Church needed acts and perhaps it had to have martyrs. A few years later, Thomas More died for his beliefs, but they were personal and not for the reform of the Church. If he had taken the lead for reform, this great humanist might have failed; he might even have died as a heretic a year or two earlier than he did; but he would have found himself less frequently in situations where he was expected to do, and often did, things inconsistent with his deepest principles. More should have been with Tyndale, not against him.

The Last Years

If the king could not tempt him on to his side, he would have William Tyndale at his mercy. Through his ambassador he demanded the handing over of this arch-heretic, and this time he did not go through the Regent, but the Emperor who was in the Netherlands

Tyndale continued to write while the hunt was on. Happily for him, the Emperor and Henry were not on the best of terms. Although Henry quoted the Treaty of Cambrai, which he said applied to Tyndale who was sending seditious literature into England, the Emperor was opposed to Henry in the question of his divorce. Henry was accusing the Emperor, Charles V, of inciting the Pope to recall the case for trial at Rome. Thus, Charles insisted upon examining the case of Tyndale himself, because he presumed he was being persecuted like so many others for his disapproval of the divorce. Since Charles refused to hand him over, Henry had to use his agents again to kidnap him. Elyot was the man this time and he had no more success than his predecessors. His bribes were of no effect. Tyndale escaped from his enemies. It is naturally difficult to discover where he lived during these last years, but he was probably never very far from Antwerp. Tyndale suffered much from the accusations against him. He cared for the goodwill of others and some of the calumny was very wounding. He did not marry and was denied a family in his exile, but was also spared the possibility of his enemies getting at him through wife or children. He writes of women with a noble tenderness which was unusual in those days:

> The preciousest gift that a man hath of God in this world is the true heart of his wife, to abide by him in wealth and woe, and to bear all his fortunes with him ... Let every man have his wife, and think her the fairest and the best-conditioned, and every woman her husband too.

That joy was denied William Tyndale by the nature of his life. The news from England was ever more disturbing. He heard of friend after friend burned at the stake or forced into an ignominious recantation. In two and a quarter years there were ten martyrdoms and five of them were friends of Tyndale. One of his dearest friends, John Frith, ventured into England and was soon arrested. A book of Tyndale's was discovered on him. After lingering in the Tower for months and a prolonged trial in which all the information that could be gleaned about Tyndale was extracted, John Frith died at the stake.

William Tyndale wrote to him and one hopes he received the letter before he perished. It would have heartened the martyr. Tyndale passed the last months of his liberty occupied with expounding the scripture and preaching, with deeds of charity and with writing. He was joined in Antwerp by John Rogers in October 1534. They were good companions. Among the scholarly work which is referred to we may be sure that he not only revised his New Testament (the second and third edition appeared in those nine months) but also worked on the Old Testament. It looked better in England too. On 19th December 1534, the Upper House of the Convocation of Canterbury passed a resolution, begging the king to have a new translation of the Bible made. Nothing came of it at the time for various reasons, but it led Tyndale to pray for the king of England.

The End

In October 1535, Coverdale's Bible was published on the continent with the approval of Thomas Cromwell and dedicated to the king. It was permitted to circulate in England. The tide was turning at last, but just at this moment of hope, Tyndale fell victim to the machination of his enemies. It was a friend who betrayed him. He lodged for about a year with Thomas Poyntz, an Englishman, who kept in Antwerp a house of merchants, among whom was the son of a customer from Poole: Henry Phillips, with his servant. He made friends with Tyndale and won his confidence. Thomas Poyntz was suspicious, but not Tyndale. Eventually, in a way colourfully told by Foxe in his *Book of Martyrs*, Tyndale was betrayed thinking that he went out to dine with his friend Henry Phillips. It was a mean trick. William Tyndale was now taken to the castle of Vilford, eighteen miles from Antwerp, in the custody of the Emperor, where he remained until his death.

The story of Henry Phillips' Judas act becomes more and more sordid as we read the papers that came to light a generation ago. He had robbed his father and ruined himself in gambling. The only way to retrieve his honour was to obtain a large sum of money. He took his bribe for betraying Tyndale, with no cause to support, but simply for the money. He had no liking for Henry and the king was probably not involved. The main engineer of the plot was almost certainly Stokesley, at that time Bishop of London. His zeal for persecution and his cruelty were well known and on his deathbed he boasted of how many heretics he had deprived of life. Henry Phillips was the miserable agent and he played the Judas to high priest Stokesley.

Tyndale was arrested on 21st May 1535. Thomas Cromwell tried to save him, but his royal master had not forgotten the snub. He remained in prison for more than sixteen months and his goods were confiscated to pay for his keep. Henry was meanwhile displeasing everybody. For five years he had been laying heavy hands upon the riches of the Church, his divorce of Catherine had touched the honour of her nephew, the Emperor, he cared nothing for reform and was definitely lukewarm in Tyndale's case. He had once been prepared to use Tyndale as a tool against the Papal party, but he would not press his cause or risk anything to save him. Fisher and More were even now about to be executed; he had sent men to Tyburn for denying the royal supremacy, others to Smithfield for heresy against the sacraments. Within a few days of Tyndale's arrest, fourteen Anabaptists had been sent to the stake in England. Thomas Cromwell was cautious. There was no intervention from England and William Tyndale was tried, degraded and burned at the stake. His last words were, 'Lord, open the king of England's eyes'. Early in October 1536, Tyndale was strangled and burnt. At the end of his book on Tyndale, Mozley recalls the bargain Tyndale drove with the king in 1531 and comments:

> In 1531 Tyndale had proposed a bargain to the king: he would be silent if the king would grant free course in his realm to an English Bible, by whosoever translated. Silent, did he say? Well he is silent now, silenced by the stern halter of the executioner; his part in the bargain is now fulfilled. But neither does the king's part tarry long; the free and open Bible stands at the door; the fight is all but won; William Tyndale has not lived and died in vain.

4. Miles Coverdale and the Great Bible

On 17th April, Sir Thomas More, the great champion of orthodoxy against all heresies and the leading contraversialist opposed to Tyndale, was arrested and committed to the Tower. He was executed in the following year on St Thomas' Eve (6th July, 1535.)

William Tyndale was arrested on 23rd May 1535, kidnapped in Antwerp. He was executed in the following year, 6th October 1536. Henry, who had once thought of using Tyndale to argue his cause, made but feeble efforts to save him. The two protagonists who had faithfully pursued their course both died in much the same manner after long imprisonment, except that More was beheaded and Tyndale strangled and burned. It was dangerous to be either a devout Catholic or a true Protestant in Henry's England. Only time-servers were safe.

The First Printed English Bible

While the two great protagonists were in prison with little hope of release, except by death, Miles Coverdale had the honour to produce the first English Printed Bible. It was a large black-letter folio, first issued in 1535 in Cologne. Conditions in England were more favourable to a Protestant Bible than 10 years before. Henry had finally broken with the Pope and the Upper House of Convocation of the Province of Canterbury had petitioned the king in December 1534 that an English translation be made by authorised translators.

Coverdale might have met Tyndale at Cambridge, but he certainly met him in Hamburg in 1529 and worked with him on the translation of the Pentateuch. He was an Augustinian, like Luther, who gave up his orders. He was a Yorkshireman like Wycliffe, educated however at Cambridge. He was born in 1488 and lived into his eighties.

Coverdale's first edition was dedicated to Henry VIII and when the second edition appeared, it was printed by an English printer, Nycolson of Southwark, it bore on the title page, 'Set forth with the Kinges most gracious licence'. That was in 1537.

Henry probably did not know how much he was licensing Tyndale, upon whom Coverdale relied heavily. In the New Testament, Tyndale's version is the basis for Coverdale's, and to a certain extent also the Pentateuch and Jonah. Coverdale revised all this with the help of Zwingli's German translation in Zurich, a Latin version by Pagninus, the Vulgate and Luther. In his preface, he disclaims any originality as a translator and he does not seem to have attempted a translation from the original languages. Dr Alfred Pollard says of him that 'the completion of an English Bible was reserved for a man of far less scholarship than Tyndale, but an equally happy style! Instead of attempting a new translation from the Hebrew and the Greek he used the available Latin, German and English versions with judgement. In those parts of the Old Testament where Tyndale had not translated, he appears to have done a direct translation from the Zurich German Bible. His one originality was to remove the non-canonical books from the Old Testament and place them in an Appendix as *The Apocrypha*'. To a generation brought up on the Authorised Version, the style of Coverdale sounds strange, although no stranger than Tyndale's. Both are easier to follow if read with a Yorkshire accent! An example often quoted is from Ecclesiastes 11: 'Send thy victuals over the waters, and so shalt thou find them again after many years', which sounds stiff compared with the AV, 'Cast thy bread upon the waters, and thou shalt find it after many days'. But perhaps it is only a matter of use, because Coverdale's Psalms sing well after centuries of *The Book of Common Prayer*.

A Career in Tudor England

The changing fortunes of a faithful Christian scholar in Tudor England are well illustrated by the long life of Miles Coverdale. He was born and brought up in the reign of Henry VII. Like Luther, he became an Augustinian and was attached to their house at Cambridge. He was there when the young Norman student, Peter de Valence, wrote his offensive graffiti on the notice advertising Indulgences. He could hardly fail to compare this with Luther's attack on Indulgences. The Augustinians had a good grapevine throughout Europe. At some stage he left the order, but we do not know when. He seems to have spent a lot of his life in exile from England. In 1528, he left Catholic England and went to Germany. It was in Hamburg that he met Tyndale and helped in his Old Testament translations. He returned in 1535, when Henry VIII had separated England from papal control and was favourable to the Protestants. For five years, which corresponded with the ascendancy of Thomas Cromwell, he lived in England. Unlike Sir Thomas More, he had no difficulty with the oath of allegiance to Henry. He denounced the authority of the Bishop of Rome over England and accepted Henry as 'immediately under Christ, the supreme head' of the Church in the realm of England. In this he was at one with Wycliffe, who was before his time, and with Tyndale his contemporary. Coverdale was seven years older than Tyndale on the usual reckoning of Tyndale's date of birth, but of course he outlived him by many years. Miles Coverdale was in England during Thomas Cromwell's activity in the suppression of the monasteries and no doubt approved, though he may have wondered how far Henry intended to go. It was not that England was becoming more liberal, simply that the Church had changed its head. The Pope's refusal to recognise the divorce of Catherine and thereby the marriage to Anne Boleyn cost him his rights in England. This is made very clear in the long text of the Oath of Allegiance (1534), which was binding upon all who held office in the Church. It included such words as:

> That from henceforth we will promise or give, or cause to be given, to no foreign emperor, king, prince, or prelate, nor to the Bishop of Rome (whom they call the Pope) fidelity or obedience in word or writing, simple or by oath; but at all times, in every case and condition, we will follow and observe, and to our power defend the parts of your royal majesty and of your successors and we will sincerely and heartily perform fidelity and obedience to your royal majesty alone, as to our supreme prince and head of the English Church.

There is much more in this vein. In his defence Henry would have maintained that he was doing no more than necessary to defend his throne. The old medieval concept of excommunication put a throne in jeopardy and the Pope had declared Henry's marriage to Catherine valid and subsequently excommunicated him.

Miles Coverdale saw the logic of this and it caused him no crisis of conscience.

During those five momentous years in England as the king took command of his church, Coverdale was safe from persecution and successful in his work of study and translation. But his sorrow as well as his triumph came in those five years. The arrest and execution of William Tyndale could not fail to give him great sorrow and also make him wonder how safe he was himself from his uncertain monarch. How far he exerted his influence to save Tyndale is not known, but Henry did make some attempt to get Tyndale to England.

Coverdale saw his own danger in 1539 when the Act for Abolishing Diversity of Opinions was passed. It was made a criminal offence, punishable by burning, for anyone to voice any denial of the old creed or any contempt for the old Mass. It was clear that Henry did not want change, except in the authority of the head, 'immediately under Christ'. He was still a supporter of the old religion. Coverdale, like Tyndale earlier, was too much of a Lutheran to live safely in a Catholic land. He therefore sought safety in exile once again.

Subsequent events showed the wisdom of his decision to leave. The Act was not a dead letter. In July 1546, a woman was burned for denying the old Mass. On Christmas Eve that same year, Henry spoke to the House of Lords and warmed to the role of 'defender of the faith'. A too familiar treatment of the Bible fell under his displeasure and Coverdale would certainly have suffered under the new Catholic regime.

Henry was unpredictable. He appeared to be restoring the old order, except for its head, but he did not make provision for a Catholic England in the future. His council which he thought would rule England after his death did not include Stephen Gardiner, the obvious choice as leader of the Catholic party. The Duke of Norfolk was in the Tower awaiting execution for high treason: his heir, the Earl of Surrey had already been executed. Both were staunch Catholics. Henry's last wife was Catherine Parr, a convinced Protestant. He knew that, at his death, his balanced council would not succeed and that he had left an heir whose mind was formed by Protestant educators. When Henry VIII died on 28th January 1547, Miles Coverdale knew that he could pack his bags for his return, because England would be Protestant under Edward VI. He was appointed Bishop of Exeter and for two years enjoyed his diocese and great influence as the translator of the Bible. Other Bibles had replaced his, *Matthew's Bible* (1535), the *Great Bible* (1539-1541) - but these were merely attempts to improve on what he had done, by more authorised translators. He was consulted about the later editions of the *Great Bible* and was happy in England so long as the Protector Somerset guided the young king Edward VI.

After rebellions in various places, Somerset fell. Warwick took the reins of power after butchering the rebels and it looked as though he would bring in a new wave of change. It was difficult to know whose side anyone was on. David Edwards in his second volume of *Christian England* quotes Sir William Paget as saying to Somerset, that 'the use of the old religion is forbidden by a law and the use of the new is not yet printed on eleven of the twelve parts in the realm'.

Archbishop Cranmer had undertaken, during the period of Coverdale's favour in England to produce a new Prayer Book and Coverdale had his part in this, which was officially authorised by Parliament in 1552. A few months later in July of that year, Cranmer produced 42 articles of belief, the parent of the 39 articles, which take the place of a Confession in the Church of England. But Coverdale was uneasy. Protestantism in England seemed to hang upon the thread of the life of the weakly young king, who was only 16 years old. The succession was in dispute and the year of Edward's death was a year of crisis. Edward VI died 6 July 1553. The succession passed briefly and tragically to Lady Jane Grey. Then Mary Tudor, from whom Protestants had most to fear succeeded to the throne. Coverdale went again into exile and was lucky to escape burning. Almost three hundred English men and women were executed as Protestants in the five years of Mary's reign. The first to die was John Rogers, one of the translators of the English Bible. He was burned at Smithfield on 4th February 1555. Coverdale did not return until Elizabeth was on the throne. He was an old man when he came home and too extreme a Puritan to be of use to Elizabeth who was intent upon uniting the nation.

The Making of the Great Bible

The king had licensed the 'English Bible' in 1537 and this left the bishops free, should they so wish, to commend it to their priests and people. Thomas Cromwell was anxious that they should do so. The first to act was Latimer, who held a visitation of his diocese in the autumn of 1537 and issued a series of injunctions.

In the spring and early summer of 1538, several bishops put out similar injunctions about the English Bible. No particular Bible was specified, but the Coverdale Bible was usually chosen. The poorer priests would prefer the Coverdale quarto, because it was cheaper than the Matthew Bible, which was larger and better printed, more suitable for reading in Church.

As the demand for English Bibles grew it became evident that large scale printing was needed and some guidance had to be given about 'comment'. The Matthew Bible in particular was printed by Grafton with lengthy Prologues to each book and there are several examples of bishops complaining that it was not always clear when the Scripture was being read and when the Prologues. For this reason it was decided to issue a recognized translation with as few comments as possible. This was to be called The Great Bible. On 5th September 1538, Thomas Cromwell, as vice-regent for the king in spiritual matters issued the most famous 'order' in the history of the English Bible:

> That ye shall provide on this side the feast of All Saints next coming, one book of the whole Bible of the largest volume in English, and

at the same set up in some convenient place within the said church that ye have cure of, where your parishioners may most commodiously resort to the same and read it; the charges of such book shall be rateably borne between you, the parson, and the parishioners aforesaid, that is to say, the one half by you and the other half by them.

Item, that ye shall discourage no man privily or apertly from the reading or hearing of the said Bible, but shall expressly provoke, stir and exhort every person to read the same, as that which is the very lively word of God, admonishing them nevertheless to avoid all contention and altercation therein and to refer the explication of obscure passages to men of higher judgement.

When he drafted the injunction, Cromwell must have had The Great Bible in mind.

Miles Coverdale was the obvious choice of editor for The Great Bible, although he was to take the Matthew Bible (which really meant Tyndale) as his basis for the new version, not his own. The printing was entrusted to Grafton and Whitchurch, who had produced the attractive edition of Matthew's Bible which Henry liked. They were chosen for their skill, but also for their devotion. This work would not be a business deal. They would have to invest a great deal of their own money in it. It was printed in Paris where better paper was more readily available and more skilled workers. Thomas Cromwell himself invested about £400 in the project. The printing was not without danger. Charges of heresy could still be brought against the printing of unauthorised material in France. Cromwell persuaded Henry to write to the king of France to permit and license one of his subjects to 'imprint the Bible in English within the University of Paris'. A copy of a licence, bearing no date, is preserved in the British Museum, granted by the king of France to Grafton and Whitchurch, empowering them to print the Bible both in Latin and English, provided that the book so printed contained no 'private or unlawful opinions'. Coverdale joined Grafton in Paris and supervised the printing. From time to time they sent sample sheets to Cromwell and occasionally sought his help against those who were seeking to hinder the enterprise. A Bible in the vernacular still had many enemies and its printing was a dangerous project. It was also costly. In June they were anxious about money and their own safety. The troubles flared up and died down. Cromwell was reluctant to act, hoping that such troubles as the printers had would soon blow over. In October Grafton sent copies of the sheets so far printed to Cromwell for safekeeping; in December he sent more by the hand of

Hereford with the request that he would be the 'defender and keeper thereof; to the intent that if these men proceed in their cruelty against us and confiscate the rest, these at least will be safe'.

Four days later the blow fell. The inquisitor of France issued an order condemning the printing of vernacular scripture on 17th December. Francis Regnault, Coverdale's printer in Paris was summoned to appear before him together with certain unnamed persons to answer the charge of printing an English Bible and forbidding them to proceed further.

This was the end of the printing in Paris, but it also meant that the whole stock of printing so far was confiscated by the French authorities.

Cromwell now tried to recover the confiscated papers and explained to the French ambassador that £400 of his own money was tied up in the enterprise. There was a diplomatic incident in which Church and State were both involved. The Church was for burning and had its way; but the State enabled the English to save some copies and the equipment, bringing these with some workers to England. And so printing began in London, but the large stock of books and sheets were not recovered at once if at all. There is some indication that they might have been recovered by November 1539, when supplies in England were available in quantity, but even this is not certain.

The Circulation of The Great Bible

Once it was available, the injunction of 1538 could be obeyed. The only problem was cost and Thomas Cromwell did his best to keep the price down to 10 shillings by giving the printers a virtual monopoly. The Bible was now available, but there were soon complaints that it was neglected. Where the priest was hostile to the vernacular scripture and there was no active lay demand for it, when few parishioners could read, there was a temptation in remote parishes to defer the purchase of an English Bible. If it was purchased for fear of royal displeasure, it could often be kept out of sight. Richard Tracy in 1546 complained that the priests and henchmen would 'pluck the bible into the quire or into some pew where poor men durst not presume to come. Yea, there is no small number of churches that hath no Bible at all'.

Edmund Bonner, the Bishop of London fulfilled the promise made at his consecration and had six Bibles set up in his Cathedral and chained to the pillars, and over each he placed a placard exhorting all men to read reverently and quietly. Other bishops followed his lead. In the spring of 1540, John Uvedale urged Cromwell to move the King to make an order that every bishop should set up two or three Bibles in his Cathedral, 'as seemly and as ornately as they can deck them, with seats and forms for men of all ages to read and study them'.

Some began to abuse this privilege and Bonner was much annoyed to find 'Protestants' reading aloud and holding services around the Bibles in his Cathedral. One John Porter was imprisoned for this in 1540 and was released later only to be re-arrested in 1542 for heresy.

John Porter died for his belief that the Bible contained the pure doctrine and that the priests had perverted its meaning. He was arrested simply because he disturbed the ordinary services. This could have been dealt with far less drastically. He demonstrated by his reading and preaching that the open Bible led to diversity of interpretations and challenged the authority of the clergy. The diversity troubled the clergy less than the challenge. Those who read the Bible discovered and proclaimed much that contradicted the doctrine and practice of the Church of their day. By the light of its teaching they condemned the mass and many other things that were said and done in the very building where the Bible was read. When Edmund Bonner threatened to withdraw the Bibles he had set up in his Cathedral it was because they had encouraged a rival authority, which threatened the dominance of the priesthood and gave to the laity a new status and a new right of judgement. By 1541, Bonner was appealing to the king to have the Bibles taken out of Churches!

When you read some of the writings of the reformers at that time you cannot help feeling that you are back in Wycliffe's time. William Turner, for example, in 1545 protests against the move made by many of the bishops to have 'English Bibles taken out of the church'. He accuses them of murdering 'one Porter in prison for no other cause but for reading the Bible'. That is a simplification of what happened, but it is a logical deduction. It was his reading which exposed the unbiblical nature of much that went on in the Church. Turner continues by saying that if all they were concerned about was the hindering of their Church services by a loud voice reading the Bible down the nave, he would answer that 'most of your services are not God's service but are made of lying legends and superstitious ceremonies, and what part of them is scripture is unprofitable to the layman, since it is read in Latin'. That was much the same as Wycliffe had said of the friars. So long as Henry reigned the conservatives gained a hold, as they waged war against the English Bible.

Henry supported the conservative bishops against the Protestants. In the end they succeeded in almost completely suppressing the lay reading of the Bible, not only in church, but at any time and place however silently.

The reaction may be said to have started with the Six Articles as early as June 1539. Coverdale with some of his friends saw the danger signs and took refuge abroad a year after this when Thomas Cromwell died. The king did not respond to the bishops' plea to remove the Bibles. Instead he called the clergy together to improve the translation. It was the Convocation of Canterbury that was asked in January 1542 to 'address themselves to the reform of religion and seek to remedy its weaknesses and errors'.

Thomas Cranmer, Archbishop of Canterbury, who had written the Preface to The Great Bible, spoke on January 27th, saying that there were in the English Bible many things needing reformation. He asked the lower house of clergy to examine the Old Testament and the bishops to study the New Testament with a view to making a better translation, free from errors.

At the third session on February 3rd, the Archbishop asked each prelate whether the English Bible could be retained 'without scandal and error and open offence to Christ's faithful people'. The majority replied that it could not. It must first be corrected from the Latin Vulgate. Thereupon they set to work to revise the English translation. Committees were set up for Old and New Testaments. Coverdale was abroad and most of those on the committees were old enemies of the translations of Erasmus and Tyndale. The conservatives were in full cry. Then the king interrupted the proceedings and, much to the disapproval of the clergy, referred the translation to the two universities. Nothing much came of this; both Oxford and Cambridge were under the influence of the conservatives who opposed the Reformation. It pleased them to keep the revision of the Bible going as long as possible while the people were denied access to their English Bible.

April 1543 was a dark month. Then the act entitled, *An Act for the Advancement of True Religion and for the Abolishment of the Contrary* was passed by parliament. It forbade 'all manner of books of the Old and New Testament in English, being of the crafty, false and untrue translation of Tyndale'. Other Bibles and New Testaments 'not being of Tyndale's translation' are not forbidden, provided all comment is cut from them. No unlicensed person may expound the Bible to others in any church or open assembly. Because, as the Act says, many of the lower sort have abused the freedom of the vernacular scripture, it was laid down that after 1st July, 'no women, nor artificers, prentices, journeymen, serving men of the degrees of yeomen and under, husbandmen nor labourers shall read the Bible or New Testament in English to himself or any other person, privately or openly'.

The penalty for this was one month in prison.

The printers of The Great Bible, Grafton and Whitchurch with six other printers appeared before the privy council and were sent to prison. This was 16th November 1538. Miles Coverdale had done well to flee the country.

In some illogical way, Henry's order for the placing of Bibles in Church was not rescinded! It did however, become more and more dangerous to possess a Bible or to read it, if it could be shown to be influenced by Tyndale or Coverdale. A proposal was made in Parliament in 1545 to limit English scripture to priests (again the shadow of Wycliffe fell over the house), but it was not passed. However, on 8th July 1546, a royal proclamation was issued ordering that after 31st August no man should have 'the text of the New Testament of Tyndale's or Coverdale's translation in English . . . '. All such books were to be handed in to the authorities and openly burned before October 1st. Some copies of The Great Bible were even taken from Churches and publicly burned. This was not according to the proclamation, but Henry died secure in the knowledge that the Catholic party within the Church of England would say masses for his soul. He was not so sure that the development under his son would follow the lines he had been following in his latter years. The old king died in January 1547. He left a divided Church, but somehow he had prevented the divisions from tearing England apart as such divisions had torn apart countries of Europe. Now his strong hand had gone. The new king was a minor and everything depended upon the Protector.

Somerset and King Edward VI

At Henry's death, Hertford rode at once to Hartford Castle where the boy King Edward was cared for and brought him on 31st January 1547 to the Tower of London where Archbishop Cranmer and others were waiting. The Council held a meeting at the Tower and decided to entrust the supreme authority and office of Protector to Hertford, who was later created Duke of Somerset. This meant that power passed to the Protestants.

Almost 8 years before, the conservatives under Gardiner had recovered their power and passed the act of Six Articles, a cruel law which endangered the lives of every true reformer. It had driven Coverdale into exile. On 30th July 1540, Thomas Cromwell had been sent to the block on Tower Hill without trial, Robert Barnes and two other reformers had been burned at the stake at Smithfield. Miles Coverdale would not have been safe. He fled overseas with many of his friends. Now that nightmare was over and he could return.

The Second Exile: 1540-1548

Miles Coverdale spent the eight years of his second exile profitably. He appears to have gone direct to Strasbourg and stayed there three years. There, he and his wife received much kindness from the wife of John Calvin, who was also in exile in that city! He spent much of his time translating books from Latin and German into English (two by Bullinger.) He also wrote a defence of his martyred friend Robert Barnes. Through a friendship with Martin Bucer's secretary, Conrad Hubert, he obtained a living in September 1545 at Bergzabern, a small town about 40 miles from Strasbourg, as assistant minister and headmaster of the town school.

In the course of these three years he appears to have taken the degree of doctor of Divinity and also paid a visit to Denmark.

As Strasbourg had no university as yet, he had to do his studies for his doctorate at Tübingen. The chief minister at Bergzabern was badly in need of an assistant and welcomed Coverdale with extravagant praise:

> I can never sufficiently thank the good and great God that by command of our prince our magistrates have given me Doctor Miles Coverdale as colleague at a good salary. He is a man of singular piety and incomparable diligence, a watchful and scrupulous performer of every duty of religion. Alleluia.

The name of this chief minister was Nicolaus Thomae and the two men formed a friendship. They both disapproved of Luther's violent attacks upon Zwingli and Oecolampadius on the Sacraments. Coverdale was ill in 1546 but seems to have been successfully treated by a Scottish doctor in Neustadt. He was much consulted by those fellow clergy who had misgivings or problems to resolve. In July 1546, he was asked to judge the propriety of an aged and widowed minister of Zweibrucken marrying a young girl. He pronounced in favour, but expressed his amusement at the determination of the young bride for whom the match had many advantages. He was an attentive headmaster, caring much for the welfare of his boys and even begging money for the fees of those who were poor. As we read his letters we soon discover how well he settled into the country of exile and how much he was trusted and respected. A letter written by a fellow exile Richard Hilles to Bullinger expresses what his English friends thought of him:

> 15th April 1545: I think you have some knowledge of him.. He is called Miles Coverdale, and indeed he is well loved and honoured by all the ministers of the word and the other learned men of this region. He is headmaster of the grammar school at Bergzabern...

where in his leisure hours, for the wider propagation of the kingdom of Christ, he translates into English various religious writings, partly yours, partly of other scholars, and this greatly benefits and promotes the salvation of those common persons who are eager for the truth. He is of the number of those who, like Moses, desire rather to suffer exile and other adversities with the people of God than to enjoy the rewards of wickedness in their native Egypt with a bad conscience.

None the less, he longed for home, but his writings put him daily in bad odour, although he was not as violent as some of his fellow exiles. He was much distressed when his books were condemned by the proclamation of the 8th July 1546 and about a dozen of them including his Bible burnt at St Paul's Cross by Bonner. When Henry VIII died, Coverdale did not at once return home. He waited to be called. The summons came on 26th March 1548. When that came he set off from Frankfurt and wrote to Calvin that he was returning home by invitation. He was in England by 24th June, when he preached the festival sermon for the Merchant Taylors. Quickly he found favour in high places. He became almoner to Queen Catherine Parr, who had taken a new husband and he continued his translation work on Erasmus' *Paraphrases* for her. When she died in September 1548 he preached the funeral sermon, with Lady Jane Grey as chief mourner. A month later we find him at Windsor as royal chaplain and writing a letter to Paul Fagius of Strasbourg, inviting him to England in the name of Cranmer and himself, to escape the persecution beginning to arise in Germany. He was a notable preacher and much in demand for special occasions. In 1549 he preached at St Paul's Cross, when the dean pulled down the sacraments of the high altar; and again a few weeks later when John Champneys, an Anabaptist, recanted.

In 1550-1, he preached two funeral sermons - for Sir John Welford at Little St Bartholomew's and for Lord Wentworth at Westminster Abbey. He was put on the Commission appointed in January 1551 to deal with Anabaptism and other heresies. At the trial of Arian, George van Parris of Mainz, he sat as judge and interpreter. He was actively engaged during the rebellion of the men of Devon and Cornwall against the new Prayer Book. He accompanied Lord Russell who had been sent to quell the rebellion and found scope for his preaching. After the victory of Woodbury Windmill he preached on the field of battle 'and caused a general thanksgiving to be made unto God'. Before the end of August 1549 the rebellion was over, but Coverdale stayed several months in the West Country, helping to pacify the people and doing the work of an absentee bishop. Coverdale earned a reputation for his work in Devon and later in Oxford, where he went to hear the lectures of Peter Martyr on Romans, and did quite a lot of preaching there himself. On 14th August 1551, the see of Exeter fell vacant and Coverdale was nominated. He was consecrated on 30th August at Croydon, enthroned in Exeter on 11th September. He was a good bishop, minding his London duties, sitting in the House of Lords and taking part in the Commission to reform the canon law; but most of his time was spent in his diocese. He was no absentee bishop.

To his servant he was a bishop who did 'most worthily perform the office committed to him; he preached continually upon every holy day, and did read most commonly twice in the week in some church or other within this city'. The servant said much more of his virtues and those of his wife; but he had enemies too. His busy life kept him away from any literary work at that time. So long as Somerset held power, Coverdale was in favour and happy. When Warwick succeeded him, things were less happy and on the death of Edward VI and the succession of Mary he was in real danger.

The Five Dark Years of Mary's Reign

On 6th July 1553 Edward died and Mary ascended the throne. Coverdale soon found himself in trouble. On 22nd August he was summoned to appear before the privy council and later put under house arrest. He was deprived of his bishopric and the absentee Bishop Veasey reinstated at Exeter. He was in extreme danger. Only the persistent entreaties of the king of Denmark saved him from being burned. On 19th February the privy council issued him a passport to Denmark.

During these months of house arrest, he had shown himself a man of courage. He answered Dr Watson's sermon against the reformers which contained the quotable statement: 'you have the word, but we have the sword'. When twelve of his captive brethren drew up a statement of their belief, he ranged himself with them and added his name: 'To these things above said do I, Miles Coverdale, late of Exon, consent and agree with my afflicted brethren, being prisoners - with mine own hand'.

Coverdale stayed no more than a few weeks in Denmark. The king was generous to him and also offered him a benefice. But he refused because of his ignorance of the language. Instead he went to Germany to serve his afflicted brethren. He was now 67 years old. At first he went to Wesel and served as chaplain to a community of Englishmen for a few months. He was invited to take up his previous work in Bergzabern and readily accepted. He left Wesel early in September and travelled via Frankfurt to arrive in Strasbourg on 22nd September 1555. He stayed for almost two years in Bergzabern.

In the spring of 1557 the Englishmen at Wesel were banished for theological reasons and made their way to Aarau in Switzerland. Coverdale joined them there. He stayed little more than a year, moving in the autumn of 1558 to Geneva where he received permission to settle on 24th October and stood as godfather to John Knox's son on 16th December.

In Geneva there is little doubt that he lent his talent to those who were working on the Geneva Bible, to appear eventually in April 1560 and to influence the Authorised Version considerably.

Queen Mary died, but Coverdale was in no hurry to return home. He did not apply to the Geneva Council for permission to leave until 14th August 1559. In England he was received by the Duchess of Suffolk, as a preacher, but also as tutor to her children.

It was soon after his return that he took part in the consecration of Archbishop Parker, wearing a black gown, though his colleagues were vested in copes. It was the same garb as he had worn at his own consecration eight years before. He was not entirely happy in Elizabethan England with its necessary compromises. For four years he remained without preferment and gave himself to preaching. At last in January 1564, he was persuaded to accept the living of St Magnus by London Bridge. But even this he resigned for some unknown reason connected with liturgical practice after about two years. Only two and a half years remained to him and these he spent preaching so long as his strength allowed. He was eagerly followed by puritans. On 20th January 1569 he died and was buried two days later in the chancel of St Bartholomew by the Exchange under the communion table.

Great crowds are said to have followed his funeral.

He died where he had lived for the last years of his life, in a house belonging to the Merchant Taylors. His widow Katherine lived on in that house, even after she remarried and until she too died on 6th April 1588.

5. Whittingham and the Geneva Bible

On 15th January 1604, the second day of the Hampton Court conference with King James, who had been crowned just six months before in Westminster Abbey, the Puritan John Reynolds approached the king and said:

'May your majesty be pleased that the Bible be new translated?'

He can hardly have approved of the king's reply, because the Puritans loved their Geneva Bible, but James set in motion the steps by which England accepted eventually her 'Authorised Version'. The king's reply was:

I profess I could never see a Bible well translated in English; but I think that of all, that of Geneva is the worst. I wish that some special pains were taken for a uniform translation; which should be done by the best learned of both universities, then revised by the bishops, presented to the Privy Council, lastly ratified by royal authority, to be read in the whole Church and no other.

With so many translations circulating, it was not surprising that James wanted one official translation used by all. The first attempt at this had been made with The Great Bible (1539), the work of Coverdale, commissioned by Archbishop Cranmer, basically a revision of the Matthew's Bible, which was substantially the work of Tyndale. For ten years it was the authorised version and continued in use long after that.

Far and away the most popular version after 1560, however, was the one to which the king referred in such derogatory language: The Geneva Bible. Peter Levi in his book *The English Bible* says that between 1560 and 1611, 'Tyndale's New Testament was reprinted five times, The Great Bible seven, the Bishops' Bible that succeeded it twenty-two, and the Geneva Bible over a hundred and twenty'. Even the Authorised Version when it appeared in 1611 failed to drive it out.

The English Refugees

The Geneva Bible should really have been dedicated to Mary Tudor! When she vigorously persecuted the protestants and thus drove them to

Geneva, she provided that city with the finest scholars in England. William Whittingham and Anthony Gilby took the lead, but there were men of talent, passion and learning to co-operate with them. The translation was from the Hebrew and Greek originals. Whittingham's New Testament appeared in 1557 and the first version of the Psalms in the same year. Geneva in the fifties was like a modern Bible Society - a new edition of the Latin Vulgate, new Greek and Hebrew texts, an Italian Bible, a Spanish and more than twenty versions in French. The English scholars found themselves simply one small part of a vast enterprise. For a scholarly translation there was no better place in all Europe.

These men who made the Geneva Bible were largely Puritans and they had much in common with Calvin and Knox. Before going to Geneva, they had fled to Frankfurt. This was a good Lutheran centre, not yet sharply divided from the Calvinists. In fact, in September 1554, the English refugees had invited John Knox to be their minister. The congregation had a history and John Knox would have done well to study it before accepting the invitation.

The first wave of refugees from Mary's fires settled at Frankfurt under the leadership of Pollanus, formerly the minister of the Church of Strangers at Glastonbury. They soon obtained permission from the magistrates of Frankfurt to establish a Church 'in the name of all such as should come out of England for the Gospel'. In June 1554, a new wave of refugees arrived, who did not speak French. They came to an amicable agreement with Pollanus and the magistrates to form a separate English-speaking congregation. It was agreed that they should subscribe to the same confession of faith as the French-speakers and more or less the same form of worship. Pollanus would have been quite happy with the *Book of Common Prayer* used in Edward's England. This seemed a good solution, because Mary Tudor had forbidden the use of this book! The English refugees were largely Puritans, they would have been glad to be rid of versicles, litany and surplice and to omit as 'superstitious and superfluous' much of the Baptismal and Communion services in that Prayer Book. They were men of the Bible.

They invited three ministers, Haddon, who was then at Strasbourg; Lever, then at Zurich; and John Knox from Geneva. Lever accepted, Haddon refused. Knox would have been well advised to follow Haddon's example! It was a quarrelsome group and Knox never understood the English situation. The main trouble was rooted in the attitude to the Prayer Book. For some of the English it represented the kind of Church they wanted and was their resistance to Mary. It was, for them, freedom to be able to use the Prayer Book of Edward VI. For Knox it was an imposed Prayer Book, linked to the secular power.

The unhappy story of Knox's failure does not belong to this book, but it can be read in Lord Eustace Percy's *John Knox*, pp 194-197.

It is pertinent however to quote Whittingham's description of Knox's last night in Frankfurt before leaving for Geneva:

> The 25th March (1555), Master Knox, the night before his departure, made a most comfortable sermon at his lodgings to fifty persons, or there about, then present; which sermon was of the death and resurrection of Christ, and of the unspeakable joys which were prepared for God's elect, which in this life suffer trouble and persecution for the testimony of His Blessed Name. The next day he was brought three or four miles on his way by some of those unto whom the night before he had made that exhortation; who with great heaviness of heart and plenty of tears committed him to the Lord.

Protestantism was losing ground in Europe. Outside Switzerland, there were only the Lutheran states and cities of Germany. Scandinavia was too remote and Denmark had proved inhospitable to some of the elect. Now Frankfurt was insecure. Knox was in Geneva only a short time before he journeyed to Scotland, but his congregation of Puritans found Frankfurt disagreeable and moved to Geneva which was more to their liking.

William Whittingham

Remembered, unfortunately as a Puritan and an iconoclast, William Whittingham is much more important as the inspiration behind the Geneva Bible. He was born in Chester, about the year 1524. Chester was a lively town with its Whitsuntide Plays and even a reputation for drunkenness and immorality. William was part of this liveliness and acquired a love of music which later earned him a wide reputation. He later used his ability on the harp and the viol for sacred purposes, but that was not how he learned them. Although not one of the most important ports in England, Chester commanded the sea route to Ireland and ships left from the Watergate for Spain and Portugal as well. William did not go to school but was brought up in the ways of a gentleman of that period. His education was in the fields and forests of Cheshire. He acquired a knowledge of falconry, of hunting the fox and wild boar, of archery, fencing and the arts of war. He went to Oxford about the same time as some of his slightly older friends, including Christopher Goodman. Their friendship blossomed at Oxford. They both went to Brasenose College.

William became a Fellow of All Souls and later joined Goodman at the newly founded Christ's College. It was a wonderful time to be at Oxford. The old university had awakened from its medieval stupor and students from all Europe filled colleges and streets. Public disputations were frequent and often on religious themes. The most distinguished name in Oxford was that of the Italian called Peter Martyr, but the influence of John Wycliffe was also rekindled. In particular, Wycliffe's view of the Sacraments was much discussed. He had attacked Transubstantiation to his great peril in the fourteenth century, now it was debated in the streets and colleges of his Oxford quite openly. In this reign of Edward VI the Protestants were in the ascendancy and Ridley's influence assured that Cranmer would devise a view of the Lord's Supper much nearer to that of Wycliffe than the old medieval view. Continental scholars also came to England which appeared the haven of Reformation. Cranmer tried to reconcile the Reformers on the Lord's Supper at this time. In 1537, he wrote to Joachim Vadian, the distinguished Protestant layman in Switzerland, urging agreement between the Reformers. Later, in a typical appeal he wrote again to Vadian:

> It cannot be told how greatly this so bloody controversy has impeded the full course of the Gospel ... especially among ourselves ... I beg, beseech, implore and adjure you to agree and unite in a Christian concord, so that we may with united strength, extend as widely as possible one sound, pure, evangelical doctrine, conformable to the discipline of the primitive church. We should easily convert even the Turks, if only we could agree among ourselves, and unite together in one holy confederacy.

Cranmer wrote as Archbishop of Canterbury in a Protestant England; his chaplain, Ridley, was most influential at Cambridge. Oxford with Peter Martyr was taking up the New Learning and to a certain extent also the Reformation. But it was not long before Oxford reduced its interest in theology and concentrated upon civil law. William Whittingham went to study abroad, because he could there qualify in law. The obvious centre for study was Orleans, but he had other interests and studies first. Italy was also famous for its knowledge of civil law and, for a romantic young man, also for its natural beauty. In the summer of 1550, he requested leave of absence from Oxford and went to France. At Lyons, he became ill and experienced a religious change. The details are not clear, but he probably came into contact with some Albigensians and was attracted by the simplicity of their doctrine, personal piety and literal adherence to the Scripture.

He gave up his plan to visit Italy and went straight to Orleans, where he spent a few years studying civil law and he married there. Not much is known about this marriage, but his wife appears to have been related to John Calvin, perhaps his sister, Maria Paludana. Orleans was a city of culture, with a reputation for civil law, the purity of its French and poetry. This was much to William's liking. His interest in language far outstripped his interest in law. From Orleans he went to Paris and at the request of the ambassador, presented himself at the French court. But primarily he was a student in Paris. After travelling in 'Germany', he ended his journeying with a visit to Geneva in the autumn of 1552.

He returned to England in the last month of Edward's reign. The ailing young king was not to last long and it was uncertain who would succeed him. An abortive attempt to put Lady Jane Grey on the throne lasted 9 days and Mary Tudor, a passionate Catholic and enemy of the Reformation, began her reign. Peter Martyr of Oxford was in danger. William Whittingham, seen more as a courtier at that time than as a theologian, appealed for Peter Martyr's right to return to his own land freely. He argued that Martyr had been received as a guest of England and, notwithstanding the change of administration, should be treated as such. Martyr was allowed to travel to London and his request to leave granted. Whittingham left England himself about October 1553, a few weeks before the Queen was proclaimed. The stories told about his 'escape' show something of the man. When his company reached Dover, the landlord of the inn was suspicious of their reasons for going overseas and threatened to take them before the magistrate. But Whittingham had led the landlord into a compromising remark. He had asked about his dog and the landlord jokingly replied, 'of the Queen's sort!'. Whittingham professed to be shocked at this reflection upon the Queen, so that the landlord dropped his intention of taking the company before the magistrate! They took ship to Calais and travelled around France, to places already known to Whittingham. Eventually he made his way to Frankfurt and by the year 1554 their troubles began. But all that was soon forgotten as they came together in Geneva.

The Geneva Bible

In the preface to his New Testament, William Whittingham refers to 'the place where God hath appointed us to dwell, and also of the store of heavenly learning and judgement, which so aboundeth in this Citie of Geneva, that justly it may be called the patron and mirrour of true religion and godlynes'. (1557.)

In that Preface, Whittingham divides humanity into three groups: the malicious despisers of the word; those who are struck with the majesty of the word, but quarrel and cavel, or deride and mock all efforts to advance the knowledge of the word; and finally, for whom the translation is intended, 'the simple lambs who partly are within the fold of Christ and so hear willingly their Shepherd's voice, or partly wandering astray by ignorance, waiting for the Shepherd to find them and bring them into his fold'.

A number of translators took part in the final issue of the Geneva Bible before it was finally published with a very clear Preface showing its purpose on 10th April 1560.

We are not told who these translators were. Gerald Hammond, in his book, *The Making of the English Bible* (1982), ventures to list the probables: the guiding spirit, certainly William Whittingham. Then, Christopher Goodman, Anthony Gilby, Thomas Sampson, William Cole - the ageing Miles Coverdale was also consulted. But it does not read like a work done by a committee. It seems likely that William Whittingham, as general editor, harmonised the style. And the dedication is to the young Queen Elizabeth.

The awful days of Mary Tudor were over and the Geneva Bible began to win the hearts of most Englishmen. No subsequent version replaced it until the AV appeared in 1611.

The Elizabethan Settlement

Queen Mary died on 17th November 1558 and Elizabeth succeeded her to the throne amidst demonstrations of great enthusiasm - not least in Geneva!. The new succession was full of hope after Mary's disastrous policy with its persecutions, its submission to Spanish influence, its unsuccessful wars and its financial failures. Elizabeth had everything going for her.

But Knox and many of those with him were not welcome in England. It caused John Knox great sorrow. He complained to Cecil that he was 'handled like a stranger', and professed 'yet was I never enemy to the quietness of England'. His two sons, baptised in Geneva were entered at St John's College, Cambridge, and later became clergymen of the Church of England. The troubles at Frankfurt put a mark on all who had been involved. Goodman also was not allowed to remain in England where he arrived on his way to Scotland.

Whittingham was not yet forty at this time. His wife had ancestral property in the neighbourhood of Orleans and his circumstances in Orleans were pleasant. He was a European with a special interest in the Reformed Churches in France. He did not hurry to return to England; but eventually decided and said farewell to the Council of Geneva on 30th May 1560. He and his friends were given honourable license to depart. They were exhorted to 'pray for us, and to act in their turn towards foreigners as we have done by them; and that they may be always disposed to look with affection upon this city, and that those who are now citizens and subjects be still regarded as such for the time to come'.

Arriving in England in the summer of 1560 he was soon accepted at court and in the following January accompanied the Earl of Bedford to France, conveying Queen Elizabeth's condolence on the death of the king. The reasons given were his perfect French and his experiences of the French court. It was not long before England was at war with France and this time it was the Earl of Warwick who requested his company as Principal Preacher. There are legends about him preaching in armour and being the first on the walls of the town they were defending if his sermons were interrupted by an alarm. There was something of the Renaissance man about him! It was the town of Le Havre they were defending and the English soldiers were smitten with plague. Whittingham discharged the office of chaplain well with the pastoral care for the sick. He remained at Le Havre until 1563 when he was appointed Dean of Durham. He was soon criticised for using the Genevan rite (forbidden by the Act of Uniformity.) He continued as a Puritan and a Calvinist at Durham. The 'Genevans' as they were called were rising into the ascendancy in the Church of England. But it did not last. A flash of lightning brought the matter to a head, March 1560. The tall spire of 'Paul's Church' was struck by lightning and the fire raged from 3 in the afternoon until the evening. Pilkington, a Puritan who had recently been appointed Bishop of Durham at the age of forty preached a sermon on the following Sunday, exhorting the people to amend their ways. It was then usual to ascribe such a stroke of lightning to the judgment of God, much as the earthquake was in Wycliffe's day. Pilkington used the occasion to call for a root and branch Reformation. He further printed and circulated his sermon text. He was attacked from many sides, including those who saw the lightning as a judgment for forsaking the old religion. The controversies raged and Whittingham joined forces with Pilkington at Durham. The Queen wanted uniformity and she insisted upon the Act of Uniformity which required all clergy to accept the Prayer Book.

Whittingham wrote to the Earl of Leicester:

> Can this be called Christian liberty, which lays a yoke upon the neck of disciples, clogs the Conscience, menaces the preachers, lays an embargo on the pulpit, leaves congregations without guides; and ties the Sacraments to an idolatrous appearance?

The Queen took a hand and ordered a Disputation between the Bishops favourable to the Roman practice and the Puritans. The Puritans were victorious in debate and there followed a new Act of Uniformity. What Elizabeth wanted was the restoration of Royal Supremacy, upon which she insisted, making no concessions to papal claims. Given that, she wanted peace and uniformity, although personally she believed in the real presence in the Eucharist and was more inclined to liturgical worship than the simple services of the Puritans. This new Act of Uniformity, which received the royal assent on 8th May 1559 was the one that Whittingham protested. It was a parliamentary Act with no real ecclesiastical authority. The new Prayer Book was ordered to be obtained by all the churches by 24th June and to be in use within three weeks. There was bound to be trouble.

In all these events, including the Disputation, Matthew Parker kept quiet in Cambridge. The Queen, Cecil and Bacon were determined that he should be Archbishop of Canterbury, but he was a most reluctant candidate! He foresaw the troubles. He was eventually consecrated on 17th December 1559.

Matthew Parker and the Bishops' Bible

He was considerably older than William Whittingham, probably twenty years older, and destined for Cambridge. Born 6th August 1504, third son of William Parker of Norwich. He was brought up like William Whittingham, as a gentleman with home tuition. But nothing is said of his training in the arts of war, although his family had the right to bear arms. His early life was an uneventful and placid preparation for an ecclesiastical career. But he was in Cambridge in lively times 'when learning and religion began to dawn there'. The opposition to the teaching of Greek had been overcome by the time he arrived in Cambridge, thanks to the eloquence of Richard Croke of King's. Erasmus' influence had been strong and his Greek New Testament was the first book to be published in Greek in England. Thomas Bilney was the leader of the reforming group, but he was not a Lutheran. He insisted that his reforming zeal came from the New Testament - Erasmus' Latin version. Bilney was a native of Norfolk like Parker, as was Thomas Arthur, the principal of St Mary's Hostel where Parker lodged. In fact, the group who made their meeting place The White Horse Inn, popularly called 'Germany', were mostly Norfolk men.

Matthew Parker began preaching in 1533 and was soon noticed as a brilliant preacher and good administrator. He rose, not out of his ambition, but from ability. However all his preferments were lost under Mary. He did not go into exile, but remained quietly and untouched. His own words show how he saw that time of retreat:

> After this I lived as a private individual, so happy before God in my conscience, and so far from being either ashamed or dejected, that the delightful literary leisure to which the good providence of God recalled me yielded me much greater and more solid enjoyments than my former busy and dangerous kind of life had ever afforded me.

That was written in October 1554. Four years later, he wanted no high office. Five years later he was Archbishop of Canterbury with the difficult task of imposing uniformity upon the Church of England. The deposed bishops, ie those who would not accept the royal supremacy and persisted in their acceptance of the authority of Rome, were Parker's care. Even those in the Tower were his pastoral concern.

The royal visitation required details to show that all was in order. Parker had little to do with this and he had no stomach for persecution. But he noted with interest and support that Elizabeth was making friendly gestures towards the Germans and even approved of the Augsburg Confession. Parker was concerned about the relation of the Church of England with other Churches in Europe which had broken with Rome. On the other hand, he had trouble with the Puritans and called for restraint. He was tolerant by nature, but with diverse views arising from among prominent leaders in the Church, he had to be on the alert.

In the autumn of 1560, it was suddenly made plain that the patience of authority with Protestant extremism was exhausted. On 19th September, the Queen issued a proclamation against the breaking or defacing of images in Churches unless they were the object of superstitious reverence. Three days later, all Anabaptists were ordered to withdraw from the realm within twenty days or face imprisonment. Parker was worried and resolved to get a clear account of all the clergy in his province. The imposing of uniformity was his duty rather than his pleasure, but he had to impose some order out of the chaos. The Queen acted again on 22nd January 1561 to order the commissioners to prepare changes in the calendar of lessons, adding complaints of 'such negligence and lack of reverence' used towards the Church and especially chancels that 'it breedeth no small offence and slander'. She was obviously determined to see that the Churches should do things decently and in order. Parker was in favour of this, as he was of most of these early efforts for order and uniformity. But he pleaded for some tolerance. This was all very different from Mary's brief and bloody reign. Apart from a few troubles of a minor kind, Parker had easy relations with the Queen and he did not hesitate to advise her with boldness.

The Convocation of 1563

In January 1563 there were meetings both of Parliament and Convocation. Both had religion high on the agenda. Parliament criticised the slackness of ministers, complained that ceremonies were conducted carelessly and that few people bothered to attend Church. Bacon expressed this in his speech, but he was clearly voicing the official or royal view. The Queen was determined to tidy up her Church, but she did not expect Parliament to do it. She referred it to the bishops. Hence the extreme importance of the meeting of Convocation. There the future shape of the Church of England would be settled and Matthew Parker saw this. In particular he was much concerned with writing the Articles of Faith, which was the equivalent in England of the German Confession. In other words, he considered the confusion within the Church of England so serious as to constitute a *status confessionis*. There is no doubt that the Articles were largely those of Parker himself. The previous Convocation had been dominated still by bishops and clergy who had served during Mary's reign. This Convocation was of Elizabeth's men. Parker was particularly concerned to conduct proceedings with impressive dignity and to maintain a continuity with the past. The Church of England had certainly rejected papal supremacy, but it was the Catholic Church still.

The existing Eleven Articles were inadequate to define the Faith. He therefore consulted other bishops and prepared a model set of Articles for discussion. Basing his draft on the earlier Articles of 1553, he removed some of the extreme vagaries of Protestantism, and expressed more firmly the differences from Rome. This is typical of his middle position. His job was to reconcile, not argue. In his book, *History of the Articles*, Hardwick points out that the rewording of Protestant positions depended more upon German than upon Swiss sources. The Augsburg Confession was his model. In this way he steered the Church of England away from Geneva, assuring that it would remain 'Catholic' but 'Reformed'. Possibly his greatest service to the Church was to have ready for discussion such a model set of Articles of Faith, as conciliatory as possible, yet clearly and firmly showing the differences from the Church of Rome and from other continental Churches. His Articles insisted upon the importance of right conduct and recognised the points of dispute. It is evident that he successfully dealt with the disputed points, so far as the majority of clergy were concerned. In fact, apart from the subsidy to the Queen, the only positive outcome of the Convocation was the Articles, substantially in the form that Parker had drafted them. They have weathered the centuries and are not very different from the present Thirty Nine Articles of the Church of England. Convocation lasted from January until April 1563.

Matthew Parker in his Diocese

Once Convocation was over, he could return to his diocese of Canterbury. There, he showed himself a great builder and lavish entertainer. He took up residence at his country manor of Bekesbourne, near Canterbury. He had already furnished Lambeth Palace and now turned to the ruinous condition of Bekesbourne. It was an historical place but had been allowed to fall into disrepair. He indulged his passion for restoration and by 1565 he was entertaining with a lavish style as befitted his high office. The Queen made good use of Bekesbourne and when an epidemic struck London, Parker was asked to entertain the bishops in the Tower. Thirlby, late of Ely, and Boxall, Dean of Peterborough, Norwich and Windsor, who had refused to accept the royal supremacy over the Church, came to live at Bekesbourne. Eventually all the bishops imprisoned in the Tower were removed, usually assigned to the keeping of legitimate bishops or with certain restrictions of residence to live in their own houses. Parker was no persecutor and he did not want to see England under Elizabeth behaving as Mary Tudor had done. So long as he was Archbishop of Canterbury, the Church was moderate in its attitude to those who still longed for the old Romish practices. The Elizabethan Settlement was not seriously challenged until 1570 after the rebellion of the Northern Earls which was easily crushed and severely punished. After that, the recrudescence of Romanism was a danger to the State. Until then, Parker was not greatly troubled and was able to watch over his diocese with much care. He was also able to give his attention to a new translation of the Bible - The Bishops' Bible.

Replacing the Great Bible

The Great Bible of 1539 was a kind of authorised version. It carried a woodcut of King Henry delivering the Word of God with his right hand to Cranmer and with his left to Thomas Cromwell. They in turn delivered it to the clergy and laity. The Great Bible was revised and reissued, but was never popular for long. It was almost neglected once the Geneva Bible became available. But the *Geneva Bible* was a Puritan Bible as its many comments made clear. Parker was anxious to replace The Great Bible by a more popular one which might fit the day of moderation. He wanted an Anglican Bible that did not smack of Geneva. Richard Cox, the Bishop of Ely suggested a new Bible. He had had many differences with Whittingham in Frankfurt and had good reasons for regretting the popularity of the Geneva Bible. The left-wing leaders among the Puritans had given the Geneva Bible a bad name, although earlier Parker had greatly approved of it and found no objections to the marginal comments.

Now it had to be superseded. The main task of organising the translation fell upon Matthew Parker. He allotted the portions among the translators, gave them guidelines to be followed and prepared it for presentation to the Queen by October 1568. Although he was not well enough at the time to present it to the Queen he sent it to Cecil with a covering letter and a list of those who had worked on the translation. He did quite a lot of it himself: Genesis, Exodus, Matthew, Mark, the Pauline Epistles except Romans and I Corinthians, and he also did Hebrews, as well as the lengthy Preface. In his covering letter to the Queen he suggests that the Bishops' Bible should be ordered to be read in churches and makes a very direct criticism of the Geneva Bible without naming it. The reason why he wanted the Bishops' Bible to be ordered for reading in churches was not to replace The Great Bible, but to replace the Geneva Bible which he says, without naming it, was being used and he refers to it as one of those translations, 'which have not been laboured in your realm, having interspersed divers prejudiced notes, which might have been also well spared'.

The Bishops' Bible was a splendid volume, clearly printed and lavishly illustrated, with the chapters divided into verses, as the Geneva Bible had introduced. But it was not a success. The Queen did not give it the sole authorisation to be read in churches. She was nearer to the people than Parker was and she was quite happy to receive a copy of the Geneva Bible as late as 1583. The revised edition of the Bishops' Bible left the Old Testament unchanged, but carefully revised the New Testament for publication in 1572. Its importance lay not so much in the acceptance which Parker had hoped for, but its influence upon the Authorised Version which would emerge triumphant when King James was on the throne. Westcott points out that much of the AV was based upon the revised edition of the Bishops' Bible.

The Bull of Excommunication

The year 1570 was a turning point in the life of the ageing Archbishop. Early in 1570, the Pope very stupidly, and ill-advised after some kind of judicial process, issued a Bull of Excommunication against Queen Elizabeth. Ignorant of the changes that had taken place in Europe since the Middle Ages gave way to a new world, he claimed full powers over all races and kingdoms. He listed a full catalogue of sins which she was supposed to have committed and denied her claim to the throne. He made life very difficult for English Catholics, who until then had been allowed to keep their Catholic faith while acknowledging Elizabeth as their Queen. The secular rulers of Europe were angry and it did not seriously shake the loyalty of the vast majority of Catholics in England. But it put them under suspicion. The Pope had called upon them to renounce their oath of allegiance to her. Matthew Parker was much distressed by this and his good counsel prevailed so that a very liberal policy was enunciated for the treatment of the followers of the old religion:

> As long as they shall openly continue in the observance of her laws, and shall not wilfully and manifestly break them by their open actions, her majesty's meaning is, not to have any of them molested by any inquisition or examination of their consciences in causes of religion.

For all her disregard of this foolish Bull, her counsellors were worried for her security. If Catholics were released from their oath of allegiance and loyalty, even encouraged to break it by the head of their Church, they were all potential traitors and even regicides, a suspect and dangerous element in society.

The Opposition of the Puritans

Parker was a moderate who had no liking for persecution. The ages of Mary Tudor, of Thomas More and even Henry belonged to the regrettable past, a hang-over from the Middle Ages. He would have liked to keep the Church of England Catholic and Reformed. But first the Pope with his inexcusable nonsense of the Bull of Excommunication had evoked the Middle Ages and in response the Puritans rose. There was trouble in Cambridge with one of the best scholars in the country, Thomas Cartwright, who had been elected to the Margaret Lectureship by sheer merit at the end of 1569. He began to lecture on the Acts of the Apostles early in 1570 and, like J B Phillips many years later, contrasted the Church organisation he found in the young Church with the present state of the Church of

England. He was brilliant, both as a scholar and also a lecturer, or rather preacher. He was implying that Parker's careful balance between Catholic and Protestant was no true Church. Cartwright was not, as many Puritans were, looking back to the Geneva model. He derived his proposed reforms entirely from the New Testament. He had never been to Geneva! What he proposed was the abolition of the episcopate and even his more moderate followers began to abuse the bishops for their enforcement of clerical attire and the Prayer Book.

In 1571, with pressure from both sides, Parker had to take responsibility for another Convocation. At the same time Parliament was called and an effort was made to have worthy members returned. None the less, it was a rowdy meeting and the Puritans attempted to force Bills through to change the nature of the Church. Bishops were abused and Parker was not exempt. Further reforms were carried through, such as those concerning the orderly distribution of benefices of which Parker approved. The oath of loyalty was also to be taken by all who were appointed to livings in the future. This was clearly designed to catch the remaining Marian clergy, who quietly retained the old rites. The Puritans wanted tougher measures to rout out the 'traitors'. They attempted to capitalise on their gains by pushing measures through Parliament, but the bishops resisted and reserved to themselves the revisions of the Articles of Faith.

Convocation was opened with a sermon by Whitgift, chosen by Parker because of his outspoken stand against Cartwright. It discussed the authority of Synods, of the enemies of the Church, 'to wit Puritans and Papists', of the use of vestments and ornaments, and of many things in need of reformation. At the second session of Convocation, Parker ordered all the members of the Lower House who had not subscribed to the Articles of 1563 to do so or be excluded. Further consideration was given to the Articles by the bishops who met at Lambeth in May. The final version was printed and distributed, to be read in Church four times a year. Every minister was to sign the Articles before ordination. Convocation was dissolved at the end of May. Its main achievements had been the Articles and the Canons agreed by the bishops.

Archbishop Parker followed up this troubled year by a stricter discipline. It was a mild repression of the 'Romanists' without giving too much sway to the Puritans. Parker proved to be the man for the hour and Bacon, Cecil and the Queen were proved right in their insistence upon appointing him. The model they had in view was a Church, Catholic and reformed, its historic roots unsevered, avoiding the errors of Rome and the excesses of Protestantism. Parker was right for this task. A weaker man would have let things slide into confusion; a more rigid man would have alienated both Romanists and Protestants. The strange new thing needed careful tending and Parker believed in it. V J K Brook concludes his careful study of Archbishop Parker with a tribute that can hardly be better phrased:

> He was gentle and conciliatory in dealing with critics either on the right hand or the left. He laboured all he could to correct abuses and to raise the standard of the clergy. And he was eminently one whose character commanded respect - without guile or duplicity, humble and without self-seeking or love of money; mild and conciliatory yet unyielding where he thought principles were concerned; honest and dominated by a real love of justice. He deserves from all Anglicans a greater measure of gratitude than he sometimes receives.

He laboured but failed to obtain an authorised version of the Bible to replace all others, especially the Geneva Bible.

King James Version

What Queen Elizabeth failed to do through Parker, her successor achieved. A simple solution might have been to cut the comments from the Geneva Bible, but they were so related to the text that the ordinance of 'no note or comment' would have been ineffective. King James was learned enough to realise that the Geneva Bible was the best translation on offer, but also diplomatic enough to rule it out as the authorised version in any form. The translators of the Bible he asked for were not ignorant of the virtues of the Geneva Bible, but they turned to the revised edition of the Bishops' Bible for their basis. And in this new translation there was to be neither note nor comment, just the text, with a Preface. The king took a hand in organising the work and the best scholars in both the universities were summoned. F F Bruce gives a clear account of how it was organised and the immense number of people involved in its six panels.

Oxford, Cambridge and Westminster produced their best men. It would take a detailed history of the ecclesiastics and scholars of the period to describe the 'Makers of the Authorised Version', but two men stand out - Miles Smith, Canon of Hereford, later Bishop of Gloucester and Thomas Bilson, Bishop of Winchester. These two saw it through the press and Miles Smith wrote the Preface. King James himself probably drew up the guidelines. The men who produced this incomparable translation deserve a separate chapter. The AV was not without its critics and James was wise enough not to authorise it as the only version to be used. Even Lancelot

Andrewes and William Laud continued to use the Geneva Bible in their preaching and it was a generation before it captured the hearts of the people. But when it did, it lasted and had no serious rivals until modern times. Throughout the English-speaking world it held a pride of place which was difficult to dislodge for more than three centuries.

6. Lancelot Andrewes and the Men of the Authorised Version

The writings of Lancelot Andrewes are included in the volumes of Anglo-Catholic theology, but he was formed in a Puritan background of London merchants and Cambridge rebels. His roots were in Puritanism and his fruits in the English Church of the seventeenth century, before Cromwell disturbed its equilibrium. His influence as stylist and translator of the Authorised Version of the Bible is crucial. More than anyone else he made it possible for the Geneva Bible to be replaced by the translation ordered by King James and he stamped it with a style that has survived with Shakespeare as the highest point of English literature.

Paul Welsby, in his carefully documented biography (1958) of Lancelot Andrewes, has succinctly summarised his life and career against the background of the history of the English Church:

> He was born in 1555, the year when the Marian persecution produced many Protestant martyrs, he was a schoolboy when Elizabeth was excommunicated, he went up to Cambridge a year after Cartwright (an extreme Puritan) had been deprived of his Professorship. In the University he found himself in the midst of the Puritan ferment and was later drawn into the controversy on predestination. After his ordination he was engaged in disputation with both Recusants and Separatists. When James became King, Andrewes was on the road to becoming a national figure. He was present at the Hampton Court Conference, he was one of the translators of the Authorised Version, he became the leading apologist against Rome, and he thus contributed to the new school of theology which was providing the Church of England with a sound historical and theological basis. He emphasised the need for order in public worship, and he had a high conception of episcopacy. At the same time, however, he was one of the foremost preachers of the divine right of kings and he was active in the Court of High Commission. He thus played his part in preparing for the rupture to come. One year after James died and Charles had begun his tragic career, Andrewes himself passed from the stage.

Puritan Origins

Lancelot Andrewes was born in London of a Suffolk family. He was one of a large family, there were thirteen children in all, and his father was a seafarer of some repute: Thomas Andrewes later became one of the Masters of Trinity House. It can safely be assumed that his father was anti-Spain and anti-Catholic, almost all the merchant class was. All that Henry Isaacson, his first biographer, says of Lancelot's parents was that they were 'honest and religious', but we may assume Puritan tendencies. Lancelot was a brilliant child and appears to have had little interest in games. He loved nothing more than his books from an early age. His first school was Cooper's Free School in Radcliffe, founded in 1538 by Nicholas Gibson, grocer and sheriff. The school was handed over to the Company of Coopers by Gibson's widow in 1552. Lancelot left Cooper's School in 1565 to go to Merchant Taylors' School, which had a reputation comparable with St Paul's. There under the mastership of Richard Mulcaster, he developed a life-long passion for languages and a good grounding in Latin and Greek.

He went to Cambridge on a Greek scholarship and studied at Pembroke College. His reputation for languages grew. To Latin, Greek and Hebrew were soon added competence in Chaldee, Syriac, Arabic and fifteen modern languages. ==He remained a scholar all his life.==

Cambridge

He came to Cambridge at a time when Calvinism with its doctrine of predestination, its dislike of ritual and vestments, and its own ideas of 'Church order' (independent or Presbyterian) was spreading in the colleges. An earlier generation had recognized the doctrines of the Reformation - Cranmer, Latimer, Ridley and Tyndale; a later generation taught Puritanism and sheltered Dissent - the Pilkingtons, Beaumont and Cartwright. Thomas Cartwright was deprived of his Lady Margaret Professorship because he attacked the Church of England for its archbishops, bishops, archdeacons and deacons, the lack of participation of the congregation in the election of clergy, the keeping of Saints Days and many other practices which he denounced as Papist. He had many followers in the University to which Andrewes came as a student.

He had been at Cambridge about a year when the news came of the horrific massacre of St Bartholomew's Eve, in August 1572. A shock of anti-Papist feeling struck the country and was most angrily expressed in Cambridge. Andrewes could recall it forty-six years later when he preached the Gunpowder Plot Sermon before James I at Whitehall in

1618. He compared the Gunpowder Plot to the massacre in Paris, when, as he said,
> it had been a heavy sight ... to have seen men trembling in their own blood here and there in the streets; nothing ... to see men torn in sunder, heads from shoulders, arms from legs, both from the body; quarters and half quarters flying about; the brains fly one way, the bowels another; blood spilt like water in the river, in the fields, in every corner of the streets.

It was the rhetoric of anti-Catholic, Puritan Cambridge, remembered many years later.

Efforts were made to administer the colleges in such a way as to keep them out of the hands of Puritans, whom Elizabeth disliked and distrusted. But the Puritan party remained strong.

On 4th February 1575, Andrewes attained his BA and in the same year was made a Fellow of Pembroke College. During his Fellowship, two events of considerable importance for the puritan cause occurred. The University Press printed a translation of *Disciplina* by Walter Travers in 1584. This book attacked the ecclesiastical authorities in England, the organisation of the Church and showed contempt for Church order. John Whitgift, then Archbishop of Canterbury ordered all the copies to be burned. But the Cambridge University Press continued to print it. Lord Burghley recommended Travers for the Mastership of the Temple! He was over-ruled and Richard Hooker was appointed.

The second event was the foundation of Emmanuel College by Sir Walter Mildmay. He made no secret of his intentions to have a college which would support the Puritan cause. There is a conversation reported of Sir Walter with the Queen, which may be apocryphal, but it was very current. Elizabeth is reported as saying, 'I hear, Sir Walter, you have been erecting a Puritan foundation'. He replied, 'No, Madam, far be it from me to countenance anything contrary to your established laws, but I have set an acorn, which when it becomes an oak, God knows what will be the fruit thereof'.

J S Mullinger, who tells that story in his history of the University of Cambridge also points out that the first Master of the College made no secret of his sympathy for the Puritan cause and that the college chapel had its own form of service and partook of the sacrament sitting.

Lancelot Andrewes was thus found in the very heart of Puritan society, but he was not of their number, except in one respect. While he had no sympathy with Puritan extremism in matters such as Church order and ceremonies, he was at one with them on Sabbatarianism. His lectures on the Commandments were very popular and that on the Fourth Commandment followed the Puritan line. He also argued that the Fourth Commandment was not part of the ceremonial law of the Old Covenant which those of the New Covenant need not feel bound to obey. 'Honour the Sabbath Day to keep it holy' was part of moral law, incumbent upon all Christians.

In 1586, Andrewes was appointed chaplain to the Earl of Huntingdon, President of the Council of the North, and accompanied him on his visits to the north to deal with recusants, priests and other supporters of the old religion. Andrewes was chosen because while sympathetic to Puritanism, he did not approve of its excesses. In particular, like the Earl himself, he was moderate in his methods of dealing with those he wished to persuade. Isaacson writes of this work in the north:

> Being in holy orders he attended the Earl ... and was employed by him in often preaching, and conference with recusants both of the clergy and laity, in which God so blessed his endeavours that he converted some of the priests and many of the laity, with great success, bringing many to the Church, and seldom losing his labour, none ever converting as many as he did.

Andrewes was on similar work in Wisbech Castle where the government had imprisoned certain Roman Catholics. A few years later, he spoke with William Weston, a Jesuit priest, who was then imprisoned in London. Weston kept an account of the interview and it shows the limits of Andrewes' Puritanism even in 1587 while he was still at Cambridge, a Fellow at Pembroke College. Weston says that when the discourse turned on sacramental confession and the interpretation of Scripture, Andrewes admitted that he could not favour the capricious private interpretation of Scripture and he did not deny the usefulness of confession which he had practised among certain Anglicans. This is very unlike the Puritan attitude to such things. Weston's comments are not far from the truth when he says:

> he was one of those Puritans who allow some form of confession, and his frame of mind, as some held, was not altogether opposed to the Catholic faith.

About this time, Andrewes was appointed chaplain to Queen Elizabeth and also to the Archbishop of Canterbury. He had some difficulty in obtaining his Doctor of Divinity because he was not puritan enough! But he obtained it eventually in 1589 and was appointed Master of Pembroke.

The Spittal Sermon of 10th April 1588
This is the earliest sermon still extant. It is more forthright than Andrewes' later sermons, less diplomatic, less restrained. It was preached at the preaching cross in the courtyard of St Mary's Hospital. At times it echoes Latimer in its forthrightness. It is a sermon against the abuse of riches. He speaks of evil creditors and corrupt lawyers ('Westminster Hall moths'), of those who 'eat up companies', of the evils of 'out-buying and out-bidding' in order that they might 'appropriate civil livings, turn common into private, the whole body's nourishment into one foregrown member'. He refers to the Papists charge that the rich in England do not 'do good' with their wealth and agrees, adding 'and thus through you and through want of doing good, the Gospel of Christ is evil spoken of among them that are without'. However, he points to works of charity and ascribes their increase to the effect of the Reformation. He turns upon the Puritan extremists, who irresponsibly criticise the Church order of the Established Church:

> If a man be grown wise and experienced well in the affairs of this world, which is also His good blessing; presently by virtue of this they take themselves to be so qualified as they be able to overrule our matters of divinity, able to prescribe Bishops how to govern and Divines how to preach; so to determine our cases as if they were professed with us; and that, many times affirming things they know not, and censuring things they have little skill of...

But despite this attack on the Puritan merchants, he leaves no doubt about his attitude to Rome:

> Seeing the Pope does as he doeth: that is, as he hath dispensed with the oath and duty of subjects to their Prince against the fifth commandment; with the murder, both violent with daggers, and secret with poison, of the sacred persons of Princes, against the sixth; with the uncleanness of the stews, and with incestuous marriages, against the seventh; so now of late, with the abomination of simony against the eighth...

But the sting is in the tail, for he continues:

> Seeing thus do the Papists, and we loath to be behind them in this gain of blood make such merchandise with this sin, of the poor Church and her patrimony, as all the world crieth shame of it; to redeem the orderly disposing of them to the Church's good, were a special way for you rich men to do good in these days.

Lancelot Andrewes was eventually appointed to the Mastership of Pembroke College on 6th September 1589 on the death of William Fulke. He was by now a man to be reckoned with and he acquired a plurality of offices, the vicarage of St Giles, Cripplegate in London, a prebend at St Paul's and another in Southwell, all within the year of his Mastership.

The gulf between Andrewes and the Puritans grew. He spoke against their refusal to take the oath *ex officio* in a theological Determination in the Divinity School. Puritans refused to take this *ex officio* oath because it was contrary to Scripture, common law, natural law and the practice of all Protestant Churches. Andrewes argued, clean contrary to most Puritans and dissenters, that the authority of the magistrates extended over the soul as well as the body, and being such it was lawful for a ruler to make a subject take the oath, that it concerned truth and must be within the competence of the person swearing it. But it was his assumption that magistrates had authority over the soul as well as the body. Twenty years later, Thomas Helwys would dare to contradict this right even to the king. His book *The Mistery of Iniquity* published in 1614 bore the dedication to King James:

> Heare O King, and despise not the counsell of the poor, and let their complaints come before thee.
> The king is a mortall man and not God, therefore hath no power over the immortall soules of his subjects, to make lawes and ordinances for them, and to set spiritual Lords over them.
> If the king have authority to make spiritual Lords and lawes, then he is an immortall God and not a mortall man.
> O king, be not seduced by deceivers to sin so against God, when thou oughtest to obey, nor against thy poor subjects who ought and will obey thee in all things with body, life and goods, or else let their lives be taken from the earth.
> God save the king.

That was the Puritan position and it led to dissent as well as reform. Lancelot Andrewes saw its danger and opposed it. Thomas Helwys of Gray's Inn was confined to Newgate where he died. He was a pioneer of the Baptists in England. Not all were as forthright as Thomas Helwys, but the Puritans had a strong resistance to the taking of oaths. Imprisonment for contempt of court did little to quench the anger of those who felt that an unjust law imposed upon their conscience the need to take an oath.

A further example of Andrewes' move away from the Puritan position came when Cambridge clashed with Lambeth in 1595. There had been a furore in Cambridge over the denial of the doctrine of predestination by

William Barrett, a fellow of Gonville and Caius, a follower of the Lady Margaret Professor of Divinity, Peter Baro. The heads of the colleges condemned William Barrett and forced him to recant. He did this in an insulting way and both sides fled to Archbishop Whitgift for support. The matter seemed to be settled. But Lambeth decided to draw up Nine Articles to prevent a similar offence occurring again. They were strongly Calvinistic in tone and content. Andrewes, although the Archbishop's chaplain, vigorously objected to them. In his *Judgement of the Lambeth Articles*, he maintained that predestination was too great a mystery to be disputed over. The Articles had firmly stated one position in an extreme form. Andrewes asserted that 'the reprobate are such not by the absolute decree of God (as the articles had affirmed) but on account of sin; that saving grace itself would be conferred upon *all* men were they not obstinate; that all men are not drawn to the Father is due not to the absolute will of God, but to the depraved will of man'.

This was not a sharp polemic. He still maintained a 'reverent agnosticism' before the mystery of God's choice.

The Dean of Westminster

In July 1601, Lancelot Andrewes was appointed Dean of Westminster Abbey. He kept all his pluralities, the vicarage of St Giles and two prebends at St Paul's and Southwell, and remained Master of Pembroke College. He resigned none of these until he was later raised to the episcopate. He was already a popular court preacher and his position at Westminster now put him at the centre of events. He lived at Chiswick and on his walks there was often accompanied by hordes of boys from Westminster School in which he took a great interest. His pluralities were not challenged except one. The Dean of St Paul's, Dr Alexander Nowell, challenged Andrewes rights to hold the prebend of St Paul's. In fact, Andrewes won the right and retained his stall in St Paul's until 1609, long after he became a bishop. He was Dean of Westminster when Queen Elizabeth died on 24th March 1603. It appears that Andrewes did not preach the funeral sermon, but he must have taken some part in the service.

James was invited to succeed Elizabeth and he made his slow progress south from Edinburgh which he left on 5th April. He was heralded all the way with avowals of loyalty, but came to a dismal London, smitten by the bubonic plague. It is said that one in ten of the population died. At St Giles, there were 2,897 burials: but it was not the Vicar who conducted them. He left the plague-ridden London for the safer air of Chiswick. The school too was dissolved and when the plague reached 2,000 cases a week, the return was further postponed until Andrewes became concerned about the enforced idleness of the boys. He seems to have been less concerned about the fate of the people in London! This was not his best moment. While in Chiswick, he preached a sermon on the plague, which attributed it not to natural causes but to the wrath of God provoked by men's sins. He specified these sins as human *inventions*, such as new meats in diet, new fashions in dress, and in the religious field he listed inventions which looked like the extremes of Puritanism! The remedy for the plague then was straightforward, a ceasing from sin. Andrewes and others who fled from the plague were criticised as one might expect. One of the critics was a man of Dissent, Henoch Clapham, who was imprisoned for his pains.

Despite the plague, James and his Queen Anne were crowned in Westminster Abbey on St James' Day (25th July, 1603.) The outdoor celebrations were, of course, muted. But James insisted upon the old rite fully performed and Andrewes was the 'abbot' for the day and stood by the king as his prompter for the whole ceremony. All the bishops were present; Archbishop Whitgift performed the ceremony and Thomas Bilson, Bishop of Winchester, preached the sermon.

On his journey south, James had been met by the Puritans in force, urging upon him a Geneva-style Church of England with the abolition of superstitious practices, such as the sign of the cross in baptism, the rite of confirmation, the use of the ring in marriage, the use of the word 'priest' and ' absolution', calling for more preaching, shorter services and less music!

All these things were discussed at the Hampton Court Conference which opened on 14th January 1604. On the first day the Puritans were excluded while James conferred with his Bishops. It was at this conference that the decision was taken to provide an acceptable translation of the Bible into English. It was on 22nd July 1604 that James set up the machinery for this massive task as already described at the end of the previous chapter and more fully by F F Bruce. Lancelot Andrewes presided over one of the panels that met at Westminster. It had a membership of ten and was responsible for a large section of the Old Testament - Genesis to II Kings. It was a learned panel, but Andrewes complains that they were negligent! He gave a great deal of time to the work of translation and cut down on other activities. But long before his task was ended he was elevated to the episcopate.

The Bishop

Lancelot Andrewes was elected Bishop of Chichester on 16th October 1605 and the election was confirmed two weeks later. This time he resigned his deanery, his London benefice and the Mastership of Pembroke College. He was allowed to retain his prebend in St Paul's until 1609 'on account of the poverty of his bishopric'. He was very careful for his financial state and in addition to keeping the prebend of St Paul's he was instituted to the benefice of Cheam in Surrey. Neither was Andrewes immune from nepotism. He advanced his relatives. The Register at Chichester has many references to his brother, Roger Andrewes, and his appointments.

In many other ways it was not a very distinguished episcopate. He was more at home in Ely which he had known in his Cambridge days. On 6th November 1609, he was confirmed as the Bishop of Ely and enthroned in Ely Cathedral on 12th December. It was a very impoverished diocese compared to what it had been. Bishop Cox had been compelled to surrender Ely House, the attractive London residence with its famous garden, to Sir Christopher Hatton for 21 years on an annual payment of one red rose, ten loads of hay and £10. When Hatton died, the Queen kept the see vacant for 18 years, with the benefice going to the crown. It was because of Elizabeth's milking of the revenue of the see and her determination to limit the powers of the Bishop of Ely over the fens that Andrewes refused the Bishopric during her reign. Despite the Reformation and the designs of the Queen, the Bishop of Ely still retained great power and prestige over Fenland. The Isle of Ely retained its distinctiveness from the rest of the country. It had its own assize and Chief Justice, its own prisons, its own rating system, and its own Chief Bailiff with powers like those of a sheriff of a shire.

Andrewes resided in the diocese only during the three summer months, because his duties in London kept him there most of the year, as was the case with many of the bishops. Moreover, the air of the fens did not agree with him. He rented part of Ely House, which should have belonged to him, for his London residence. He was best known as a preacher at court. His sermons were not topical, but calculated to inspire devotion, as indeed they did.

The Preacher

In her brief biography of Lancelot Andrewes (1952), Florence Higham has a fascinating chapter on Andrewes as a preacher. She describes the effect of his preaching, making mention of a particular Christmas Day sermon in 1609 which so impressed the king that he asked for the preacher's notes to put under his pillow. For thirty years Andrewes held the dissolute court of James I in thrall. Florence Higham expresses the effect well:

> Across the grandeur and futility, the selfish scheming and the empty love affairs of the Palace of Whitehall the Bishop's words fell like the clear, cool notes of a bell calling the world to prayer.

Even today, when you read these sermons, the quality of language is evident. Every phrase seems to have been fashioned with care. Some found this careful phrasing too much. Florence Higham quotes a Scot who heard him in 1617 on the northern journey:

> he takes up a thing and tosses and plays with it and then he takes up another and plays with it a little. Here's a pretty thing and here's a pretty thing.

But these playings with words, foreign to those who had been brought up on the fire of John Knox, were usually to make sure of the exegesis and always led to a vigorous spiritual appeal. Or, at the very moment when his academic treatment of the text, and he was a supremely competent linguist, seemed to leave the hearer with dry bones, the wind of the Spirit blew, and the scholar became the saint, speaking simply and directly to the hearts of his hearers. His most moving sermons are the 17 Christmas sermons. His memorable phrases come mostly from the thought of God incarnate, 'a little child's flesh, not a span long'. He could have preached 17,000 sermons on the Incarnation and never part from his theme. The sermon on the 'wise men' gave T S Eliot the opening lines of his poem on *The Magi* - 'a cold coming they had of it'.

Florence Higham picks out other phrases and a book of quotations could be compiled from a morning's reading of his collected sermons:

> 'a stable for his cradle, poor clouts for his array', 'We blame them that this day received him in a stable; take heed we do not worse ourselves'. 'And for that, men may talk what they will, but sure there is no joy in the world like to the joy of a man saved .... In danger of perishing by sickness, to hear of one will make him alive again; by sentence of the law, of one with a pardon to save his life; by enemies, of one who will rescue or set him in safety... And it may be, we need not any of these; we are not presently sick, in no fear of the law, in no danger of enemies ... But that which he came for, that saving we need all; and none but he can help us to it'.

As a preacher, he was less oratorical than John Donne, who stirred the hearts of his hearers with uneasy emotions; but he spoke to the age of

Shakespeare and of the Authorised Version. In fact, you can almost hear him preaching in some of the Genesis passages, although he used the Geneva Bible for his sermons even after 1611.

Although his Christmas sermons make the most immediate appeal to us, there are some moving passages in the sermons he preached on the Holy Spirit at Whitsuntide. It was in one of these that Andrewes pleaded for unity and accord in men's individual souls as in the life of the community. Perhaps this was the sermon the Scot objected to! It was preached in Holyrood House in 1617. He took his text from Luke's account of the sermon of Jesus at Nazareth. He spoke with tenderness of Christ's commission to 'cure the broken hearts and release the prisoners'. He referred to the poor: 'They are not much troubled with much worldly good news; seldom come there any posts to them with such. But the good news of the Gospel reachest even the meanest', and of the captives he said, those most truly captive were held in slavery to sin and Satan. He had a vivid sense of sin and expressed his conviction that only those whose hearts are broken by the sight of their sins could hope to hear the word of God.

His homely similes must have made his preaching so much more effective. He compares the working of the Holy Spirit to an anointing:

> An ointment is a composition we know; the ingredients of it oil and sweet odours. By virtue of the oil it sinks even into the bones, saith the Psalm; but it works upon the joints and sinews sensibly, making them supple and lithe, and so the more fresh and active to bestir themselves. By virtue of the sweet odours mixed with it, it works upon the spirits and senses; cheers him and makes him glad that is anointed with it. And not him alone, but all that are about and near him ... that take delight in his company, to go and to run with him, and all for the fragrant sweet scent they feel to come from him.

One could go on. We have already noted that from his Puritan origins he retained his strong Sabbatarianism; but equally he retained his sense of the importance of preaching.

Not Canterbury but Winchester

In November 1610, Richard Bancroft, Archbishop of Canterbury died and it was widely expected that Andrewes, despite the short period he had been at Ely, would succeed him. Clarendon, in his *History of the Great Rebellion* goes so far as to say, looking back over the centuries, that if he had been appointed he might have stemmed the rising tide of Puritanism.

Be that as it may, Andrewes was not appointed. Instead, George Abbot, then Bishop of London was. He was James' choice on the recommendation of the Earl of Dunbar, who died before the appointment. James had no qualms about appointing his friends nor did he doubt that Andrewes was the better man, but he chose this strong Puritan on personal grounds:

It is thought that there could have been another reason. Andrewes had a very high view of episcopacy as divinely appointed. James was equally sure that bishops were necessary, but for utilitarian reasons, 'no Bishop, no King'. Abbot fitted far better into this view of the political value of episcopacy as Crown appointment. But it was a disastrous appointment. Bancroft had been a reformer; Abbot was negligent, lax and very much a secular prelate.

Andrewes continued with his duties at Ely and with his wider interests, like all Bishops, in London and at the court. His preaching went on much as before. He was in no way soured, nor did he complain. Until 1618, when the king's son-in-law accepted the crown of Bohemia, life was pleasant for a scholar at the court in London. The strains of the Reformation, the nationalism of Elizabethan England, the anxieties about the succession had all mellowed with a king who loved learning and a secure succession - two sons. Princes and prelates provided a cultural nexus to which scholars from Oxford and Cambridge were welcome. The life at court may have been morally dissolute, but it was not uncultured. Lancelot Andrewes was a beloved and familiar figure at the very heart of this scholarly nexus.

He also had good relations with continental scholars who gravitated towards him when they were in England, partly because of his command of languages. The eminent classicist, Isaac Casauban was among these. They met in the autumn of 1610 when Casauban was in England and the friendship continued until the latter's death four years later. Casauban was a Huguenot, who had lived for many years in Geneva and eventually migrated to Paris where he served Henry IV. They conversed in Latin and French, because Casauban's English was slight. Andrewes and he had much the same academic interests and were both concerned to find a way for a Protestant Church to avoid the extremes of Calvinism.

The Closing Years

At the court of King James, ambitious families like the Howards fell out of favour and new men arose. As James aged and it was evident that Charles would be the next King, a young man replaced all the others in influence - George Villiers, who became Duke of Buckingham in 1617.

A year earlier, both Francis Bacon and Lancelot Andrewes were appointed Privy Councillors. They had little power at court, but were respected as venerable advisers from an earlier age. Andrewes hardly minded, but Bacon was severely disappointed. He had longed for power, while Andrewes was content to be allowed to preach and avoid factions or any affairs of State which had no bearing on the Church. He was never an ambitious man. He did what was required of him in the Court of High Commission. As Royal Almoner he behaved shrewdly, was generous and showed great compassion. But he always regarded his preaching as the main reason why he was at court.

Andrewes' health deteriorated and he suffered much. When King James was ill, almost on the point of death, he could not be with him. And it looked as though he and the king whom he served would die about the same time. In fact, Andrewes outlived his king by a year.

The new king respected him, but he wanted younger men about him. There were many who compared the young king to Rehoboam, who foolishly listened to his young advisers rather than the older men who supported his father. William Laud replaced Lancelot Andrewes, who quietly gave himself to his devotions and died on 25th September 1626.

Men of the Authorised Version

We have seen how Lancelot Andrewes played his part in the translation and from Genesis to II Kings we may detect his hand. But he was not the most prominent among the forty-seven who had their part to play in the final version.

John Reynolds (1549-1607) made the proposal to the King that there be a translation and the main work on the Prophetic Books was done in his rooms at Corpus Christi, Oxford. John Reynolds, often spelled Rainolds, was president of Corpus Christi College, where he went as a scholarship student from Merton College. His family was closely associated with Oxford; he graduated BA in 1568. About that time he was employed as tutor to Richard Hooker. His career was much involved with Oxford, although he remained throughout a staunch partisan, even declining a bishopric rather than leave Oxford. He was rebuked by Queen Elizabeth and enjoined to 'follow her laws and not run before them'. He was a brilliant Greek scholar and at one time 'Greek Reader'. His first speciality was in Aristotle. He was at Queens' College for a while, appointed in 1586 as 'Temporary Lecturer for the Confutation of Romish tenets', sponsored by Sir Francis Walsingham, with a stipend of £20 a year! For a few years he was Dean of Lincoln, but returned to Oxford to become president of his old college, Corpus Christi, in 1598. It was at that time that he refused a bishopric. His Puritan tendencies were doctrinal rather than practical. He died of consumption when he was barely 58 on 21st May 1607. He was without doubt one of the greatest scholars of his day.

Thomas Bilson (1546-1616) was one of the two who saw the final version through the press. Born in Winchester and eventually Bishop, he too was an Oxford man. His career was similar to others who served James well in the work upon the Authorised Version, but he had already achieved before that meeting in 1603 at Hampton Court. A scholar at Oxford, New College, he was awarded his doctorate on 24th January 1581. Over the next sixteen years he was appointed to a prebend at Winchester, became Warden of New College, Bishop of Worcester and then 13th May 1597, Bishop of Winchester. Queen Elizabeth made good use of him in stirring up the Protestants in the Netherlands. His work, *The True Difference between Christian Subjection and Christian Rebellion* may have justified Protestant rebellion against Spain, but it could also have prepared the way for the fall of Charles. A contemporary commented: 'Bilson gave strange liberty, in many cases, especially concerning religion, for subjects to cast off their obedience'.

Miles Smith (died 1624) was at the time, Canon of Hereford and was later appointed Bishop of Gloucester. He was born in Hereford, the son of a butcher, around 1568 although the date is not certain. He too was an Oxford man, Corpus Christi and later Brasenose. In 1575 he was appointed chaplain, or petty canon at Christchurch. He was a classical scholar and an orientalist with much the same qualifications as John Reynolds. He was, of course, very much younger and only a canon; but his work earned him promotion and he was appointed Bishop of Gloucester on 20th September 1612.

He worked with John Reynolds on the Prophetic Books and with Thomas Bilson in reviewing the whole of the Old Testament before publication. When this was done and the New Testament collected, largely from Cambridge, they left it to the younger man to see it all through the press and write the very informative preface, 'The Translators to the Readers'. Later issues of the Authorised Version, while they contained the dedication, often omitted this preface. It is seldom found today in any issue. F F Bruce has expressed his regret at this and I would agree with him. There is a very valuable summary of its contents and style in F F Bruce's *History of the English Bible* and it need not therefore be repeated here.

The forty-seven men who accomplished this remarkable task of a translation of the Bible - Old Testament, Apocrypha and New Testament - which stood the test of centuries were the leading biblical scholars in England. They also, happily, possessed a style of writing which is still the glory of English literature. Their names are known and listed in earlier editions, but the personal roles of the scholars and the processes followed in using earlier versions, annotating and editing for style is still a subject for further study.

The Authorised Version, although published in 1611 was not immediately taken to the heart of the people of England. Wycliffe was still treasured by some, the Geneva Bible, as we have said, remained the most popular, particularly throughout the Civil War and Commonwealth period. It was not until the Restoration of the Monarchy in 1660 that the AV really became the Bible of England. From then on, it was rarely challenged until our present century, except by devout Catholics who continued to regard it as a Protestant and, therefore, unauthorised version.

7. An Acceptable Catholic Version

Among the 300 Protestant martyrs who were executed during Queen Mary's short reign of four years was John Rogers, one of the translators of the English Bible. He was burned to death at Smithfield on 4th February 1555. David Edwards, at the beginning of the second volume of his most readable *Christian England*, has given us a vivid account of his trial as described by John Rogers himself in papers which his widow collected from his prison cell. It was an account of his examination before some of Queen Mary's leading councillors:

> According to this document, there had been an argument about the authority of the Bible. 'Thou canst prove nothing by Scripture', John Rogers had been assured. 'The Scripture is dead; it must have a lively exposition'. The man thus prepared to patronise the Bible was Stephen Gardner, Lord Chancellor of England and Bishop of Winchester... 'No', John Rogers had replied, 'the Scripture is alive ...'. 'Thou wilt not burn in that gear when it cometh to the purpose', Sir Richard Southwell had sneered.

The account is, of course, from John Rogers' point of view, but he wrote it down and went to the stake, because he was sure that his faith in the Bible as a living Word of God would be stronger than the pain of death by burning, and so it proved.

When Elizabeth succeeded to the throne in 1558, the revulsion against so much cruelty and persecution favoured the Protestant wind and England once again declared independence from Rome. This time the opposition of Rome was fiercer than under Henry, because for four years England had been 'saved'. The young Queen was instantly condemned, her acceptance of the title 'Supreme Governor of the Church' in England declared monstrous and she was excommunicated. Philip II of Spain was the self-appointed champion to carry out the execution. The Elizabethan Settlement was debated and many concessions made to opinions from all sides, but once fixed it had to be maintained as much for the safety of the realm as for the truth of doctrine. Elizabeth executed Catholics and Dissenters. In particular, her regime was hardest on those missionary priests who came over from Douai and from Rheims, as well as Rome, Englishmen who had fled and trained and bravely returned to win England back to the faith. *The Memoirs of Missionary Priests,* which the Roman Catholic Bishop Challoner wrote nearly two hundred years later is as moving and as heroic as Foxe's *Book of Martyrs.* But to be fair to Elizabeth, there were more executions in Mary's four years than in her forty!

Not all Catholics agreed with Stephen Gardner when he replied to John Rogers that, 'The Scripture is dead', although most would have preferred it to be accompanied by a 'lively exposition', lest heresy be derived from it by capricious, private interpretation.

Catholics fled from Elizabeth's England to Flanders and there established a seminary for the training of priests who would one day return to England and save her for the true Church. One of the products of that seminary was a version of the Bible in English, acceptable to Catholics.

The Seminary

Elizabeth did not have it all her own way, but she was determined to survive on the throne! Within a year of her succession, the Acts of Supremacy and Uniformity were passed in defiance of the Bishops in the House of Lords.

The only Bishop who can be found agreeing with it was the Bishop of Llandaff. It was also carried through with the knowledge that the clergy, meeting in the Convocation of Canterbury earlier in the year (1559) were solidly in favour of the old religion. She was still dealing with Mary's Bishops and Mary's clergy. The Protestants had largely fled, been eliminated or deposed. Elizabeth was quite sincere in her beliefs and genuinely concerned for the survival of the throne of England as independent. This was confirmed when Pius V deposed her in 1570 as Queen of England. David Edwards has a shrewd summary of her attitude to those who opposed her in Church and state:

> Although she consented to very severe punishments for real or alleged treason, it is impossible to think of her as an implacable persecutor like her sister, who executed hundreds never accused of treason. There is no reason to doubt her agonies of mind when she had to order the death of the Duke of Norfolk or Mary Queen of Scots were genuine, although politically she had no choice.

The Catholics certainly saw it as a religious persecution and many fled the country. They lived on the stories of heroic Catholic martyrs and the walls of their seminaries were hung with pictures of torture chambers and martyrs at the stake. Challoner's *Memoirs of Missionary Priests* gives a vivid account of the suffering of those who risked their lives in the venture. An edition of Challoner's *Memoirs* of 1803 is in Sion College Library and it has many blank pages where innumerable notes have been written in a very legible hand in Latin and English. One entry records:

Mr Barton was the first Seminary Priest from Douay College,

And then adds:

> In the beginning of Q Elizabeth's Persecution, many Catholics retired beyond the seas, says Father Persons, and for the most part to Louvain. Others soon after began to live in the University of Douay. Dr Allen and other leading Englishmen there seeing that sundry young men were moved by God in like manner to come over and to leave their country and commodities of study there for enjoying the benefit of Catholick Religion thought it best to live together in form of a College than dispersedly, though as yet there was no intention at all (and often I have heard Dr Allen affirm) of the end to returning again to the country to teach and preach Catholick Religion.

That quote would appear to be a contemporary comment and from one whose family was much involved in the setting up of the College in Douai.

William Allen

Born into a wealthy family, brought up in Lancashire and taught in Oxford, where he was a Fellow of Oriel College, he refused to accept the Elizabethan Settlement and fled to Flanders in 1568. He founded the College at Douai for English refugees, who wished to be trained for the priesthood. His initial plan was simply to wait and have a band of trained priests ready when England returned to the true faith. He soon saw that there was an urgent need of missionaries to work for the restoration of Catholicism rather than just wait. At first Spain saw the mission as part of its crusade and supported the College financially. Then anti-English feeling developed in Douai and the College had to move to Rheims in 1578. This had the advantage that the Duke of Guise took an interest in the College (or Seminary as it was now called) and financial problems were eased. However, it was not only money that troubled Dr Allen. Some very inferior candidates came across the water, their theology was confused and they had no experience of disciplined teaching. He established Douai on the basis of an Oxford College and tried to keep that standard. It was extraordinary what he did with the material he had. He made them into priests and his seminary an example for posterity. Again, it is David Edwards who most clearly captures the atmosphere of Douai training priests and martyrs:

> Most were trained for a mission of constant discomfort and tension, riding from house to house with a one-in-two chance of arrest and a one-in-seven chance of execution, braving a certainty which to many a Tudor Englishman was probably as worrying as the risk of a painful death: official condemnation and public execration as traitors.

But before long, Allen's extraordinary seminary was too small for popular demand and some students had to be sent elsewhere. He went to Rome and established the English College there, leaving Richard Bristow in charge of the Seminary in Rheims. Bristow was also an Oxford man, from Exeter College. William Allen died in 1594 and his last message tells a great deal about the man. He forbade Catholics to worship with Protestants, but added that those who did, because they were afraid for their families, were to be treated with great compassion and mercy. He died a cardinal and a short time before his death he was appointed Archbishop of Malines.

Gregory Martin

The Seminary soon discovered that, despite the many and persuasive pamphlets and books written by Willian Allen, the missionary priests would not make much headway in Elizabeth's England without an English version of the Bible. They were unable to use the Geneva Bible, because it was anathema to them, and all other existing translations were likewise 'Protestant'. Apart from Wycliffe's translation which was unacceptable for other reasons they were all translated from the Hebrew and Greek.

The Council of Trent had declared the true text of the Bible to be the Latin Vulgate. What they required was a translation of the specific Latin text derived from Jerome, which the Council of Trent had authorised. The man to do this was Gregory Martin. He was also an Oxford man, from St John's College. It is not quite certain when he was born, but it was in Sussex and he was nominated in the first batch of scholarship students to St John's College in 1557. He was the college companion of Edmund Campion for 13 years.

His first appointment outside Oxford was as a tutor in the Howard household, to Philip who was a nephew of the Duke of Norfolk. Something of Gregory Martin's reputation can be gathered from a speech made to the Duke of Norfolk when he visited St John's College, Oxford. The orator referred to Martin's place in the Howard household when he said: 'Thou hast, O illustrious Duke, our Hebraist, our Grecian, our poet, our honour and our glory'. That seemed to make him a good candidate for translating the Bible although it was a pity he was restricted to the Latin version!

When the Duke was sent to the Tower in 1570, Gregory Martin went to Douai, where he was welcomed by William Allen and by many other old companions from Oxford. He was ordained priest in 1573 and took his licentiate in Theology in 1575. He was employed at the Seminary to teach Hebrew and lecture on the Scripture. In 1577, he went to Rome with the first overflow of students, but he returned shortly afterwards. He removed to Rheims with the Seminary after civil commotions which virtually drove them out of Douai. It was at Rheims that he published the New Testament and it was thereafter known as the Rheims New Testament.

Gregory Martin was a very methodical man. Of his scholarship there can be no doubt and of his loyalty to the old religion. In the Howard household he would be encouraged in his devotion and for a time protected. The Duke of Norfolk was a powerful man and Gregory Martin must have felt himself quite safe as he followed the dictates of his Catholic faith.

As a young man going up to Oxford in 1557, he was in Mary's England, which presented few problems to a scholarly young Catholic. He was never politically involved and he was not ordained during his long spell at Oxford. The Acts of Supremacy and Uniformity may have worried him, but they proved dangerous only to his priest friends after 1559. He would have read with little sympathy John Foxe's *Book of Martyrs* when it appeared in 1563 and followed the new Archbishop Matthew Parker with some curiosity as his 'Advertisements' caused trouble with the Puritans. Like Wycliffe before him, he was protected in Oxford and there was not yet the bitter attitude to Catholics that later years brought when they were all thought to be agents of the King of Spain and traitors to the Queen. He lived the sheltered life of a scholar with very much in common with the Protestant scholars. His study of Hebrew is interesting, considering that his Church while he was still a child, had specified that the authentic text of the Scripture was the Latin Vulgate. He could only have studied Hebrew with the Hebrew text of the Old Testament. Of course he knew Latin, but it was as an Hebraist and a Grecian that he was known.

The little that we can learn about him at Oxford suggests a man whose ideas were not very far from those of Erasmus. His friendship with

Edmund Campion, however, and the 'persecutions' fired in him also a crusading spirit. This would not be quenched in the Howard household. Why the Duke of Norfolk invited him to serve as tutor is not clear. It may be that the Duke had plans to gather a formidable group of scholars around him for the day when England would return to Rome. But all hopes of a peaceful return were shattered when the foolish Pope Pius V claimed to depose Elizabeth of England. The news troubled Catholics far more than it troubled Protestants. It was a manifestly absurd action and it put all Catholics who accepted the Pope as Vicar of Christ and thus head of the Church Universal into the category of traitors.

Events followed rapidly and in the same year, the Duke of Norfolk was arrested and committed to the Tower. Gregory Martin no longer felt safe in England and he fled to Flanders. The training was strongly Jesuit with the thoroughness that accompanies everything the Jesuits do. Gregory Martin would have been completely at home in this atmosphere and soon absorbed himself in study and teaching. The Bible was his theme and he taught Hebrew, faithful to his Church in regarding the official Vulgate text as authoritative, but introducing his students to the Hebrew text of the Old Testament and the Greek text of the New. He was thoroughly conversant with the Bible in its original languages and this was bound to affect his teaching of Scripture. The students who came from his seminars and lectures would be able to hold their own with Protestants who based their opposition to the Catholic Faith on the Bible. He was without doubt a key figure at Douai. But what was lacking was a version of the Bible in English which could be as accurate as the Geneva Bible (or Tyndale's, or Coverdale's, The Great Bible or the Bishops' Bible) and accuracy would not be enough. It would have to be acceptable in style. Any translation from the Latin Vulgate was in danger of seeming stiff and latinate. Gregory Martin had one other gift. He was a stylist of high quality. The Douai Bible that we are accustomed to is stiff and no match for the splendour of the later King James, but that was not the Bible of Gregory Martin.

Translator and Polemicist

As a translator, Gregory Martin was most thorough. He began with the Old Testament which he rigorously translated from the Latin, although his mind must often have wandered to the Hebrew! He tried not to paraphrase, because he did not want to 'restrain the sense of the Holy Spirit to our fancy'. When he translated a difficult passage with which readers might scarcely believe, he would put the Latin words in the margin to justify his

English text. F F Bruce tells us that he worked systematically, 'at the rate of two chapters a day and as each section was completed it was revised by his colleagues Allen and Bristow'. F F Bruce has a careful discussion of his style from the point of view of a biblical scholar.

An interesting assessment by a Catholic stylist and classical scholar is found in the book by the Oxford Professor of Poetry, Peter Levi, on *The English Bible*. He deplores the subsequent revisions of Martin's translation culminating in the 'massacre' by Challoner, which turned it into a predecessor of the Good News Bible. Of the original translation, he says:

> It has an astonishing life as English, its prose is somewhat Latinate and based on Latin, but wonderfully musical, fresh and sweet-smelling. It is natural in its idiom and completely convincing in its rhythms. Its language is within ten years the English of the generation of Shakespeare, and this of course is its strength.

Gregory Martin did not publish his translation of the Old Testament, but went right on through the New Testament. The work was interrupted when the seminary had to leave Douai in 1578, shortly after Martin returned from his brief visit to Rome. He was in no way tempted to stay in Rome. William Allen did and became a cardinal. But Gregory Martin was a scholar without ambition.

On his return to Douai, the civil disturbances grew worse and the 'English' were more and more unpopular. The move to Rheims was right. It secured better financial support and gave Martin peace to continue his translation. In 1582, he published two books: the translation of the New Testament, which is properly called the Rheims New Testament and a polemic against Protestant translations *A Discoverie of the Manifold Corruptions of the Holy Scriptures*. He found the Latin Vulgate much nearer to the Hebrew and complained that English translations had not rendered the original honestly. It is no part of this book to go into detail about mistranslations. But to take one - 'Sheol' (and Martin rendered this in the Hebrew letters) was wrongly translated 'grave' where 'Hell' would have been nearer. Of course in the New Testament he complained of 'congregation' for 'Church'. This was the stock in trade of Catholic criticism since the days of Thomas More against Tyndale, but Martin's polemic was much more scholarly and showed a much greater command of the Hebrew. Thomas More confined his comments usually to Greek mistranslations, but Martin was equally at home with Hebrew.

His book shows that he was still revising his Old Testament. Peter Levi is of the opinion that he translated the whole of the Old Testament, with the Apocrypha where Catholics usually included it following the order of the Septuagint with the canon of the Old Testament. He must have had assistants in this work and the revisions of Allen and Bristow must have changed some parts. But Levi writes with conviction: 'It was written, I myself believe, completely by Gregory Martin except perhaps for Maccabees, and overseen by two or three of his colleagues'.

His teaching and writing continued at Rheims and news from England raised his hopes and dashed them again. Martin became more and more a crusader as his friends perished in the flames and his students found themselves in prison. In 1581, Edmund Campion was executed - a severe blow to Martin. The rise of the Puritans and Archbishop Whitgift's attempt to suppress them was followed with interest. The Spanish Armada in 1588 was a cause for hope and its disaster for despair.

The succession after the death of Elizabeth gave him little joy and the discovery of the Gunpowder Plot in 1605 spelled doom for his students, now missionary priests. The Seminary, which was by now regarded as a nest of traitors in England, moved back to Douai. News of the preparation of the Authorised Version of the Bible in England may have led the seminary to publish its Bible ahead of time. Martin had completed his revisions before he died of consumption on 26th October 1582. Now the Seminary felt that it must publish the whole Bible and did so as soon as possible after returning to Douai in 1609. The Douai-Rheims Bible was published 1609-1610. Later, however, it suffered from revisions in a way that Martin would have hated.

Revision

It is difficult to leave a good translation alone. Time brings changes in language and also ideas about new renderings of familiar texts. Preachers do it regularly! But to publish a revision of a classic is a very serious step. However, it is often with the best of intentions - some important passages are obscure, a new manuscript or more detailed textual criticism gives a better knowledge of the original, the meaning of certain words and phrases have changed or become associated with a particular set of ideas so as to render the translation misleading, etc. But one intention is always to make the Bible speak more directly to a new generation. When such a situation arises, the decision has to be taken whether it is better to do a new translation or to revise the ancient and honoured one. This problem will occur again and again. Jerome was much revised and in later years the Authorised Version would have its share of revisions. Few have suffered more from revision than the Douai Bible. The chief offender was the

Roman Catholic Bishop Challoner in the 18th century. Peter Levi calls his work a 'massacre'. The unadorned descriptions of what he did to this Shakespearian classic is contained in the Introduction to the 1977 edition of the New Testament: The Douai Catholic Version. It is written by Laurence Bright, who obviously does not feel so offended by its style:

> In the form familiar to us it (The Douay Version) is almost entirely the work of Bishop Challoner, who in this as in other ways did so much to give English Catholicism its present shape. Though he worked on the version produced in recusant days by members of the English College at Douay, the modifications he made were drastic enough to amount to a new translation.

The slight revisions during the seventeenth century were harmless enough, simply clarifying here and there. The major revisions undertaken by Richard Challoner totally changed it and unfortunately became the standard edition. In order to read the original Gregory Martin translations, it is necessary to visit a museum or a specialised library, such as that at Heythrop College, London.

Richard Challoner (1691-1781)

Born in Sussex on 29th September 1691, his father was a wine cooper and a rigid Dissenter. His mother was probably a practising Catholic. When she was widowed while quite young and Richard still in his infancy, she went into service nearby with a staunch Catholic and Jacobite family - the Gages. They were most unlikely to have employed any but a Catholic in their domestic service. However, Challoner claims to have been brought up an Anglican until his thirteenth year. About that time, his mother became housekeeper to Lady Anastasia and Richard came under the influence of her chaplain, an evangelising Roman Catholic, John Gother, who before he died in 1704, saw to it that Richard Challoner was not only a Catholic but on his way to Douai to train for the priesthood.

When Richard Challoner arrived in Douai, financed by a fund for poor boys, the College was at a low ebb. The president was Dr Edward Paston, who had some problems with discipline and his experiments in simpler courses for boys of lower intelligence were not appreciated. He was an ineffective character, a would-be reformer, but without discretion. He did not realise how 'English' the College was! He tried to base the education on a French model and was soon controlled by higher powers! Some of the senior staff were also suspected of Jansenist sympathies. These Jansenist troubles dominated the College for Challoner's first ten years. The effect was a very wary attitude to Jesuits which persisted through his life. From the staff, the strongest influence on the young Richard was Edward Dicconson, a Lancashire man, who at the time of his arrival was College procurator and professor of syntax.

From 1714, when Robert Witham became president, things improved greatly and for the rest of his time, Challoner was at a College vigorously reconstructing and reforming. He remained at Douai until 1730.

Robert Witham was a Yorkshireman, a vigorous Jacobite and a strict disciplinarian. The fear of Jansenism led to stricter control of theological opinions and a certain amount of anti-intellectualism. Most Douai priests could be described as are two in the Douai Papers:

> John Brand, a very vertuous and good man, of an indifferent capacity but by extraordinary diligence he made good use of his time here;
>
> John Reeves, a zealous, laborious and obedient missioner, but is not eloquent, nor can he sing.

By August 1730, Challoner had resigned all his Douai offices and went to London to begin his mission. There were about 20,000 Catholics in London at that time and among them many very poor. Challoner began among the poor. It was work that he loved best and in later years looked back with nostalgia. In a letter written nearly thirty years later, when he was harassed by the duties of a bishop, he looked back longingly to when he was 'absolutely released from all kinds of superiority and left in a lower station to preach to the poor'.

Challoner's Writings

Even while he was preaching to the poor 'in a lower station', he had time to write and his constant concern was the eradication of Protestant errors. In 1732, he published the first of his many controversial books: *The Unerring Authority of the Catholic Church*, followed a year later by *A Short History of the First Beginning and Progress of the Protestant Religion*. In 1734 came *The Touchstone of the New Religion*. Many books have contained an assessment of the quality of this controversial writing. It will suffice to quote Eamon Duffy in his essay which opens the collection he edited on *Challoner and his Church*:

> The writings ... are clear, scriptural, tightly argued, but never original, the work of a first-rate jobbing carpenter in command of his tools but disapproving of imaginative frills. Relentlessly he chipped away at the rock of Protestant obduracy, and his fellow Catholics at least were impressed.

His controversial writings came at a time when English Protestants were very sensitive to the obvious growth of Catholicism. There was undoubtedly an extraordinary growth and Challoner was partly responsible. It led him into conflict with Conyers Middleton who published his anti-Catholic tract *Letter from Rome* in March 1737. The Catholics were profiting from the tolerance of the eighteenth century. Eamon Duffy has convincingly shown that Challoner in no way suffered any unpleasant consequences from his outspoken attacks upon Protestantism - despite the many legends!

The Bishop of Debra

When Robert Witham, the ageing president of the College at Douai knew that his end was near, he nominated Challoner as his successor. The Vicar Apostolic would have none of it, because he needed Challoner. Benjamin Petre was not a very efficient Vicar Apostolic, holding high office more because of his aristocratic background than his scholarship or administrative abilities. Challoner was already dealing with his more difficult clergy for him. Petre did everything to keep him even to the extent of offering his resignation if Challoner should be forced from him by his superiors. Challoner in his view was the most important priest in the mission and was essential to Catholic strategy in London. Petre succeeded and Challoner was consecrated Bishop of Debra. The Catholic strategy at the time was through aristocratic Catholic families like the Norfolks at Arundel or the Southcotes at Witham - and many of these were declining. Challoner now had episcopal jurisdiction over the London district which extended over ten counties - from Kent to Hampshire, including the Isle of Wight and the Channel Islands. Theoretically, Petre was in charge, but he had sunk into inactivity once Challoner was appointed.

Challoner now began to order his life as became a bishop and fixed a pattern which would remain for the whole of his episcopate: He rose at 6 o'clock, praying as he dressed. An hour in meditation. Private Mass was at 8 o'clock and then on Sundays and Holy Days he celebrated for a congregation at 9 o'clock. During the week, he breakfasted at 9 o'clock and then recited his breviary. From then on until 1 o'clock, he saw visitors, answered letters and worked at his writing, 'an endless stream of devotional, instructional and hagiographical books'. At 1 o'clock more breviary. At 2 o'clock, lunch with his chaplain and half an hour's relaxed conversation. In the afternoon, he went with a chaplain to visit friends or walk in the woods north of Holborn. He was back at home between 5 and 6, once more receiving visitors, hearing confessions, attending to business. The rest of his time until 9 o'clock supper was spent in reading and meditation, completing his Office. After supper and a little conversation, he retired to bed. He kept to this pattern as part of the requirements of a faithful priest, believing that discipline, regularity and poverty are fundamental to a priestly life. This discipline with which he held his own priestly life together gave him more credibility when he attempted to discipline the unsatisfactory clergy with whom he had to deal. He had good grounds for disciplining some of his clergy and he has some hard words to say about the religious orders. He did not spare the laity either, however important they may be. He saw the spiritual life of the Catholics as lax and opposed the liberalising tendencies of the age. He understood his people and could be very compassionate, but he saw that the growth of Catholicism would be halted in England if clergy, religious and laity did not maintain the highest standards of behaviour and piety.

His writing proceeded apace and was designed to promote an *English* piety. He translated spiritual classics like à Kempis and Francis de Sales. He wrote the *Memoirs of Missionary Priests* to awaken the epic age of heroism and kindle a sanctified patriotism. Catholicism needed its heroes; but he also saw what the Bible meant to Protestants and how much more it should mean to Catholics. With this in mind, he attempted a simplified form of translation. The classical Douai translation was admired by scholars and stylists, but unintelligible to the ordinary Catholic. His results were flat but easy to understand. He brought out his first revised New Testament in 1749 (slightly changed and with the Old Testament added in 1750). In 1752, another edition contained 2,000 changes. He added notes on certain controversial passages. One or other of his versions completely replaced the original Douai, which even today is hard to find.

The Gordon Riots

Challoner lived to a great age for his period, as he grew older he saw Catholics winning their rights as citizens and recognised as loyal. The triumph of his life should have been the Catholic Relief Act of 1778. He was glad to see Catholics accepted as first-class citizens, but it was not a happy ending. William Payne had instigated prosecutions before the Act and often been successful. After the Act, this was no longer possible, but on 2nd June 1780 the Protestant Association, 60,000 strong, led by an unbalanced Scottish nobleman, Lord George Gordon, gathered in Southwark to present a monster petition for the repeal of the Act. The march to parliament got out of hand. The crowds broke up into detachments and one went to the Sardinian Embassy which was ransacked and set alight. The Bavarian Embassy also suffered looting. A week of violence followed in which the military and the police were quite unable to control the destruction of lives and property. On the worst night, 7th June, the distillery of a wealthy Catholic was set on fire with 120,000 gallons of spirit. The fire spread to the neighbourhood and rioters burned the prisons at King's Bench, Newgate, Southwark, the Fleet, and the Marshalsea and prisoners were turned loose. Catholic houses were burned and Mass houses pulled down. Only the force of 10,000 soldiers at last brought the Gordon riots under control. In that week, 285 people had been killed. George Gordon was tried for treason and acquitted; 62 rioters were sentenced to death, of whom 25 were executed. Challoner was rescued from a mob, shaken, but ready to return to London when the worst of the riots were over.

He took up the threads of his ministry after the riots and held a confirmation on 5th October. He weakened, suffered a stroke and eventually died just before midnight on 12th January 1781.

He was a legend in his own day. He was a monument to what he called the 'old religion'. He was a man of many limitations. He had not a shred of imagination, not a trace of poetry. He had no interests outside religion, no Protestant friends except potential converts. Yet his narrowness was the narrowness of total dedication and an inner vision. Eamon Duffy sums him up in one penetrating sentence:

> Through clear, tired eyes Challoner looked out on the world and thought it a poor enough place, but loved the God who made it and the men who were in it and gave his life to their service.

It was a pity that so unimaginative and unpoetic a mind should be brought to bear upon the English version of the Bible that was to serve Catholics for the next century and a half.

8. Revising a Classic

The Authorised Version formed the spirituality of the English-speaking world in such a way that its style became the language of piety and prayer. *The Book of Common Prayer* with its similar style made a language of worship which could hardly be challenged. For a long time, the library of a Protestant Christian was the *Bible* and *Pilgrim's Progress*. The Catholics, of course had a different language of devotion, formed by the Latin Mass, or Challoner's 'revision' of the Douai Version, as well as his translation of Thomas à Kempis.

It was the scholars who revised the Authorised Version, and they were careful not to change the style. The first serious attempt to provide a substantial version to succeed the AV was the Revised Version. The initiative came from Samuel Wilberforce, Bishop of Winchester, who submitted the following motion to the Upper House of Convocation of the Province of Canterbury on 10th February 1870:

> That a committee of both Houses be appointed, with power to confer with any Committee that may be appointed by the Northern Province, to report upon the desirableness of a revision of the Authorised Version of the New Testament, whether by marginal notes or otherwise, in all those passages where *plain and clear errors*, whether in the Hebrew or Greek text originally adopted by the translators, or in the translation made from the same, shall, on due investigation, be found to exist.

The motion was tidied up by Dr Ollivant, Bishop of Llandaff who proposed extending 'the New Testament' to 'the Old and New Testament' The Biblical scholars of Britain and America were eventually involved in large numbers in the task, but three names stand out from the beginning: F H A Scrivener, B F Westcott and F J A Hort. These were not men seeking a new language, but a more accurate text.

Samuel Wilberforce

His father, William Wilberforce was the 'liberator of the slaves'; Samuel was his third son. He married a relative, Emily, the daughter of John

Sargent, whose wife was his father's cousin. The Clapham 'saints' found it hard to live with outsiders who did not share their puritanical approach to life or their strict moral codes. The Evangelicanism which William Wilberforce had worked to instil into his sons was becoming diluted by success and Samuel was aware of this. At Oxford he had heard enough that might have encouraged him to follow his brother and many of his friends along the path to Rome. But he resisted this. He supported the Evangelical Church Missionary Society, which was newly formed. For him, it was his favourite society, 'so thoroughly Church of England, so eminently active and spiritual', although he grew more and more dissatisfied with the Evangelicals. Before long it was evident that he was neither an Evangelical nor a Tractarian, (ie an Anglo-Catholic), but he was firmly rooted in the Church of England.

Robert and his younger brother Henry were both intoxicated by the Tractarians. In a sermon given by Samuel Wilberforce in 1839 he clearly describes his attitude, so different from the Tractarians. He believed that clergymen preached and wrote tracts to bring men into the Church and thus into communion with their Saviour. This was the 'leading idea' to seize upon; anything else that hindered this expression was beside the point. He could not see the importance of the minutiae over which the Tractarians agonised.

The Tractarian Controversy

The Oxford Movement, which developed an Anglo-Catholic wing of the Church of England in opposition to the Evangelicals, was born of a series of *Tracts for Our Time*. The champions of the Movement were Pusey, Keble, Newman, Froude and included Samuel's brother Robert Wilberforce. These were all friends of Samuel Wilberforce, but they were not sure where he stood. They were coming to the conclusion that Samuel had his eye on advancement. Both the Queen and Prime Minister disapproved of the Oxford reformers. There may be a little in the accusation that he kept himself free from party in order to win a bishopric, but the evidence tends more to show that he was genuinely concerned that the Church of England should hold together and there was much of an Evangelical in him still. Like many others he found fault with Newman for 'denying God the power to work within the souls of men at his own pace and by his own will'. His objections to Newman were also very practical. Any theology which emphasised 'the chains of duty' and 'the details of obedience', Samuel maintained, ran the risk of driving men with 'timid conscientious minds' out of the Church altogether. He also attacked Pusey's tract defending the sacrament of baptism from Protestant heresies. Again, it was a practical point, concerning sin after baptism. Pusey had argued that sin after baptism 'is not only a step towards final impenitence, but weakens the Baptismal grace, and tends to deprive the individual of the ordinary means of restoration'. Once having sinned, man could never be completely restored to favour in God's eyes. It was this *Tract LXVII* which drew from Wilberforce a public answer which declared his dissatisfaction with the Tractarians.

The Bishop of Oxford

On 10th March 1841, his wife Emily died in childbirth. Samuel never completely recovered from this blow. He was then Rector of Alverstone and Archdeacon of Surrey. These heavy duties absorbed his time and his grief. He went little to Oxford and even cancelled the Bampton Lectures he was due to give in that year. A few years later, he was offered the Deanery of Westminster, but hesitated to accept. After consulting Prince Albert's secretary and learning that the Queen wished him to accept, he did so on 28th March 1845. He viewed the task with trepidation, but he had little time to undertake it, because in the autumn of the same year he was appointed Bishop of Oxford.

Wilberforce entered upon his duties resolved to think of nothing but the service he might perform for God and the Church. He was aware of the dangers this new position held for one so active - and so worldly. He was a good bishop, concerned primarily with his pastoral office, particularly towards his clergy, but there were inevitably public offices to perform. He was also a reforming bishop and much concerned with the proper training of the clergy.

After Emily's death, Samuel Wilberforce determined that however strenuous the work of the diocese, he would not neglect his children. He vowed to show the affection he felt for them and give them all the time and attention he could. His mother-in-law, Mary Sargent, agreed to live with them and help him raise the children. She was 63 at the time of Emily's death and had spent the past 12 years watching at the deathbed of her husband and four of her children. She accepted the new burden as a duty, although she would have preferred a more tranquil life. They lived mostly at Cuddesdon and the children were well looked after. They did not lack affection and Samuel kept his vow. He was an attentive father. He took the boys on rides and to the zoo. When they were sick he fretted over them. When they left for school, he pined for them. His sense of the loss of Emily intensified as the family grew up.

The Defence against Rome

As Bishop of Oxford, Samuel Wilberforce had one clear objective, to find a *modus vivendi* for the Church of England between the two extremes of those rushing headlong back to Rome and those who as 'Evangelicals' were inclined to throw away the advantages of the Established Church, Catholic and Reformed. He had sympathy with both sides and was anxious that the strength of both be retained within the Church of England. This meant supporting the emphasis upon the authority of the Bible without denigrating the authority of the Church. At the same time it meant maintaining the place of the Church of England within the historical Catholic Church without submitting to the authority of the Bishop of Rome. What he had no sympathy with was the Broad Church Movement, which today we should call 'Liberal'.

In the years 1845 to 1860, his most troublesome opponents were those who wished to guide the Church of England back to submission to the Roman see. Wilberforce hated controversy within the Church and it was his long term ambition to bring Tractarians happily together within the family of the Church of England. He was an Evangelical at heart, but suspect, because he had great sympathy with the Tractarians who were his natural allies. The problem arose from indiscretions on both sides. The focus of his concern about the Tractarians rested upon Pusey. The younger clergy were attracted to Pusey and Keble, introducing into their churches practices they had learned from them - confession, the rosary, prayers to the saints etc. Wilberforce wanted to be tolerant, telling his clergy that 'what we deem errors in others are often different views of the same truth, imperfect on the one side as our own probably are on the other'.

After 1852, relations between Wilberforce and Pusey improved and they joined forces against Rome, supported by Gladstone as Prime Minister and with the approval of the Queen. A bill went through Parliament which sought to halt the papal 'aggression' in the form of a re-established Roman Hierarchy: 'The Ecclesiastical Titles Bill', which ruled out as illegal the use of Roman titles. The Bill had little effect and was only mildly supported by Wilberforce, who wrote to Gladstone recommending a more tolerant course.

He was acting under an almost unbearable strain. First his younger brother, Henry, married to a Roman Catholic went over to Rome, followed by one of Samuel's closest friends Henry Manning, and finally his elder brother Robert. These losses almost broke his heart. Robert died in Rome where he was preparing for Orders as a Roman priest in February 1857.

Wilberforce was determined the more now to deal firmly with ritualism and creeping Romanism within the Church of England when he thought it dangerous, but for all his bitterness and hatred of those who had robbed him of his brothers, he did not allow his private grief to influence his public office. He continued sympathetic to the sensibilities of the ritualists and Anglo-Catholics under his charge. As the years passed, Wilberforce grew tolerant of different views within the Church. Extremists on both sides complained that he had no position of his own. He welcomed and encouraged clergy, Evangelicals and Anglo-Catholics, insisting that diversity and variety meant life and for that reason were to be welcomed. This tolerance was not extended to the growing school of Broad Churchmen. In the fifties and sixties, Wilberforce became the champion of orthodoxy against the double threat of higher criticism and evolutionary theory.

Evolutionary Theory and Higher Criticism

'The divinely ordered limits beyond which man had no right to go', were rudely trespassed by *The Origin of Species* in 1859 and Wilberforce was asked to review it for the *Quarterly*. This led eventually to the infamous debate between Wilberforce and T H Huxley at the meetings of the British Association for the Advancement of Science which were held in Oxford in 1860. Unfortunately Wilberforce is best known for his somewhat pathetic defence in that debate. It was not his greatest moment! What he was defending was the authority of the Bible and the superiority of knowledge obtained by revelation over that obtained by scientific observation. He was not alone in being concerned about the inroads being made both by higher criticism and by scientific enquiry into belief in the Bible as the inerrant Word of God. It was this deep concern which later led him to seek a revision of the Authorised Version of the Bible, free from 'plain and clear errors'. The Word of God could not err, but the translators could.

A far greater threat to the Church than Darwin came a year later with the publication of a collection of essays, which seemed to Wilberforce to pervert the doctrines of the Church. The essays were written by six clergymen and one lay-man, who was a distinguished scholar. The conception of the book was due to Benjamin Jowett and Frederick Temple.

Essays and Reviews was published in the autumn of 1860 and by February Wilberforce was agitating for its condemnation. He was given an opportunity to comment upon it in the *Quarterly* where he expressed regret that men of such 'earnestness, piety of spirit and high moral object' should have written this book. Their character made it all the more dangerous to the young men who would be led astray by it.

This review came under fire from many directions. Yet he stuck to his main position, which was that revelation may be substantiated by other evidence but not probed and criticised. Such an activity is to encourage doubt in a loving God. Revelation must be accepted and all that science can do is show how wondrously true it is. In particular, he attacked those clergymen who were appointed to teach. It was none of their duty to encourage questioning of the truth of what they had to teach. The Bible was inerrant and must be accepted. He did however admit that there was room for scholarship to expound the meaning of the Bible from the original texts and to provide more accurate translations.

In 1869, Gladstone secured for him the see of Winchester. There were not lacking those who said that he was promoted for services rendered, but Winchester was not much of a prize, except in prestige. Briefly he hoped for something higher when the Archbishop of Canterbury fell seriously ill. But Tait recovered and Wilberforce remained for the rest of his life, Bishop of Winchester.

He was not so successful at Winchester as he had been at Oxford. The diocese was too large and the clergy less inclined to be reconciled. It was while he was Bishop of Winchester that he proposed the revision of the Authorised Version of the Bible and continued as the permanent chairman of the committee set up by the Convocation to undertake the task of biblical revision. Wilberforce wanted 'plain and clear errors' removed and the best possible original text determined, but he did not want to lose the 'ring of familiarity'.

He took little part in the work of the committee. He was no scholar and had little enthusiasm for the task, but he was conscientious and a bit of a nuisance. The chairman of the New Testament panel, Dr Ellicott, who was a scholar and pursued his task with enthusiasm, commented to the Archbishop:

> My only care now is to keep Winchester as much out of the chair as can cleverly be done. He has not criticism enough for it, and he gave mortal offence to some during his short tenure of the chair. I received private notice that resignations would be sent in if I did not continue.

He may have been exaggerating. He was not above ambition. But Wilberforce himself sensed some displeasure and left the work to others while he concentrated upon his diocese which was proving much more demanding than Oxford. His health began to fail, he had two heart attacks and finally while riding from Leatherhead station to Lavington, he fell from his horse and died in 1873.

The Scholars

Samuel Wilberforce did not revise the Authorised Version, but he was persistent in his advocacy of revision. He had neither time nor ability to play any substantial part in the task, but he recognised the men who could do it. There were two tasks:

1. A more reliable text, particularly for the New Testament, which was as near to the original as possible. This required textual critics of the highest qualification, and the time was ripe. Textual criticism was coming into its own. The discovery by Tischendorf of the Codex Sinaiticus in St Catherine's Monastery on Mount Sinai was a headline story and for textual critics it provided a new impetus.

2. An accurate translation of the best text possible. This was a more difficult task and eventually had to be left to a later generation. If the time was ripe to accept a new and more accurate text, there was no support for changing the sound of the Authorised Version. It must be an accurate translation of the best text, but not sound like a modern translation! The Authorised Version must be altered as little as possible and only because a better knowledge of the text required it. Hence the important people in the preparation of the Revised Version were not the translators, but the textual critics. The makers of the Revised Version were those who laboured at textual criticism to discover as far as they could the original text as it left the hands of the sacred writers.

There were those who queried this, such as J N Darby, who wrote in the Preface to his translation of the New Testament which he had prepared for his community of Plymouth Brethren:

> In the translation I could feel delight - it gave us the word and mind of God more accurately: in the critical details there is much labour and little food.

None of the scholars thought Darby's translation was very successful and they regretted that he held the accuracy of the original text so lightly. The first priority then, for the Revised Version was to be the text from which the translation, or rather revision, was made and this was successfully achieved, although not without controversy. The scholars chosen for this work were: F H A Scrivener, S P Tregelles, B F Westcott and F J A Hort. Tregelles was not well enough to take any part in the revision of the text, but the other three were very active. They represented the best in textual criticism that this country could produce. Westcott and Hort were closely related in the work and usually in agreement. Scrivener, when he disagreed was almost always outvoted! They were three very different people.

Frederick Henry Ambrose Scrivener

Scrivener's father was a tradesman, a stationer, who lived in Bermondsey. His son was born on the 29th September 1813 and little is known of the family. It was F H A Scrivener, who made the name known by his industrious work on the text of the New Testament. It was his life long concern that clergy and preachers, scholars and serious students of the Bible should have confidence in the text.

As a boy he was educated at St Olave's School, Southwark, until the age of 18. His ability with the Classical languages was noted at an early age and he was encouraged to proceed to Cambridge. He enrolled at Trinity College and did well. He was elected a Scholar on 3rd April 1834, ie in his 21st year. He looked set for an academic career and had the temperament for it. But there was no precedent in his family and he became neither a Fellow nor a Professor. That kind of career would have provided him with resources and stimulus to continue his early passion for textual studies. Despite that, he became the Master of Textual Criticism by other than a University route. He had before him the choice of school master or clergyman. He managed to achieve both and do his academic work with the text of the New Testament.

In 1835, he was appointed Assistant Master at Sherborne School and learned his craft of teaching there over a period of almost three years. Then, having obtained his MA, he was ordained and appointed curate at Sandford Orcas in Somerset. There on 21st July 1840 he married Anne Blofeld. She helped him in his pastoral work and encouraged him to pursue his textual studies. Quietly supportive, she lived with him until her death in 1877. Together they brought much life to the Church at Sandford Orcas. It was a remote place and his duties were not heavy. He had leisure to read and work away at reproductions of manuscripts. But a long curacy in a remote country parish was not very satisfying and in 1846, he was appointed Headmaster at Falmouth School with a perpetual curacy at Penwerris. During his headship, which lasted for twelve years, he followed with growing interest the discovery and study of the Codex Sinaiticus by Tischendorf.

Something of the excitement of this recovery of a fourth-century codex of the New Testament, with parts of the Old in Greek, can be recognised years later when he published an account of Tischendorf's contribution to textual criticism. The description occurs in his introduction to a work which he prepared while still a curate at Penwerris, although by 1865 he had found the pressure of work as Headmaster of Falmouth School too great for his growing concern with textual criticism. The work was published first in connection with Archdeacon Wordsworth's edition of the Greek New Testament, but appeared in 1864 as a separate publication under the title: *A Full Collation of the Codex Sinaiticus with the Received Text of the New Testament.*

> While Tischendorf was travelling in 1844 in search of ancient manuscripts under the patronage of his own sovereign, King Frederick Augustus of Saxony, he was so fortunate as to pick out of a basket of papers, destined to light the stove in the convent of St Catherine on Mount Sinai, forty-three *vellum* leaves containing portions of the Septuagint version, chiefly from I Chronicles and Jeremiah, with Nehemiah and Esther complete, bearing every mark of extreme antiquity, in oblong folio with four columns on each page.

Scrivener goes on to tell how Tischendorf explained that the vellum leaves were part of a codex of the fourth century. Once the monastery realised their value, he was not allowed to take any more. Eventually he persuaded the monks to present the Codex to the Czar of Russia who was their patron, on the occasion of the millennium of the Russian Empire. Scrivener never lost his interest in that Codex and when the time came to decide upon the text for the Revised Version, he constantly pushed the virtues of Codex Sinaiticus. This led him also to champion the Greek text which the translators of the Authorised Version had used, the *Received Text*. His conservative attitude to this text separated him from Westcott and Hort, who as we shall see, were not content to edit the Received Text, but wanted a thorough revision.

Before resigning as Headmaster of Falmouth School, he had shown his ability to handle texts by publishing a collation of twenty different manuscripts of the Gospels. The meticulous attention to texts and their variants soon earned him a reputation; but it needed time which he could not give with the heavy responsibilities of the School. The collation of the Gospel texts was done while he was still headmaster as was the careful work on *A Supplement to the English Authorised Version of the New Testament*, published as early as 1845.

After leaving the School in 1856, he continued to publish technical works on the Greek text of the New Testament, *The Greek Testament* 1858, and *Codex Augiensis and Contributions to New Testament Criticism* 1859. His major work, however, of this period was *A Plain Introduction to the Criticism of the New Testament*, which soon became a standard work and throughout his life time ran into second and third editions.

Before he died, he had done most of the work for the fourth edition which was published posthumously in 1894. The meticulous examination of texts and manuscripts can be illustrated by the very number of manuscripts he dealt with and the way in which they grew in subsequent editions. The first edition in 1861 dealt with 1,170 manuscripts; the fourth edition in 1894, with more than 3,000! Much of this work was done after his move from Falmouth.

The Rector

In 1862, Scrivener was given the Rectory of St Gerrans in Cornwall. This was a very fruitful period for him. He not only worked away at the manuscripts and developed some of the permanent principles of textual criticism, turning it from an amateur interest in various readings of the text, into a scientific method by which to arrive at the most probable original. He laboured at a time when many found the subject of textual criticism dull. He attempted to popularise it and delivered six lectures 'chiefly addressed to those who do not read Greek'. These lectures were published while he was still at St Gerrans in 1875. It may well have been the reputation of those lectures before they were published or his growing stature as the Master of Textual Criticism, which in 1874 led to his appointment as prebend in Exeter Cathedral. There could have been another reason. In May 1870, the invitations had been sent out to those who would be expected to revise the Authorised Version. Traditionally, it was expected that such a committee would be drawn from the two Universities, Westminster and the Bishops. Scrivener came under none of these headings, but he could not be ignored as the leading exponent of textual criticism and a stout defender of the Received Text. A rector in Cornwall would not have been a very obvious choice. A prebend of Exeter Cathedral was at least somewhere among the honours! His contributions to biblical criticism had already been recognised by the award of a civil pension of £100 in 1872. Apart from the recognition of his contribution to biblical criticism the award was said to 'aid publication'.

Certainly the publications continued. Apart from revising the standard work on *Introduction to the Criticism of the New Testament*, there was another work during his time at St Gerrans, which made his reputation. 1870-1873, he published in three volumes, the *Cambridge Paragraph Bible of the Authorised Version*. The text was in paragraphs and verse numbering in the margin. But more important than the arrangement of the printing was his extensive introduction. It dealt with most of the problems of the Authorised Version, but argued for the retention of the translation as far as possible. He was to be the most conservative of the members of the NT Company for the Revised Version. During this publication, he was given his first doctorate, LL D, from St Andrews. The one volume edition in 1873 thus carried on its title page, Rector of St Gerrans, MA, LL D., and 'One of the New Testament Company of the Revision of the Authorised Version'. A list of the contents of that extensive introduction will give some idea of his thoroughness:

1. History of the Text of the Authorised Version
2. Marginal Notes
3. The use of Italic type
4. Punctuation adopted in 1611 and modified
5. Grammatical peculiarities and the use of Capitals
6. Marginal parallel texts
7. Miscellaneous comments on the present text

There were also five appendices dealing with the passages in which his edition departs from the AV, the two issues of the 1611 Bible, passages which have been restored from earlier versions of the AV, a report of the work of translation and some details of the Greek text of the AV in the New Testament. There is also a Translator's Preface included and a Dedicatory Epistle. One gets the feeling that he was producing his own conservative 'Revised Version' of the New Testament ahead of the appointed company! But Westcott and Hort were later supported when he differed from them and despite his immense scholarship his judgements have not stood the test of time. The text adopted was not his revision of the Received Text, but that of Westcott and Hort which has survived the century since it was prepared.

The Vicar of Hendon

It was probably to bring him nearer to London that Scrivener was moved from St Gerrans in Cornwall to Hendon in Middlesex. He was appointed Vicar of Hendon in 1876. It was not a wise decision. Oxford honoured him with a DCL that year, but Hendon was a parish of 5,500 and made considerable demands upon him. He was trying to prepare his third and later fourth edition of *Criticism of the New Testament*. His wife died in 1877, Hendon was growing and preparation had to be made for extra work at the church. The strain was too much for him. He suffered a paralytic stroke and died at Hendon on 30th October 1891. His continuing influence is largely due to his major work, *A Plain Introduction to the Criticism of the New Testament*. His own assessment of the work is contained in a Dedication to 'Edward, Lord Archbishop of Canterbury' in the Third Edition, dated Whitsuntide 1883.

> Nearly forty years ago, under encouragement from your venerated predecessor Archbishop Howley, and with the friendly help of his librarian, Dr Maitland, I entered upon the work of collating manuscripts of the Greek New Testament by examining the copies brought from the East by Professor Carlyle, and purchased for the Lambeth Library in 1805. I was soon called away from this employment to less congenial duties in that remote county (Cornwall). What I have since been able to accomplish in the pursuits of sacred criticism, although very much less than I once anticipated, has proved I would fain hope, not without its use to those who love Holy Scripture, and the studies which help to the understanding of the same.

The other work, which for a time proved most influential and set the pattern for many similar writings into our own century was the six lectures on the text of the New Testament 'chiefly addressed to those who do not read Greek'. Those lectures greatly widened his readership and prepared those who were not scholars for the Revised Version.

Brooke Foss Westcott

Born in Birmingham, 12th January 1825, an industrious little boy both with his private tutor, a curate at Erdington, and at King Edward VI's School in Birmingham; Westcott was most meticulous in his records. His first Latin Dictionary contains on its blank page a list of his career from first at school, Easter 1837, to Durham 1889. As a boy he took a keen interest in the Chartist Movement. The popular presentations of the sufferings of the masses deeply affected his imagination and never faded from his mind. He was greatly influenced by one of his teachers at King Edward VI's School and continued to pay tribute for many years to James Prince Lee, 'superior, as I believe, among the great masters of his time'.

Westcott went up to Cambridge, October 1844. He registered at Trinity and had lodgings in Jesus Lane, overlooking the gardens of Sidney

Sussex. He had a very distinguished record at Cambridge; following his First in the Classical Tripos, he remained up as a graduate with a considerable amount of private tutoring until 1851. In that year, on Trinity Sunday, 15th June, he was ordained deacon in the parish church of Prestwich by his old teacher, Dr J Prince Lee, by then Bishop of Manchester. He was disappointed by the coldness of the ceremony. In the same year, 21st December, the Bishop ordained him priest in the church of Bolton-le-Moors. Although the ceremony seemed cold his own reactions were warm enough.

Westcott continued at Cambridge until he was ordained and gathered a circle of friends who regretted his decision to leave for some other educational post. He wanted to marry and share his work with Mary a friend from his childhood. His first thought was a headship at Exeter Grammar School, but was dissuaded; then the principalship of Victoria College, Jersey, a new institution seeking its first principal. He would probably have been appointed to either; but he chose instead to be an assistant master at Harrow.

Harrow

It was the most junior of the possibilities that he had chosen, commenting to J B Lightfoot, he said, 'For this, my youth and power is better fitted than for the office of governor'. Westcott settled into a little house opposite the gates of The Park early in 1852. He was quickly happy at his work.

He married on 23rd December 1852 in St Philip's Church, Bristol. After the Christmas holidays they settled down at 'The Butts'. His Cambridge pupils gave him a very handsome silver inkstand which he greatly valued, but vowed he would not dare to use it until he could sign other than his own name. When he became a bishop the family filled up the inkwell and insisted upon his using it!

Westcott made a very interesting visit to the Auvergne in August 1854 and his son preserved a copy of his report which shows how deeply he was affected by that volcanic area and his visit to France as a whole. In Paris, at the end of his tour, he spent most of his time in the *Bibliothèque Nationale* studying manuscripts. Back in Cambridge briefly in 1855 he met the famous German textual critic Tischendorf and was not much impressed! He complained that the man had only one idea - 'palimpsests and codices'. In the same year, 1854, Westcott brought out his *General Survey of the History of the Canon of the New Testament*. That was the first edition.

He also had a passion for geology, but his last indulgence of it was Easter of 1856. His letters to his wife show him so involved that you would judge him to be a man obsessed with nothing else but fossils and dry bones! He had postponed his proposed visit to Bonn to learn German for this trip to Lamb's Close quarry near Farringdon and then to Chippenham. He never lost that love of geology but that was his last field trip. In the summer of 1858 he went to Dresden to learn German, but most of his letters home are about pictures in the Art Gallery. His visit to Dresden was with Mr R M Hensley (later Sir Robert Hensley, Chairman of the Metropolitan Asylum Board). From Dresden, having completed their German lessons, they went to Prague. There he was greatly impressed by the singing in the Catholic Church and expressed his longing for the same devotion in the Church of England. More than once he contrasts the life of the Catholic Church with the poverty of enthusiasm in his own:

> It makes me almost feel angry to hear sounds so deeply moving, which ought also to express our feelings, and yet I know that we must remain silent when we should in turn raise full swelling hymns. The same sort of feeling came over me also yesterday when I saw that the Pope had at once directed two bishops, one with twenty missionaries, to proceed at once to China in consequence of a new treaty. We shall barely follow with two or three perhaps. What marvellous power the organisation of the Roman Church gives to its leaders, and is it wrong? Oh, Marie, how often I wonder what we *do* for our religion.

Westcott had written a scholarly book in his *History of the New Testament* and its value was recognised, but something was needed for the general reader. He, therefore, spent his summer holidays in 1863 at Seaton with the family, working on a popular version called *The Bible in the Church*. In this more popular work he decided to give some account also of the compilation of the Old Testament Scriptures.

Early in 1864 the Norrisian Professorship of Divinity at Cambridge became vacant and Westcott thought to apply. It was not to be. A subsidy hitherto given to the professorship was withdrawn and left its income at only £100 with which Westcott could hardly support a family!

Westcott kept a large correspondence going with his former pupils and it is from this that we learn most of his intellectual development and his writings. In a letter to Lightfoot, for example, in January 1865, he refers to a strange essay, which he says contains 'some very old thoughts to which I feel bound to give expression in the present crisis'. The crisis is presumably that initiated by *Essays and Reviews* which so troubled

Wilberforce. It rumbled on for many years, together with the Church's problems of coming to terms with Darwin. Controversy was in the air and Westcott was reluctant to enter into it. His essay was 'some very old thoughts', which his son interpreted as thoughts that had brought him comfort in his undergraduate days, when he suffered so much from a torturing scepticism. The essay was composed late in 1864 and sent to a number of friends for their comments before publishing. It was eventually published in 1865 as *The Gospel of the Resurrection*. Among his little works (ie apart from his massive and learned works on the text of the New Testament) this was the one he cared about most, as he said to Macmillan when preparing an edition of it as late as 1873.

What he wanted to work on, however, was a formative study of St John. For this he was never able to find time.

In the summer of 1865, Westcott visited La Salette, near Grenoble and was impressed by the miracles performed there by the Virgin. He wrote a paper on this and intended to publish it, but Lightfoot dissuaded him. He feared that it might bring upon him the charge of mariolatry and prejudice his chances of a professorship at Cambridge. He withdrew it, but had a few copies printed for private circulation only. By this time, Westcott was a power at Harrow. On the death of Mr Oxenham in 1863, he had come over from his 'Small House' to take charge of the 'Large House'. The Headmaster, later to become Master of Trinity, wrote of his management of that House: 'His house was from the first pre-eminent for its intellectual and general vigour, and no small part of this result was due to the new Master.' Unless this be misunderstood, he added, 'No learned man was ever less of a pedant. No great student of books could be more genial and even playful'. He supported this by stories of his fun with the boys. But Westcott could not stay for ever at Harrow.

Peterborough

In June 1870, Bishop Magee offered him the Archdeaconry of Northampton. He had left Harrow by then and was installed as a canon in Peterborough, where he went at the beginning of 1869 and was reluctant to give it up. He asked Lightfoot for his advice and as was to be expected, Lightfoot advised him to refuse. He continued happily at Peterborough, throwing himself into the work of the Cathedral. He also attracted promising theological students and gladly directed their studies. One of these was Canon Scott Holland who gives his impressions of this studious man of prayer:

We had never before seen such an identification of study with prayer. He read and worked in the very mind in which he prayed; and his prayer was of singular intensity. It might be only the elements of textual criticism with which he was dealing; but, still, it was all steeped in the atmosphere of awe, and devotion, and mystery, and consecration. He taught us as one who ministered at the Altar; and the details of the Sacred Text were to him as the Ritual of some Sacramental Action.

Westcott loved Peterborough Cathedral, frequently sitting in the darkness of the night and realising the presence of the past. He was powerfully sensitive to the Communion of Saints. He also enjoyed the preparation of great services, Sunday evening in Advent and Lent and in the summer almost every Sunday a special occasion. He was busy and happy preparing and delivering Congress addresses and many of these found their way to publication. Collections of his sermons in 1881 produced the very influential, *The Revelation of the Risen Lord*, as the previous year had produced *The Historic Faith*.

In 1875, he was appointed Honorary Chaplain to the Queen and succeeded in 1879 to Chaplain-in-Ordinary. There were many other such appointments and his work on St John was hindered by them. Even when he agreed to write the Commentary on St John for the Speakers' Bible he was aware that that meant putting to one side his work on the 'tripartite commentary', part of which was to be a commentary on the Greek text of the Fourth Gospel.

By 1883, his many activities had caused some concern to Bishop Magee, because he felt that Westcott was neglecting his duties as examining chaplain. The result was an abrupt resignation from Peterborough in May of that year.

Regius Professor of Divinity, Cambridge

It is hardly surprising that Bishop Magee felt himself neglected by his examining chaplain, whose residence at Peterborough was only in the summer months. As early as 1870, Westcott had been appointed Regius Professor at Cambridge by a large majority. He applied himself to his task at Cambridge vigorously from the outset, seeking to give real value to the University's divinity degree. His former students, particularly J B Lightfoot were delighted at his return to Cambridge and they were equally offended when he was virtually dismissed from Peterborough.

The work at Cambridge made it possible to hold other offices such as that at Peterborough and it was not long before another canonry was offered him. Gladstone who saw the value of Westcott, suggested first a deanery and then, realising his devotion to Cambridge, offered to obtain for him a canonry which he could hold together with his Cambridge work. He was appointed Canon of Westminster in succession to Canon Barry who became Bishop of Sydney, on 2nd February 1884. His first sermon at Westminster was on behalf of the Church Missionary Society.

Westcott's base remained Cambridge, where after the opening of the Divinity School in 1879 he had his rooms. They became the centre of a powerful theological influence, which could be defined as biblical and devotional. Westcott put his stamp upon it. Lightfoot, who became Lady Margaret Professor in 1875, was of course a frequent visitor. Students were equally encouraged there as they had been in his Trinity rooms. But the 'trio' who became famous long before the Divinity School was opened continued - Westcott, Hort and Lightfoot. Westcott did magnificent work at Cambridge, raising the level of academic work in theology and deepening the spiritual life of the university.

The Revision of the New Testament

It was as early as May 1870 that Westcott, Hort and Lightfoot were all invited to join the Company appointed by Convocation for the Revision of the New Testament. None of them was very happy about this. Westcott was convinced that the text of the New Testament needed to be more accurately determined before anything could be done about a new or revised translation. He wrote to Hort complaining that 'Convocation is not competent to initiate such a measure', but that 'we three' should get together and 'make the best of it'. He suggested to Lightfoot a conference of the three before the first meeting for the Revision.

Westcott was clear from the beginning that doctrinal matters did not concern them. They had to determine what was written and the best rendering in English. But quite early in the proceedings, he was deeply offended by the bishops who had broken their word about allowing the translation companies the deciding voice.

Convocation tried to retain a control on what was done. The correspondence shows a very worried Westcott, but he persisted and hardly ever missed a meeting. He took careful notes and filled 21 quarto volumes with them.

Behind the revision of the English Version lay the monumental work of Westcott and Hort in producing the Cambridge text of the Greek New Testament. This was his and Hort's greatest achievement. It was begun and ended at Cambridge.

Two Fellows of Trinity - Westcott, aged twenty eight and Hort, aged twenty five - started in the spring of 1853 to systematise New Testament criticism. They were dissatisfied with the *textus receptus* at the time and not much impressed by Lachmann and Tischendorf. They started to work on the Greek text of the New Testament, collecting all the variations for what was eventually to become their masterpiece. Westcott was less involved in the Old Testament translation and his main work was therefore finished by May 1881 when the New Testament appeared and during that period, he was much involved in other matters.

Westminster

J B Lightfoot was already at Durham, installed as bishop, when Westcott became Canon of Westminster. Almost immediately after he had settled into the Abbey Church, Westcott had the joy of three sons ready for ordination. The choice of bishop to ordain was obvious. In Advent 1884, he went to Bishop Auckland to be present at the ordination of these three eldest sons by Bishop Lightfoot.

As at Peterborough, Westcott threw himself into the life of the Abbey, arranging special services and making suggestions for the improvement of the music. He was so involved that the combination of Cambridge and Westminster seemed perfect. Gladstone could not tempt him away to rest in a deanery, not even Lincoln.

His chief work at Westminster was in connection with the Sunday afternoon sermons. There were large congregations and Westcott was well aware of the responsibility and his sermons were prepared with a special concern for the needs of the time. One collection of these sermons had the title, 'Special Aspects of Christianity'. In the Preface to that volume, he was confident enough to write:

> Of all the places in the world, 'the Abbey', I think, proclaims the social Gospel of Christ with most touching eloquence.

As is still the custom to this day, he entertained the preacher to tea and invited people to meet him. He would do this also when he was preaching himself, despite the considerable strain preaching made upon him. It was in that same preface to the volume of Westminster sermons that he paid tribute to his two mentors in *The Social Gospel* - Comte and Maurice. Comte's *Politique Positive* greatly impressed him, he wrote, when he worked through it in 1867. There he found many salient features of what he had long held to be the true social embodiment of the Gospel. He added, 'a social idea which faith in Christ is alone able to realise'. Two years later he read F D Maurice's *Social Morality* and paid glowing tribute to its worth and its influence upon him.

There were, of course, many Westminster sermons and many collections. Apart from Sunday services, he delivered many lectures on weekday afternoons. A series of such lectures on the Revised Version was published in *The Expositor* and subsequently collected in a volume called *Some lessons of the Revised Version of the New Testament*.

He was not always preaching and lecturing. He loved nothing more than to take crowds of visitors around the Abbey and especially enjoyed August bank holiday. He also fulfilled his duties on great occasions such as the Queen's Jubilee service on 21st June 1887. But one thing Westminster did for him above all else was to develop his deep concern for social problems. He took a special interest in the application of the lessons of the Gospel to international life and was most concerned about the steady building up of armaments among the European nations. On 5th April 1889, a Conference of Christians representing many Protestant denominations met at his residence in the Abbey Gardens. He chaired this conference and was asked to report it for *The Guardian*. He pointed out the danger of growing armaments inevitably leading to war, he deplored the mistrust among nations and saw that the main cause was the failure of Christians to accept their responsibility as peace-makers. He recalled a letter, written to *The Times* some fifteen years before by another hand, which pointed out the danger then, but put the blame on the leaders of the nations. This conference put the blame on Christians and in particular English Christians, 'who have been, and are, in a position to claim an impartial hearing from the Continental powers'. The failure of Christians to speak with one voice because of 'our unhappy divisions' has hidden the grandeur, the power and the obligations of 'our common faith in Christ'.

It was a moving report. The conference included such outstanding Non-Conformist ministers as John Clifford and F B Meyer. The list is impressive. A Provisional Committee was formed, of which Westcott was chairman and the name of the organisation determined as The Christian Union for Promoting International Concord. Westcott's 'pacifism', if it can rightly be called that, was firmly based upon the Incarnation, as he made perfectly clear in his public addresses. He believed that disarmament would be a natural consequence of the acceptance of a rational and legal method of settling national disputes, but he had deeper reasons for wanting nations to discover their common destiny in the peace of the Nativity:

'The question of international relations', he said, 'Has not hitherto been considered in the light of the Incarnation, and till this has been done, I do not see that we can look for the establishment of that peace which was heralded at the Nativity'.

He himself considered all things in the light of the Incarnation. While the issue of peace occupied his attention, Westcott did not neglect his New Testament studies and published his Commentary on *The Epistle to the Hebrews* towards the end of 1889. His last year at Westminster was much clouded by the serious illness and death of his friend, Bishop Lightfoot, the first of the 'trio' to go.

Durham

After Lightfoot's death, the see of Durham remained vacant for several months, but eventually Westcott was appointed. After his consecration on 1st May 1890 he left Westminster with reluctance. He had made a name for himself and was embarrassingly popular. On 13th May, he did homage to the Queen at Windsor and then on the next day left for his diocese. He was welcomed first at Darlington Station by the Mayor and Corporation. That evening he drove through the gaily decorated streets of Bishop Auckland and then to the Castle. He was enthroned on Ascension Day and took as the text for his sermon: 'Brethren, pray for us'.

It was the same Festival at which Bishop Lightfoot had been enthroned eleven years before and Westcott could not let that pass without a reference. The see of Durham gave him a seat in the House of Lords and he used that position wisely to promote peace and put down such social evils as gambling. He was soon involved in the International Parliamentary Peace Congress and shortly after taking his seat in the House of Lords, he addressed the Congress. He felt that it was right to give clear expression to the Christian view and commented 'the audience, chiefly French and German, listened kindly'. He said he tried to read them the parable of Durham. He was particularly attached to this. A few lines will suffice to show why:

> A Bishop of Durham could not look upon the two great buildings immemoriably connected with his office - the Castle and the Cathedral, rising side by side, parts of one whole - without knowing that for him, ecclesiastical and civil duties were inseparably combined.

He took the keenest interest in the welfare of the people of his diocese, encouraging the development of the Co-operative Movement and working incessantly for the support of those who were poorly treated. Apart from the lectures he gave in London from time to time on Peace and Social Justice, he arranged conferences at Auckland Castle on National Insurance and other safeguards for the working people in his diocese. He was not able to write much more in the busy life at Durham but he prepared *The Gospel of Life* for the press in 1891.

Over the next ten years, he maintained a heavy programme in Durham and in London, with failing health. His last public engagement was a sermon to the miners at their annual service in the Cathedral. He seemed aware that this was his last public address and used the occasion to explain what he had tried to do as Bishop - setting forward quietness, love and peace among all men. There was no doubt that he had worked hard for the improvement of the conditions of the miners and had tried to maintain a spirit of concord:

> 'So I have been enabled to watch with joy', he said at the end of his sermon, 'a steady improvement in the conditions, and also, I trust, in the spirit of labour among us. At the present time Durham offers to the world the highest type of industrial concord which has yet been fashioned. Much, no doubt, remains to be done; but the true paths of progress are familiar to our workers and our leaders, and are well trodden'.

A week later on 27th July 1901, Westcott died.

Fenton John Anthony Hort

It is all too easy to feel that when you have dealt with Westcott there is little left to say about Hort. Certainly, Westcott was the senior partner. Fenton John Anthony Hort was born in April 1828 in Dublin. There is some mystery about why the family left Ireland. They moved to Cheltenham when Fenton was nine. At the age of ten, they were in Boulogne, where Fenton went to school and developed rapidly in classical studies. They returned to Cheltenham and the young Fenton never saw Ireland again until he received an honorary doctorate in 1888 from Dublin University. He came of Nonconformist stock; his great grandfather was a lifelong friend of Isaac Watts and his schoolfellow at a Nonconformist Academy. After a time, he conformed to the Church of England and went to Clare College, Cambridge in 1709. He crossed to Ireland as chaplain to Earl Wharton, the Lord Lieutenant, and later became Archbishop of Tuam. He died in 1751.

Anne Collett

Although Hort retained a very loving memory of his father, it was to his mother that he looked for guidance. Anne Collett was the daughter of a Suffolk clergyman and a descendant of Dean Colet. She was a woman of great mental power, extremely well educated, with a beautiful and exact command of the English language. She transmitted to her sons a value for thoroughness and scrupulous accuracy. She was an Evangelical with a fear of the Oxford Movement and what it might do to her sons. It was his theological views which eventually put a barrier between them. But her influence remained. She ruled the household, determining its discipline and making sure that her children knew the Bible thoroughly and had learned its lessons of truthfulness and responsibility. It was a happy childhood for Fenton who was tenderly cared for and gently disciplined. He became a studious boy and did very well at the preparatory school of the Reverend John Buckland at Laleham when they were living in Cheltenham.

One who remembered him as a child gave a charming picture of him in few words:

> he was so fond of reading that he generally buried himself in some nook with a book, and his mother often laughed at his gravity and studious habits. He was reserved and silent, always kind and amiable in manner and unselfish, but we were all surprised in the way he came out in conversation; as a young man he could talk on any topic, and his company was a real treat.

Rugby School

Fenton Hort entered Rugby in October 1841, his entry delayed by many factors including fever at Rugby. He thus had January to October 1841 at home, attending Cheltenham College as a day boy with Arthur, who seemed very close to him. But Arthur died of measles in the following May, 1842. The death of this younger brother at the age of ten was a stunning shock from which he could hardly recover and it overwhelmed the life of his mother too. His brother's memory was kept sacred and he would hardly ever want to talk about it. A little later, Dr Arnold died. This was a shock of a different kind, but a shock none the less and it affected him like a staggering blow. At Rugby it was Mr Bonamy Price whom he singled out as having taught him more than any one else: 'To him I owe all scholarship and New Testament criticism,' he said in 1871. The new headmaster, Dr Tait, regarded him very highly when he went to the Sixth Form and had great hopes for him. He was never distinguished at games, however, and regretted this, but he enjoyed Rugby and played football as well as he could. His achievements were mostly in the academic field and there they were considerable. He showed evidence of leadership and did much for his House. He was at Rugby until the second half year of 1846 and then went up to Trinity College Cambridge.

Cambridge University

At first, Fenton did not do too well at Cambridge. He tried unsuccessfully for the University scholarships and his classical compositions were said to be rather weak. But he was a very accurate scholar.

Like most students he used his university years for more than studying his chosen subjects of classics and mathematics. He had a wide ranging intellect and revelled in the opportunities of Cambridge to interest himself in many subjects. His religious involvement also was important. His two headmasters at Rugby had of course influenced him. Arnold and Tait were both men of broad religious interests. When he came to Cambridge he sought out the Evangelicals to whom he belonged by upbringing. In any case, that represented the strongest religious tradition at Cambridge. The decisive influence at this stage however was that of F D Maurice. But he reached him by way of Coleridge, the dates of whose birth and death he had recorded carefully in his diary for 1847. It was the breadth of Coleridge's intellectual interest combined with his spiritual earnestness that attracted and continued to attract for some time. But F D Maurice satisfied many a want that had until then distressed him. Before he had read Maurice, he was already feeling the influence of the Oxford Movement, much to his mother's distress. He was very much a churchman and offended by the ugly and bare churches that were at that time prevalent. Although he regarded the ritual as secondary, he did need a careful and orderly conduct of worship. The simplicity of the Evangelicals bordered upon carelessness and disregard for sacred things.

F D Maurice

The year 1848 was a stirring time for all students throughout Europe and Hort was caught up in the excitement. He entered into all the liberal discussions which swept Cambridge and took sides, but was not carried away by any cause. He continued his absorbing passion for botany and could describe some of the disputes with the humour of an onlooker.

What is obvious from his letters is that he viewed all the movements of the time in connection with theology. He required a theology which was a living reality and any system which did not have a direct bearing on life was to him unsatisfactory. The Evangelical position seemed to him without firm foundation in life. It was in F D Maurice that he found his first glimpse of a religious teacher who seemed to bring the doctrines and sacraments of the Church into relation with the needs of individual and social life. One particular point attracted him at once. He had hesitated before the 'anti-liberalism' of the Oxford Movement, but in Maurice he did not find that distrust of human reason. He was working from Maurice's writings only. He did not know the man nor had he met any of Maurice's disciples, but he followed the controversies of the day and found himself more and more in agreement with 'Politics for the People', a remarkable venture in journalism which survived for the three summer months of 1848.

In the Long Vacation of 1849, after Hort had obtained his scholarship at Trinity, he went for long walks in the Lakes and wrestled with his theological difficulties. His perplexities led him into deep depression and on his return to Cambridge, he wrote to Maurice a long letter on Eternal Punishment and Redemption, to which Maurice replied with a very detailed and helpful letter. That letter led to a friendship which lasted until Maurice's death.

A Graduate at Cambridge

In 1851, Cambridge introduced the 'new Triposes' in Moral and Natural Sciences. Hort entered for both and in each he obtained a First Class. He won the Moral Philosophy prize and was listed 'distinguished' in Physiology and Botany. He was now in the thick of things and he was accepted as one of the influential thinkers at Cambridge. He became a member of what must be called a 'secret society' and before accepting the invitation consulted Maurice. The society is properly called, 'the Cambridge Conversazione Society', although it has usually been known as 'The Apostles'. Some of the most distinguished men of Cambridge have been members of this curiously silent 'Club'. They met for the reading of papers and discussion. Hort frequently read papers, which had to be controversial and lead to discussion.

Two other societies were started in the same year, of which Hort seems to have been the moving spirit: a small club for the practice of choral music, and the 'Ghostly Guild', a society for collecting examples of psychic phenomena. In this he anticipated Sir Alister Hardy at Oxford by almost a century. He obtained a fellowship in 1852 at the same time as J B Lightfoot. Westcott joined his 'Ghostly Guild' and they began to see a great deal of each other. Hort realised that his life was to be that of a scholar and he had to decide upon his field. It was either the Greek Text of the New Testament or Early Church History. Westcott seems to have helped him to decide by recommending that he get hold of a copy of Bagster's *Critical Greek Testament*. Something of his excitement can be gathered from a letter to John Ellerton, by now a clergyman:

> Every night after prayers I lug down a big pile of books - Bruder's Concordance, Olshausen, De Wette, Tischendorf's text, Bagster's Critical Greek Testament, and a German dictionary - and work at St Paul chronologically. I have been two nights at II Thess 11 and have at last got some light, which has much pleased me and encouraged me; I find it altogether a most interesting and all-ways profitable study.

And he goes on at length about the Textus Receptus, Tischendorf etc. A month later he is writing to Westcott about II Thess 11.

The correspondence in 1852 with Westcott included a discussion on the Oxford Movement and Newman: 'the perfect clearness and keenness of Newman always gives me pleasure; at the same time it is rather like a very pure knife edge of ice. I believe he has really a warm heart, but he has put it to school in a truly diabolic way.'

In 1853, Hort suffered from a troublesome skin disease, probably the result of his scarlet fever in undergraduate days. He tried unsuccessfully the water cure at Umberslade Hydropathic establishment, near Knowle. That stay had one momentous consequence for him. In the course of a walk with Westcott who was visiting him, they agreed to do a joint revision of the Greek Text of the New Testament. The story of that life work has been told in Bruce's book and enough has been said in Westcott's section of this book. It bound them together as Westcott and Hort.

Ordination and Marriage

Hort was soon preparing himself for ordination and asked for a curacy. One was offered, but he was persuaded to remain at Cambridge. There he was much involved, but another reason soon arose to end his Fellowship and make some kind of living necessary. He broke the news to Westcott in typical fashion in a letter dated, 23rd February 1857:

> In spite of the vagueness of my last note you will perhaps have been looking for me before this time. I may therefore say at once that the 'business' which has detained me has been of a tolerably engrossing character. The result of it is that I am going to get married.

However he assured Westcott that it need not interfere with his literary plans and that he intended to continue with the New Testament text from his new living rather than from Cambridge.

The ordination was not a matter of course for him. Eight years before when he was a boy at Rugby, he was convinced that he had a 'call' to holy orders. He prepared diligently for it. His letters reveal his deep concern amidst all this at the dismissal of F D Maurice from his place in King's College, condemned exclusively he says on two counts - that he threw a cloudiness about the meaning of the word 'eternal'; and that he seemed to tend towards the belief that the wicked might perhaps find mercy at last. Maurice was asked to resign quietly, but he refused. He was convinced that a Professor of King's College should not have to resign, subjected to a test of orthodoxy beyond the Creeds, Prayer Book and Articles, all of which he cheerfully accepted. He compelled the Council to *expel* him. Many came to his defence, but he was expelled. The shame fell on King's rather than Maurice. There is today at King's College an F D Maurice Memorial Lecture annually.

Fenton Hort was ordained at Oxford in March 1854, at the age of 25. There was no reason for him to resign his fellowship because he was still single. But marriage preoccupied his mind. He was of a very reserved nature and thought for a long time about the possibility and desirability of marriage. He had made a special study of marriage from the point of view of society and of the complete life of the person. His conclusion was almost academic as a series of private letters show. He reached the conclusion that no life of man or woman attains its full purpose in the single condition. This was not Paul's, 'It is better to marry than to burn', but a much more sober and considered conclusion. Romantic love does not come into his consideration, but that was soon changed when he met a real girl! She was already known to the family and it was not so much his careful study as his overwhelming love for her that led him to propose marriage. They were engaged in February 1857 and that meant that he would have to give up his fellowship. Fellows of Cambridge Colleges were not monks who had taken vows, but they had to be single so long as they held their fellowship.

The real girl was Miss Fanny Dyson Holland, whose family were closely associated with mutual friends in Cheltenham. Someone must have worked hard and skilfully to get Fenton Hort to propose! A few days after his engagement, he was presented with the country living of St Ippolyts-cum-Great Wymondly, near Hitchin, and there he settled in June 1857 with his wife. He now had what he had always longed for, a home.

College rooms were, to use his own words, 'the best substitute for a home, but nothing in any wise like a home'.

A Country Parson

Many must have thought that it would only be a few years before this brilliant young scholar who had made such an impact on the university would be back at Cambridge. Surely he would be wasted in parochial work of this kind. In fact he continued for fifteen years in parochial work. He never considered himself wasted on a village congregation. Hort regarded the care of his parishioners as a work second in dignity to no other. He took up his charge with enthusiasm and his interest never abated. The work itself was one for which he felt he had been prepared over the years and which from his earliest days he had made his deliberate choice. He was a keen gardener and soon brought a disordered ground under control. His principal academic work during these years was the revision of the Greek New Testament. All spare hours of every day were devoted to it and occasionally Westcott came to stay for a few days and they worked together for several hours continuously every day.

Introduction to the Greek Testament

For two years in his mid-thirties (1863-1865) Fenton Hort was unable, in fact forbidden, on medical grounds to do any parish work. They were spent at Cheltenham with long pilgrimages to the Alps. He was not forbidden to work. In the Alps he pursued his botanical studies and at Cheltenham he worked on the New Testament and drafted the introduction. The two occupations overlapped and in fact an important turning point in his Greek text work came when he was staying alone in the region of Mont Cenis. It was 1864 and for some time his Alpine sojourns had taken him into systematic work on the Greek text. He completed his draft of the introduction. This was not the final version which F F Bruce and others have praised so much; but it was important for him. It enabled him to put down the principles which had guided him and Westcott during the first decade of their work. The publisher began to wonder if and when this work would be finished. He feared it might not be until the millennium. At best, he thought that it looked like taking until 1890 and he was not far wrong. Hort played his part, but was aware that both in the Alps and in Cheltenham he had to spend most of the day outdoors. Only in the evenings could he work away at the text and the introduction. Westcott was restless. He feared Hort had exchanged geology for theology. At the same time Westcott was debating whether he should stand for the

Norrisian Professorship of Divinity at Cambridge. Hort wrote urging that he was needed more at Cambridge than at Harrow. In all this, the confidant of them both was J B Lightfoot. He was producing his valuable *Commentaries on Paul's Epistles* at the time and both Westcott and Hort followed their progress with great interest. Separated as they were, the trio were trying to work in harmony and were mutually helpful.

There is a continuing ambiguity in Hort's attitude to Rome and to Newman. Of course, he found the controversy with Charles Kingsley unattractive. It still mars the book. His main criticism of the writings of Newman is still that he has a seductive, if cold style, which masks irrationality and suppresses personal experience. He had more than once shocked his friends with his poor view of Protestantism. He even quoted Irving with approval and said that Protestantism was 'parenthetical' and 'temporary'. He was however not prepared to go back to what he called 'The elements of the world'. Anglican he remained and was content to put up 'with comparative formlessness for I know not how many generations'.

Return to Parish Work

In November 1865, Hort returned to his parish, able to work, but still far from strong. He was to remain there for another seven years and no doubt did his work faithfully, but he longed for Cambridge and tried every way he knew to get back. The work that absorbed him was clearly the Greek text of the New Testament and he could do that much more easily in the university. Westcott was at that time in Harrow and later became Canon of Peterborough, constantly urged by his friends including Hort to return to Cambridge, which eventually he did. All three had Cambridge in their sights! Hort stood unsuccessfully for one post after another. In 1871, he examined in Natural Science in the Trinity Fellowship examinations, and also in the Natural Science Tripos. He was Hulsean lecturer in the same year. These lectures were on Christian philosophy and gave him an opportunity to express his thoughts on the great issues of the Christian faith and take him away from the minutiae of textual criticism. They were published under the title, *The Way, the Truth, the Life*. They were his chief contribution to theological thought.

At last, in December 1871 came the invitation to a Fellowship and lectureship in Theology at Emmanuel College, Cambridge. He resigned his living and was in Cambridge in 1872. By then Westcott had been nearly two years at Cambridge as Regius Professor. Lightfoot was already there and the trio were united. He was also a near neighbour of F D Maurice.

College Lectures

For six years, Fenton Hort lectured to theological students at Emmanuel. That lecturing was largely on the New Testament and early Apostolic Fathers, with series on Origen and Irenaeus. This did not occupy his entire time, he was much involved in university affairs and continued the work with Westcott. He did not publish much, but in 1876 he brought out two Dissertations, the one of the received text of John 1.18 and the other on the early creeds. They were not popular works, but showed the quality of his scholarship. The second dissertation earned him his doctorate in 1875. The Master of Trinity praised the dissertations as 'epoch-making in the history of the Divinity School'. Even Newman praised them.

Hort was a painstaking writer and often his articles in Dictionaries held up publication. But all recognised his extraordinary care. This came out in his lectures which continued to be popular, although difficult.

Hulsean Professor

In 1878, Hort succeeded Dr J J S Perowne as Hulsean Professor of Divinity. He continued to lecture and collaborated with Lightfoot in work on his Commentaries. But, to his regret, in 1879 Lightfoot was removed to the see of Durham. The trio were represented at the consecration of the new Bishop, Westcott preached the sermon. About the same time Clerk Maxwell died and Hort lost a close friend with whom he had shared his scientific interests. His tribute to him quoted a proverb which Clerk Maxwell kept always before him, 'The lip of truth shall be established for ever'.

The new Divinity School was opened and Hort found his room also there, chiefly used to house his growing library.

The revision both of the Greek text and the English version of the New Testament was now almost finished. The last meeting of the New Testament Company was held in November 1880. The next step was the Apocrypha and to the Cambridge committee was assigned *II Maccabees* and *Wisdom*. Apart from some notes by Dr Roberts, the work was done by Hort, Moulton and Westcott. They started in March 1881 and met regularly. Westcott moved to Durham in 1890 and he continued by correspondence. Moulton and Hort worked through at Cambridge and they were finished by the summer of 1892. Some points reserved for later decision were his last work. By then he had been appointed Lady Margaret Professor. One further task he fulfilled with his failing strength was his contribution of an article to the *Dictionary of National Biography* on

"Lightfoot". This was completed on his return from Switzerland on November 10th 1892.

He died on November 30th and was buried from Emmanuel College, Cambridge.

9. A New Language

The production of a new Bible always raises the question of whether it should revise the old, correcting both text and translation, or make a completely new translation. The Established Church of England in the nineteenth century decided for 'revision' and produced as good a Bible as the scholarship of the time allowed. It was a success on both sides of the Atlantic. American variants were put into the appendix at first and then later incorporated into the text to form 'The American Standard Version'. There were those who felt that a new generation needed a Bible in their own language. As the nineteenth century drew to a close, it became evident that the English language, even in England, was changing. And although a younger generation may have understood the text of the RV it sounded archaic and not relevant to the new century.

In 1902, *The Twentieth Century New Testament: A Translation into Modern English from the Original Greek* (Westcott & Hort's Text) was published in one volume. It had previously appeared in three parts in 1898, 1900 and 1901. The story of its evolution from 1891, when the editor of *Review and Reviews* received two letters calling for such a version, to the time of its publication and the ultimate revealing of the names of the translators is told by F F Bruce and need not be repeated here.

Richard Francis Weymouth (1822-1902)

One of the scholars consulted from time to time by the translators was a schoolmaster, recently retired from the post of Headmaster of Mill Hill School (a public school with nonconformist foundation). Dr Weymouth was almost an exact contemporary of Westcott and Hort.

He was born in Stoke Dameral, Devonport (then called Plymouth Dock) on 26th October 1822. His father was a Naval Commander and a Baptist. Young Richard Francis went to a private school and was then educated for two years in France. He had no prospect of entering Oxford or Cambridge, because those universities were not open to Nonconformists. But in 1826, University College, London, was founded by lovers of religious toleration to provide a university education for non-Anglicans.

The founders were Lord Brougham, Thomas Campbell and James Mill. Opponents of such tolerance called it 'the godless college in Gower St', where it still stands. The foundation stone was laid in 1827; it received a charter in 1836 and was incorporated in the University of London in 1907.

This was the only possibility for Richard Francis to obtain a university education in this country. He therefore matriculated there in 1843 and studied classics. He was awarded BA in 1846 and MA in 1849.

His philological studies continued throughout his life. He joined the Philological Society in 1851 and was an enthusiastic supporter. He edited many of its publications from 1864 onwards. His knowledge of languages was very wide, including Anglo-Saxon, Icelandic, French, as well as the classical languages. He was the first to be awarded the Doctor of Literature degree at University College and this after a gruelling examination in Anglo-Saxon, Icelandic and English and French Literature. He won his doctorate in 1868, but it was not officially conferred upon him until 1879! By then he had already been a Fellow of University College for ten years and was a highly respected Headmaster of Mill Hill School.

He was well known as a zealous Baptist. In Plymouth, he was a deacon of the old Baptist Church in George Street (founded in 1620) but now replaced by a modern church called Catherine Street Baptist Church, although the adjoining buildings are still referred to as Old George Street.

When he moved into the Home Counties he soon became a Committee Member of the Essex Baptist Union.

The School Master

Weymouth's first appointment was as an assistant to Joseph Payne, the educational expert at Mansion House School at Leatherhead. This gave him some experience of managing a school and before long he opened his own in Plymouth. It was a private school, Porthead Grammar School and by all reports he made a great success of it. His major appointment came in 1869 when he was chosen as Head Master for the newly refashioned Mill Hill School. The *Daily News* announcing that appointment on 23rd July 1968, refers to his success in Plymouth - 'For many years he has conducted with great ability the Portland Grammar School. Plymouth'. The paper also reports his recent honour as the first Doctor of Literature in the University of London. He was to remain as Head at Mill Hill for seventeen years. The character of the man can therefore best be judged in terms of his work at Mill Hill.

Protestant Dissenters' Grammar School

The school was founded in 1807 for the sons of Protestant Dissenters, because they were disadvantaged. The public schools and universities were practically closed to them, since as was said, 'No degree can be taken before the candidate has subscribed articles for which Protestant Dissenters can trace no sanction in the Scriptures'. For this reason a number of influential London merchants, always a rich source of Nonconformists, founded a grammar school. It had its ups and downs over the years and was in a parlous state some eight years before Weymouth was appointed. That was the old foundation and thanks to the persistence of the treasurer, Thomas Scrutton, it was founded on a new basis as a public School: Mill Hill School. To this new foundation Dr Weymouth was invited as Head. He was on a short list of two from seventy applicants. The provisional committee had to choose between these two and their first choice was Mr A S Wilkins, MA London, BA Cambridge. Almost at the same time, he had an offer from Owen's College and accepted that. The committee, who had great difficulty choosing between the two were not troubled. They invited Dr R F Weymouth, MA, D Litt, both of London. He accepted and fashioned the new foundation.

Almost at once, Weymouth made his mark. That same report in the *Daily News* telling of his appointment and commenting on his success at Plymouth also adds, 'The selection he has made of the gentlemen by whom he will be assisted indicates the high character of education he intends to maintain'. It was an impressive list including J H Taylor, MA Oxford and BA, Cambridge.

A student who was at Mill Hill in the seventies left his assessment of the Head Master who served from 1869 to 1886 and laid the foundation of its subsequent character:

> Dr Weymouth was a man with an unmistakable genius for teaching and ruling boys, and if only he had been of a more sympathetic disposition and had possessed a keener insight into human nature, and more consideration for human nature's little weaknesses and imperfections, he would have been nearer to the ideal Headmaster. Thanks to his scholarly attainments, splendid courtesy, and rare dignity of manners, the school had now for seventeen years a singularly interesting figure head, who inspired parents and the outside public with respect and confidence, and the boys whether small or great, with a becoming awe. But it was of course as a disciplinarian and practical administrator that Dr Weymouth accomplished the main part of his great work for Mill Hill, whereby the school was enabled for the first time, to take a really worthy place among the public schools of the country.

He was a born teacher and a man of energy and untiring industry. He hated laziness and would not tolerate it in his pupils. When he taught Greek or Latin or English he generated enthusiasm, while his passion for accuracy was remembered by all who were taught by him. It left an indelible mark, as one student said, 'finding as they did, how heavy a trial to their master's soul a false quantity was, or a wrong accent, or the misplacing of a comma'.

The full opening of the ancient universities to Free Churchmen came in 1870, just a year after Weymouth's appointment. It was a happy chance and he found excellent lieutenants on his staff to prepare for this: Mr Hurley, Dr Murray and J M Lightwood. The team soon won its place by producing boys who could more than hold their own at the universities, with an exceptionally high number of firsts and fellowships. Dr Murray was a keen philologist and eventually became the first editor of the Oxford English Dictionary. Dr Weymouth encouraged him to work at this at Mill Hill until he left for special premises in Oxford.

The Disciplinarian

If Weymouth governed his own life with strict discipline he certainly required this of the boys. Many complained that he was not always fair. When there was disorder, he invariably put the responsibility for it on the oldest boy rather than seek out the most culpable. But one habit every boy of this period reports is that of requiring five minutes' complete silence after any disorder that was reprimanded. He would stand firmly before the class with his gold watch in his hand watching the seconds tick by and if there was a shuffle or a whisper before the five minutes was up, he would repeat in unemotional terms, 'The five minutes will now begin all over again'.

The discipline that he had learned from his father seemed right to him and no doubt it helped the boys who had no liking for it at the time. It brought much unpopularity and he was rather feared than loved. Discipline was probably part of his religion and he was certainly a powerful religious influence upon the school. More than one scholar, remembering the discipline with little warmth admits that he learned the value of moral and spiritual standards. He did not often preach, but when he did, they were powerful sermons. At the Bible class he frequently led on Sunday afternoons he appealed for decision. He warned of the misery and ruin that followed wrong-doing. He did not hesitate to appeal and work for 'surrender to Christ and purity and nobility of life'.

The tone of the school was austere, and that tone was set by Weymouth, for whom moral rectitude and faith in Christ were of the stuff of life itself. The majority of the boys were from Nonconformist families who approved of Weymouth's strictness. This was a Puritan school and no one was ashamed of that. It was also a very successful school.

Growth

From the very start of his headmastership, Weymouth saw the school grow, J H Murray came to Mill Hill in 1870 and the Reverend Robert Harley two years later. The first report of the Headmaster to the Governors was enthusiastically received and plans accepted for expansion. The house called 'Sunnyside' opposite 'The Three Hammers' was bought for Mr Murray, who lived there for the 15 years he spent at the school. When he moved to Oxford to complete his great work on the *Dictionary*, he gave his Oxford home the same name, and it was open house for all Mill Hill boys who came to Oxford.

After a few years. Weymouth saw the opportunities for real expansion and he aimed to make Mill Hill a worthy public school. At first his ideas seemed a little grandiose, but he gradually convinced the governors that growth must be accompanied by the acceptance of a larger vision. In 1874 a boarding school was built at Burton Bank. It was built on similar lines to some of the houses at Harrow and designed to hold 35 boys. Good grounds were purchased at the same time. Weymouth was always to the fore in new ideas and at times put his own resources into his schemes. For example, he saw the need for a new chapel and he put £200 of his own money at the disposal of the governors to provide a nucleus for the chapel fund. That scheme was not at once appreciated and the governors decided upon a swimming pool instead.

Dr Weymouth, particularly in his early years proved a very wise and perceptive Head. He made good use of his staff and recognised the importance of their stature for the reputation of the School. A good example is his relations with Mr (later Sir James) Murray. At the very beginning he saw the value of this man and greatly encouraged him in his philological studies, in which he was personally interested, allowing the Scriptorium to be used for the daily collection of thousands of paper slips for the proposed Oxford English Dictionary. He also encouraged Dr Murray's other wide-ranging interests and allowed him to develop them - the Debating Society, the Natural History Society, the School Magazine. Dr Murray was a great resource with his almost unlimited energy until he had to leave in 1885 for Oxford to supervise the editing of the *Dictionary* and devote all his time to it.

With careful use of the strength of his staff and judicious contacts with public figures, Weymouth guided the school into an unprecedented period of growth.

Discipline Remembered

It was in connection with one of the illegal offshoots of the Natural History Society that the interference of Dr Weymouth was remembered by all involved. The Society had arranged a number of field trips and eventually required a museum at the school. Dr Weymouth saw the value of this and obtained permission for the boys to enjoy the nearby grounds of Moat Mount, which belonged to a friend of the school, Mr Serjeant Cox. The boys were not beyond poaching to supplement their meagre meals with succulent rabbit. But when they began bird nesting there was trouble. One Midsummer term, the 'Handy Gang', as a small group of boys called themselves, discovered several good nests in the grounds of Moat Mount. They tied a handkerchief to the nearest tree and came back next day to collect their spoil. Someone had been there before them. They had lost the eggs, but also the incriminating handkerchief. On the following day, word was passed round, 'All the boys in the Large'. When the boys had assembled, Dr Weymouth came in frowning, as one boy remembered vividly, and looking as black as thunder! He could remember almost word for word what he said, many years later: 'No doubt you are all aware that through the kindness of Mr Serjeant Cox you are permitted to walk in the beautiful grounds of Highwood Hill. But this permission does not extend to trespassing or birdnesting in his preserved woods. I am sorry to say that the keeper has found this handkerchief at the top of a tree in the woods near the lake'.

The culprit and his friends were soon detected through the handkerchief. The heavy thunder continued as he added: 'I thank you gentlemen for your endeavours to raise the school character, and I feel that the rest of the boys also thank you for depriving them of the privilege of enjoying the beauties of Mr Serjeant Cox's grounds, as he has withdrawn the privilege from this day'.

As was his custom he selected the oldest boy from the 'Handy Gang' and gave him the task of writing out one hundred French irregular verbs, adding 'and I shall only take good writing'. Three of the other boys were 'gated' for a month.

The Perception to Choose Men

Weymouth had a rare gift for choosing exactly the right person for the post in Mill Hill School. After securing the academic reputation of the school by bringing the first Oxford and Cambridge teachers to Mill Hill, he saw the need for teachers of another type. He appointed two without degrees. It was a brilliant choice for the dynamic growth of Mill Hill under his leadership. They were Henry Judson Tucker, who built up the athletic life of the school, introduced Rugby and cricket, and eventually producing county players in both games, and J A H Murray. The latter was a brilliant choice and Weymouth knew it. At the time of their meeting at the Philological Society, Murray was a foreign correspondence clerk of the Chartered Bank of India, China and Hongkong. He invited him to come to Mill Hill as an English teacher and gave him separate accommodation free from house duties and at liberty to pursue his philological research. Three years later the whole field of dialect studies was revolutionised by Murray's *Dialects of the Southern Counties of Scotland*, which brought him an honorary doctorate from Edinburgh in 1874. Murray followed this with the brilliant articles on the *English Language* in the Encyclopaedia Britannica. Weymouth also continued his philological work and Mill Hill became a well-known centre of philological progress throughout the English-speaking world. Weymouth's own work included a study of Homer's Greek, the Resultant Greek New Testament (of which more later) and the pronunciation of Chaucer's English. In 1879, Murray received the invitation to edit what is now called the *Oxford English Dictionary*.

This perception extended beyond the choice of staff. He knew how to choose guest speakers who would draw attention to the school! He was a superb figure-head and he had a flair for attracting attention, not to himself, but to the school. The first guest for Prize Day was Thomas Hughes, author of *Tom Brown's Schooldays*. This book had brought a great deal of sympathy for public schools and Mill Hill was aspiring to that rank with its New Foundation. Thomas Hughes came twice. In 1879 he secured Gladstone. Something of Weymouth's difficulty at growing out of his background comes out in the invitation to the Grand Old Man. Weymouth informed him about the School saying, 'Mill Hill virtually represented the Congregational and Baptist Churches though by the terms of its foundation it was undenominational and the religious training was so also.' It was left to his successor to reject the negatives and once and for all declare Mill Hill - inter-denominational.

But he secured Gladstone and at a time when he was out of office and no longer leader of the Liberal Party. It maybe saying too much that 'His noble speech at Mill Hill, fully reported in the Magazine in July 1879, drew the attention of the country to the fact that the Grand Old Man was still very much alive' or that 'it proved to be a prelude to the Midlothian campaign'. But it certainly drew a wide circle into considering Mill Hill as a place to be reckoned with as a public school to which they might send their sons. The visit of Mr and Mrs Gladstone was in every way a red-letter day for Mill Hill School and everybody saw it as such.

But Weymouth's weakness of management began to show. When things were going well he could exercise his perception and draw attention to the school, but in adversity these gifts did not take the place of tact and management skills. Burton Bank, where the boarding boys lived, was owned by Mr Harley. This was a mistake from the beginning, but only in the later years showed up as an unwise decision. That a member of staff should own the boarding house was clearly unwise. Eventually, there was trouble, Mr Harley resigned and sold the house to the governors, making quite a good profit. Harley had rightly assumed that he was essential at the School. Personality clashes led to friction. When he left, Weymouth was equally good at choosing a successor, but there is no doubt that Harley had attracted many boys to the School.

Decline

The number of boys was already falling. Its height had been 183, which fell to 140. Harley's connections in Yorkshire had been very good and that was a centre of robust non-conformity. The Charity Commissioners became troublesome and questioned the very high price paid for Burton Bank. Finances were crippled by this large outlay and it took years to recover. The School managed to recover its position slightly, but a bad year followed with outbreaks of chicken pox, scarlet fever and measles. Numbers fell. There was no Foundation Day in 1883 and Mr William Summers, MP who had been invited came in the winter term. It was plain that the School was declining. The only remaining sign of former glories was the first notice of the publication of the English Dictionary in 1882 and the evident signs of labour which almost buried Dr Murray in paper. Three tons of paper slips with quotations on them had been sent in from many parts of the English-speaking world, but that also meant that Mill Hill had to lose Dr Murray. That too had an effect upon the numbers of boys sent to the school. In 1883 there had been 104 boys in the school-house, and at the end of 1884 there were still 91; but by December 1885 when Dr Murray's resignation had taken effect there were only 63. Dr Weymouth could not handle decline, and when the School showed no signs of recovery he handed in his resignation in March 1886. The governors expressed their regret and recognised his ability and were grateful for his long and admirable services, but in view of the decline of the School, they felt they must accept his resignation. A new era had come and needed a new type of Head.

The Resultant Greek New Testament

Norman Brett-James, who wrote the history of Mill Hill School, is critical of Weymouth for not preparing the boys adequately for the older universities - Oxford and Cambridge - but being set in the mould of London University. His judgement of Weymouth is that his approach 'made for the development of personality, for the teaching of boys to think and hold opinions, rather than for high scholastic acquirements or educational finish'. He gave prominence to classical studies, but they were not, according to Brett-James pursued with success or thoroughness. 'Dr Weymouth, though learned', he adds, 'was not in the technical sense a "scholar", save in New Testament Greek'. There, he most certainly was a scholar and even Brett-James admits that, 'There are many now who look back to hours ... with Dr Weymouth on the Second Aorist in Greek, as among the most stimulating of their earlier mental efforts'.

The School did not give Weymouth the time to become the 'scholar' that he could have become. The space he made for Dr Murray he did not make for himself. Yet it was while at Mill Hill that he did his work on *The Resultant Greek Testament*. This was a careful collation of all the different readings of the Greek text, compared and contrasted until he could reach what he regarded as the majority opinion in every disputed case. F F Bruce describes this 'resultant' text as exhibiting 'the text representing the greatest measure of agreement among the leading nineteenth-century editors'. That text together with its elaborate critical apparatus must have required the detailed attention that Murray expended on his *Dictionary*.

The Resultant Greek Testament was published in the year of his retirement from Mill Hill. The Bishop of Worcester provided a preface and it was printed several times, remaining as Bruce says 'a useful edition of the Greek Testament'.

Retirement

Dr and Mrs Weymouth retired from Mill Hill School in July 1886 and it was clear that Weymouth would pursue his Greek studies. He also continued to edit some publications of the Philological Society. Mrs Weymouth, Louisa Sarah, daughter of Robert Marten, whom he married in 1852, died in the year 1891. We hear very little about her at Mill Hill School and it is probable that she was content to be the wife of Richard Francis Weymouth. It was a steady uneventful marriage with no children except the boys at Mill Hill, who succeeded the boys at Porthead Grammar School. Their life together was divided between these two schools and it encompassed both of them. After his wife died, he remarried in October 1892, another Louisa, the daughter of Samuel Salter of Watford. She brought with her three sons and three daughters. His retirement was then to a family and, austere as he was, he enjoyed it. But the classical studies to which he said he would devote his years of retirement were not neglected. In 1894, he published *The Rendering into English of the Greek Aorist and Perfect* (with an appendix.) There are many hints that this subject not only interested him, but he could stimulate boys also to find it exciting. It was certainly a good preparation for the work by which he is best remembered, his translation, *The New Testament in Modern Speech*. F F Bruce gives almost five pages to Weymouth and has one intriguing comment relative to this 1894 work, 'his treatment of Greek tenses, for example, marks an improvement over the Revised Version'. His translation was of his *Resultant Greek Testament*. He brought no theological bias to his work, but set himself to render the best Greek text into dignified modern English. He did not see it in print, because although it was finished before his death, it needed some editing and was prepared for the publisher by E Hampden-Cook. It was published in 1903 and frequently reprinted. Hampden-Cook was a Congregational minister and also one of the translators of the *Twentieth Century New Testament*. In 1924, when it was a very popular modern translation, Professor James Alexander Robertson of Aberdeen revised it. To this day it is the preferred modern version by some people. After his second marriage in 1892 a new house was needed and he and his wife moved to Collaton House in Brentwood, Essex. A year earlier he had been given the distinguished honour of a civil service pension of £100 per year. He died on 17th December 1902.

James Moffatt (1870-1944)
Although many attempts were made to translate the New Testament into appropriate modern English, Weymouth had few serious rivals until the eve of the First World War. That gave him a clear run of ten years and he would not have been surprised to find another scholar prepared to try his hand at improving his translation. It was revised several times. But its first competitor was Moffatt's, which soon became a household word and eclipsed all other modern translations.

James Moffatt was a Scot, his family belonged to the Free Church of Scotland and he was brought up in the same. His father, George Moffatt was a chartered accountant. James, was born in Glasgow on 4th July 1870. His father intended him to have a good education and he went to the best school in Glasgow, the Glasgow Academy. From there, he went to Glasgow University and took an Honours Degree in Classics in 1890. He was a brilliant student and few could have been surprised that he decided to become a minister of his kirk. In Scotland at the end of the last century, education was highly valued for its own sake and an educated young man either left Scotland to compete in whatever field he chose or remained in Scotland to serve the Church. The very high standard of the theological training of the Scottish ministry meant that most scholars remained in Scotland if they wanted to do theological work. This often meant taking a small rural parish and compiling some of the standard reference books used by theological students in the English-speaking world. The Hastings Dictionaries were a good example.

There was nothing provincial about theological studies in Scotland. The extraordinary level of theological studies in Scotland was known from America to Hungary and both sent their best students to one or other of the four ancient universities of Scotland. James Moffatt studied in Glasgow and when he decided upon the Ministry he had no need to go to an English university to get the best. He studied his theology at the Glasgow College of the Free Church of Scotland. This was before the Union of the principal Presbyterian Churches into the Church of Scotland. He was not a 'Wee Free', those who stayed out of the Union. In fact, later he was very active in the affairs of the Union and died a loyal Minister of the Church of Scotland. But that is to anticipate.

The strongest influence upon him at theological college was Alexander Bruce. He introduced him to New Testament criticism.

James Moffatt was ordained in 1896 and in the same year he married Mary, a girl from Aberdeen. He settled as a minister at the Free Church in Dundonald, Ayrshire. He continued his studies.

Alexander Bruce showed him the importance of reading the books of the New Testament in their historical context. He now set himself the task in the midst of his pastoral duties and the preparation of weekly sermons, to follow this method and read through all the writings of the New Testament in their setting. His studies led him to produce his first published book: *The Historical New Testament*. It was an original piece of research, examining each of the NT writings in the light of their chronology. Many have done this since, but his was the book that set the pattern and he published it in 1901 while he was still minister at his first church in Dundonald. It was immediately recognised as of high academic standard and valuable for biblical studies and preaching. The University of St Andrews awarded him an honorary DD for it in 1902. He was just 32 and never before had St Andrews awarded a doctorate of this kind to so young a person.

For five more years he continued his ministry at Dundonald and there is a good report of his faithful pastoral care and the high quality of his preaching. It was perhaps a little above the heads of his congregation, but they loved it. The Scots expected sermons with meat in them in those days.

The Second Pastorate

In 1907, after serving eleven years in his first pastorate he accepted a call to Broughty Ferry, to become minister of the United Free Church there. It was a holiday resort for the growing city of Dundee and further afield. His preaching was popular and he attracted large congregations. But he remained a scholar rather than a popular preacher. He was not an extrovert, but preferred the quiet excitement of the scholar in his study uncovering new truths and fresh insights. In the four years that he stayed at Broughty Ferry he produced one standard work which for years remained the constant reference book of countless students of the New Testament and preachers: *Introduction to the Literature of the New Testament* (1911) and started a service for all theological students in the *Hibbert Journal* which continued for thirty years. The reference book was really written while he was at Dundonald and followed naturally upon his earlier work on *The Historical New Testament*. These were two major works and he made his mark with them. It was not long before publishers and universities took note of this new light coming from the parish of Broughty Ferry. The editor of the *Hibbert Journal* needed someone to draw attention to the more important religious books being published and invited him to write for that prestigious journal. That invitation probably came after Moffatt had delivered the Jowett Lecture in London, or on reading some of the numerous articles that he was producing for several journals. Moffatt accepted and for thirty years wrote a quarterly survey of current religious books.

Oxford

Some of the leading Free Church scholars have over the years been attracted to Mansfield College, Oxford. It was established in Oxford, though not a college or hall of the university, for the training of Congregational Ministers. In subsequent years, New Testament scholars of the calibre of C H Dodd, T W Manson and A M Hunter taught there, and the Old Testament scholar, H Wheeler Robinson. A very long list of scholars, prominent in their field could be compiled. Later it became a hall of the university and matriculated its own students. In 1911, it had students who might but were not obliged to take the university examinations. If they wished to register they could do so through St Catherine's Society. This remained so until the Second World War. Later, Baptist students joined the Congregational students and Mansfield pioneered the way with a woman student. All this lay in the future. James Moffatt was invited to become Professor of Greek and New Testament studies at Mansfield College. He was aware that his developing interest in academic work required an academic post. And he had in mind the translation of the New Testament for which he was amply qualified. Much of the work was already done when he moved to Oxford in 1911. *The New Testament: A New Translation* was published in 1913. It rapidly became popular and James Moffatt was a name. As Ronald Knox once said, 'A Bible translator suddenly loses all his Christian names and becomes, in my case, plain Knox'. It was so with Moffatt. F F Bruce records that on a later visit to America, Moffatt was billed on the public hoardings as 'Author of Bible will Lecture To-night'. A similar thing happened years later to J B Phillips when the blurb on the jacket of his translation of the Book of Revelations had him billed as 'Author of the Gospels'. The error was noticed in time and changed. It was this kind of fame that greeted Moffatt in 1913. In Mansfield College, he also had an important pulpit. Free Churchmen had only been in Oxford for forty years and they still tended to group together. Whatever their College, Mansfield became a natural gathering point, especially the chapel services, to which famous preachers were regularly invited. Moffatt took his share of staff preaching and for years after he left Oxford he was invited back to preach in a chapel he learnt to love. But he was never an Oxford man, even though Oxford honoured him with a DD in 1915 when he left to return to Glasgow.

Glasgow College of the Free Church of Scotland

In 1915, Moffatt was invited back to his old college to become Professor of Church History. He remained twelve years in that chair and was very active with the Union that led to the formation of the Church of Scotland, as it now is. The nineteenth century in Scotland had been a time of division into innumerable Free Presbyterian Churches. Moffatt's own Church had been formed by a union of some of these in 1900. He welcomed and supported actively the moves towards a union of his United Free Church of Scotland with the Church of Scotland which was effected eventually in 1929. That left the National Church overwhelmingly the Church of the Nation, as the Church of England had not been for more than a Century. E F Scott, who knew him best, wrote two brief descriptions in the *Dictionary of National Biography* that helped to bring the scholar alive:

> He was a man of simple and beautiful character, who endeared himself to a multitude of friends. Although a tireless student he had a great variety of interests: an athlete in his youth, a lifelong enthusiast for football and golf. A musician: 'Ultimo' is in our hymn books.

The entry makes clear that he was an all-round man, but of course it is his theological contribution that makes him memorable:

> A new attitude to the Bible had become imperative and he showed that nothing essential was lost when it was frankly adopted. To his interpretation of the ancient writings, he brought a profound scholarship, a rare power of judgement and a genuine religious sympathy. He rendered this in a language which enabled the common reader to study the Bible intelligently in the best light of modern knowledge.

He did not stay in Scotland until the Union was complete, but in 1927 accepted a post in Union Theological Seminary New York.

The American Period

Union Theological Seminary was gathering a galaxy of talent and anxious to be international. Among the outstanding British scholars they could hardly miss James Moffatt. In 1924 his translation of the Old Testament had been published and he had written forty theological works, was a regular contributor to the *Hibbert Journal*, as well as occasional contributor to almost every other technical journal in his field. In 1928, a one volume edition of the Bible appeared: *A New Translation of the Bible*. The vigour of his translation and his free style appealed to the Americans and they forgave the Scotticisms! He was invited and accepted, to the Washbourne Chair of Church History at Union Theological Seminary in 1927. He felt that he had done enough biblical study and wanted to broaden his field. He even went outside the theological field in writing introductions to an edition of Shakespeare and one detective novel, *A Tangled Web* in 1929. He could not easily shake off his association with the New Testament studies and was soon involved in the American revisions of the Standard Version. But in 1938, he managed to publish a considerable work of church history, *The First Five Centuries of the Church* and a book on Tertullian.

James Moffatt retired in 1939 but continued to live in New York, where he died on 27th June 1944. His wife lived on for two more years and he was succeeded by two sons and one daughter. His eldest son had died in boyhood. The name of Moffatt will always be associated with his pioneering work in providing a popular and scholarly translation of the Bible into English.

Edgar Goodspeed

F F Bruce regards the Goodspeed Version as the American counterpart to Moffatt. He quotes Dr Goodspeed as saying that American readers 'have had to depend so long upon versions made in Great Britain' that 'there is room for a New Testament free from expressions which however familiar in England or Scotland are strange in American ears'. The 'or Scotland' is a plain reference to Moffatt, although no mention is made of him by name. Dr Edgar J Goodspeed published *The New Testament: An American Translation* in 1923, just ten years after Moffatt's. He was a contemporary of James Moffatt.

Edgar Goodspeed began his study of Greek at the age of twelve at the old University of Chicago. His father Thomas Wakefield Goodspeed was largely instrumental in founding the New University of Chicago, to which Edgar returned for graduate work in its first year, after studying at Denison University and specialising in languages at Yale. It was a return home in two senses, to his earliest university and to one that had become very much his father's pride. He received his first doctorate from Chicago and then travelled in Europe for two years. While in Greece, he joined an archaeological party and unearthed a mass of invaluable Greek papyri. This later influenced his translations of the New Testament. He was one of the earliest to show the relation between the New Testament Greek and the Greek of the papyri. He returned to Chicago and did not repeat his archaeological expeditions, he joined the staff of Chicago University and served the faculty all his working life, ie 1898-1936. When he retired, he taught at the University of California, in Los Angeles, wrote books on Greek and the problems of translation and broadcast. His retirement home was in Bel-Air, Los Angeles.

Details of the Goodspeed translation are given in Bruce's book with a generous assessment of its value. Goodspeed did not feel competent to translate the Old Testament, but entrusted it to Dr J M Powis Smith. It appeared four years after the New Testament in 1927. But Dr Goodspeed returned to his task once he retired and translated the Apocrypha, which appeared in 1938. This was included in *The Complete Bible* which was published in 1939. Goodspeed's work was done and it remained for many years the most popular Bible in America.

10. Catholic Modern Translations

Catholics had long recognised that the Douai-Rheims-Challoner translation, used by almost all Catholics, was unsatisfactory. Attempts were made to revise it and the *Confraternity Version* (or *New American Version*) had some success. At least it showed that with the new atmosphere created by the Second Vatican Council it was possible for Catholic and Protestant scholars to work together. There were two outstanding modern translations by Catholic scholars produced in the twentieth century - The Knox Version and The Jerusalem Bible. The former was the work of one man, worthy to be put side by side with Weymouth or Moffatt; the latter was the product of a remarkable biblical school, which decisively influenced English Catholic scholars and a publisher! This latter is now generally accepted as the version to be used in Catholic services of worship. And it already has a revised version - The New Jerusalem Bible.

Ronald Arbuthnott Knox

Ronald was the youngest of the family, born in 1888 with three older brothers and two sisters. The family was Anglican, his father Edmund Arbuthnott Knox, later became Bishop of Manchester and leader of the Evangelical Party in the Church of England. Both his grandfathers were Anglican clergymen, Evangelicals who served in India and were closely associated with the Church Missionary Society. His mother's father, Thomas Valpy French was Bishop of Lahore. Ronald knew neither grandfather because they died when he was about three, but he heard much about them and their evangelical fervour influenced his early life at home. The more colourful of the two lives which must often have been related to the young Ronald was that of his mother's father. When he retired from Lahore, he found the Church Missionary Society unsympathetic and no work to satisfy his vocation in England. His knowledge of Urdu was considerable and he had translated the *Book of Common Prayer* into that language. He now felt the call to the Arab World. He set his sights on Muscat, wandering about the Arab World as a holy man, refusing the comforts of the British consul and eventually dying there. Evelyn Waugh vividly describes his mission and compares him to Charles de Foucauld.

'He has borne witness as his vocation led him', he adds, 'far beyond the horizon of George Knox'.

This George Knox is the other grandfather. He also served in India, but among the English community and he returned to England to become Central Association Secretary of the Church Missionary Society. He was a strict Calvinist and brought up his family with austerity which bordered upon privation; not because they were poor, but because the father decided that such was morally good for the children. He became more and more extreme and even disapproved of Bishop French because of his very slight inclination towards the Tractarians in later life. George Knox was more or less compelled to resign his secretaryship but a living was found for him in Rutland and he continued as editor of the *Church Missionary Intelligence*. He had the qualities of a good public relations officer.

Edmund Arbuthnott Knox, Ronald's father, seems not to have suffered too much from his austere life. In fact, he pays tribute to his father that 'his children all remained steadfast in the faith of their school-room.' Edmund won his way by scholarships to St Paul's School which he entered in October 1857. From there, he went to Corpus Christi, Oxford. He became a Fellow of Merton and advanced steadily in the Church. He was brilliant and set his heart on Holy Orders, against his father's wishes. He was uncompromising in his religious opinions, rejecting the Puritanism of his father, fearless in his opposition to those dissenters and agnostics who were moving into high places, and unwavering in the belief that the Church of England was the Church of the Reformation in the sixteenth century. He was worried by the higher criticism of the Bible, which made him slightly modify his theory of verbal inspiration. It was, however, the Prayer Book to which he clung tenaciously, 'as being both the legal charter of the Church of England and the monument of national liberation from the tyranny and corruption of Rome'. Edmund became engaged to the daughter of Bishop Thomas French, whom he had known slightly before, but met again when she came to St Ebbe's in Oxford with his family. Merton amended its statutes in 1876 so that four of its Fellows could marry, which meant that Edmund would not have to give up his Fellowship when he married Ellen. When Chavasse was appointed to Wycliffe Hall, Edmund did not feel the need to stay in Oxford to defend the Evangelical cause. Oxford was not good for Ellen and so Edmund accepted the living of Kibworth in Leicestershire. There between 1880 and 1888, four sons and two daughters were born, the youngest being Ronald on 17th February 1888.

The Attraction of Eton

Ronald had a very pleasant childhood, despite the tragedies enacted around him. Kibworth Rectory was the most pleasant home the family ever lived in, but the parish was dull for one so intellectually active as Edmund Knox. It also bored his wife. He had hopes of a deanery; Manchester was almost promised, but they wanted a man with more accommodating views. He eventually accepted the large and very difficult parish of Ashton-juxta-Birmingham. After Kibworth, the vicarage and the parish seemed dark and forbidding, but they were happy. Mrs Knox, who had been ill every winter at Kibworth seemed strangely better in Birmingham, but it did not last. She died in August 1892. Edmund threw himself into his work and achieved miracles. His sister came to look after the children, but her health did not last and the children had to be dispersed. The older children suffered considerably. But the two little boys, Wilfred and Ronald, went to their Uncle Lindsey at Creeton, near Grantham. They were there for nearly four years and were very happy. No doubt both suffered from a motherless childhood, because Uncle Lindsey was a bachelor. His love of children covered up this defect for the boys, who thoroughly enjoyed the freedom of the place. Their education was in his hands at first. Then Ronald went to Summer Fields in 1896 and liked the school. In his last year, he became head boy and a prefect. Dr Williams prepared him well and he won his place at Eton where he went in September 1900. He loved Eton and always remembered it as the happiest period of his life. It was there that he was first drawn towards Catholicism. The story of his conversion from the Anglicanism of his family and forebears is told by him in *A Spiritual Aeneid*.

There is little doubt that the attraction of Catholicism contributed much to his enjoyment of Eton. He knew that he had a hard road ahead of him, but he did not attempt to tackle all his problems at once. He gently coasted. Ronald was an attractive boy and retained that attraction into adult life. He had humour and intelligence, sympathy with those who held different views, but as he moved towards Catholicism he was not swayed much by arguments. His heart was attracted to the new faith. It is interesting that the book which started him on this course was R H Benson's *The Light Invisible*, written by an Anglican who later became a Catholic. It was the reading of that somewhat indifferent book which led him to the Virgin Mary as a central figure of devotion. He had not decided upon the priesthood when he took his own private view of celibacy. His account of that is all we need to recall, a decisive moment in his journey to the Catholic priesthood:

I think I could still point to the precise place on 'Chamber Stairs' where I knelt down at the age of seventeen one evening and bound myself to a vow of celibacy. The uppermost thought in my mind was not that of virginity. I was not fleeing from the wickedness of the world I saw round me . . . I was just beginning to form close and intimate friendships. I was just beginning also to realise that in many cases such friendships were likely to be dissolved through circumstances of separation after leaving school. And, conscious for the first time how much my nature craved for human sympathy and support, I though it my obvious duty to deny myself that tenderest sympathy and support which a happy marriage would bring. I must have 'power to attend upon the Lord without impediment'.

Ronald's literary career began before he left Eton, articles in various magazines and verse; one poem in the Cornhill magazine and a book of verse in English, Latin and Greek. The book took its title from Lucretius, *Stigma Severa*, and contained verse written from July 1903 to May 1906. It was published by Spottiswood. It went into six editions. With such a reputation he and a throng of contemporaries went up to Balliol College, Oxford in 1906. Ronald was eighteen and looked young for his years. His father was by now Bishop of Manchester. Their views were already diverse, but they kept arguments about 'high' and 'low' within the bounds of good humour.

The Conversion to Rome

It did not occur to the Bishop that his favourite son would ever desert the Church of England and neither was that in Ronald's mind. He had a brilliant undergraduate career, president of the Union, and at the end became a tutor and fellow of Trinity in 1910. He was ordained into Anglican orders, which he regarded as valid and passed through the stages of deacon and priest, becoming chaplain at Trinity. He was temporarily a schoolmaster at Shrewsbury and then during the war worked as a clergyman in the Ministry of Information section of the War Office. It was during this period that Ronald made up his mind that he must become a Catholic. There had long been growing tension between his views and those of his father. Once the decision was made the relationship of father to favourite son was tragically disrupted; but not broken entirely. Ronald Knox was surprised at the kindness of replies to his letters of information to many Anglican friends, including Bishop Gore. The reply from his father shows the depth of love and the quality of both men - father and son:

First I must acknowledge faithfully the affectionate spirit in which your letter was written, and express my satisfaction that you will not be required to repudiate your baptism.

Next I will say what I said to both the clergy from this diocese who went over, that when the time came for their return they might be sure of a most hearty welcome. In both cases the desire to return has been expressed, but the correspondence has never gone beyond my letter in reply. I need not say what your return would be to me though I am conscious that my hopes of it must reckon with difficulties almost insurmountable. Still it is only on this side that I shall dwell. I am enclosing a copy of a prayer which I have been offering and shall continue to offer on your behalf. There is little, if anything, in it which you could not use. The day will come when we shall know as we are known.

I suppose that I must address my letters to you as a layman. You cannot know what that means to a father.

But *Fiat Voluntas Tua* (Thy will be done)

Ronald made up his mind away from controversy in the Abbey at Farnborough. The precise dates are in the guestmaster's diary. He decided on 19th September 1917 and he was received into the Church three days later by the Abbot.

He did not leave his work at the War Office, but continued to work as a layman. His life was now divided clearly into two: 9am-3.30pm, at the Office; after 3.30pm, writing.

A Catholic Priest

Having written his apologia in *A Spiritual Aeneid* tracing in a style so different from his later writings the progress from the religion of his home to that of his heart, he laid aside his pen and wrote no important book for several years. He was a Catholic layman, but had no doubt about his vocation to the secular priesthood. Cardinal Bourne instructed him. He did not take a full theological course but continued with his work at the War Office, lived at the Oratory, read in the library and shared in the life of a Catholic community. The Cardinal thought two years of this would be sufficient. Brilliant as he was intellectually, Ronald Knox suffered from the lack of a rigorous theological training, and he knew it. His duties at the War Office ended in December 1918. His next job was to be at St Edmund's, Old Hall, near Ware in Hertfordshire. He was ordained subdeacon on 22nd June 1919, a deacon shortly afterwards and finally a Catholic priest at Old Hall, on October 5th. There, at St Edmund's he was assistant master and continued in this modest post after 1922 when he was appointed Professor of the Old Testament at the seminary. He is remembered in this latter office for having recommended the Greek New Testament as a useful crib for the Douai version!

It can be said that Ronald Knox led a double life. He was immersed in the life of St Edmund's inspiring classes and sport with his humour. He also took a great interest in the school magazine. But he was preaching often, lecturing, writing and noted as one of the outstanding Catholics of the day. Writers recognised a master. He tried his hand at many forms including the devising of *Acrostics* for *The Illustrated Review* and published the first of his detective stories, *The Viaduct Murder* in 1935.

The Oxford Chaplaincy

Ronald Knox remained at St Edmund's until 1926, when he moved to Oxford to become Chaplain to Catholic Undergraduates. Now, for the first time since he had entered the Catholic Church he had a home and a cure of souls. He was already well known and a good choice for young men who needed their faith nurturing by a wise and friendly person of wide knowledge. His broad and tolerant views did not extend to serious doubts about the Catholic faith as such, but he was prepared to discuss many details and understand the difficulty of acceptance. His home was on the corner of Rose Place in St Aldate's. It was called The Old Palace, but it was really a reconstruction of some old houses of various periods. Dominicans and Franciscans had used the houses in the past. Ronald Knox took delight in giving it the atmosphere of home for four generations of Oxford undergraduates. Women were not admitted to the chaplaincy until the Second World War when Knox's successor came. Ronald's last year was 1938-1939. He was the fifth Catholic Chaplain at Oxford since the Reformation. The others had styled themselves, 'Catholic Chaplain to the University'. He changed the title to 'Chaplain to the Catholic Undergraduates'. By this time, the Anglican hold on the university had loosened and Catholics were no longer afraid of the influence of Nonconformists as they had been in Cardinal Manning's time. Ronald Knox clearly was not happy about women. Catholics in the women's colleges were really the concern of Cherwell Edge (a Catholic hostel for women students) or St Aloysius. He was glad to be able to tell women who came too frequently that he was not supposed to poach on their preserve! His written direction for male students on how to behave if women came was:

> If women turn up at the undergraduates' Mass they should be made to sit close to the wall; no male will sit on either side of them for fear of looking responsible for them.

Evelyn Waugh quotes the assessment of Knox's influence on the men. Knox had invited him to leave his Christchurch rooms and live in the Old Palace. He refused at first, but eventually accepted. He sums up the life of the Old Palace by saying:

> In some indefinable way his influence was, in dozens of cases, retrospective. It was only when we looked *back* that we realised how much this hopelessly shy, quiet creature had affected our thinking ... What happened was that Ronnie took quite a long time to sink into us; and by the time that he did we were stockbrokers, journalists or Inverness sheep farmers ... We were full of inhibitions about him when we were there, and perhaps he was too, about us, but we in the long run, drew all the dividends. We gave him damn-all; he gave us a lot.

He wrote a great deal during his Oxford period, but mostly small books of lesser importance. The only book of substance to appear in this period was at the very end, *Let Dons Delight*. But he preached and helped Douglas Woodruff restore *The Tablet* after a period of serious decline.

Daphne Strutt

In his youth, Ronald formed a very close alliance with Guy Lawrence, who sustained him in many times of depression. Their relationship was intimate and profound. When Lawrence died he was numbed. For nineteen years he was without this 'fructifying intimacy of affection which was essential to his growth'. All these long years, his heart stood empty. In the summer of 1937 it was filled by a remarkable young married woman, Daphne Strutt, daughter of Lord Rayleigh. She married Lord Acton. She had no attachment to the Church, although nominally Anglican. Her brothers were fiercely anti-Catholic and were worried about her marrying a Catholic. When she married she was entirely hostile to her husband's faith. Douglas Woodruff seems to have aroused her interest and within five years of marriage she declared that she was to become a Catholic. Her family was worried and persuaded her to wait a year. Douglas Woodruff introduced her to a full course of theological, devotional and liturgical studies. So when, in 1937 realising that she needed a priest he introduced her to Ronald Knox.

When they were introduced, she insisted that they should not talk about religion! This pleased Ronald, because he was reluctant to persuade anyone, least of all a beautiful young woman, to become a Catholic against the wishes of her family. He was shy too, but she soon brought out the best in him. She was intelligent, beautiful and full of vitality. Mind responded to mind and for the rest of his life she was his soul companion and he her priest. There was no scandal in it, but it is hard to rule out love as the basis of their relationship. They refined that love into a spiritual relationship by the disciplines of their church. She brought Ronald Knox alive and sustained him through years of difficulties. He had from her the intellectual, spiritual and inter-personal relationships that he needed; she had the like from him, which her husband could not supply. Lord Acton, her husband was a light-hearted, sweet-tempered man, the grandson of the historian, a good Catholic.

For his last two years at Oxford, Knox spent the greater part of the long vacation at Aldenham and his friendship with Lady Acton touched every part of both their lives. They were not always concerned with religious matters and Ronald was much more than a priest to her. When they were apart they wrote to one another with daily information of what they were doing, whom they were meeting and what they were reading. At Aldenham he was part of the family, concerned also with Lord Acton's horses and his business affairs.

Let Dons Delight, his best book from the Oxford period, he freely acknowledges was due to her prodding. She forbade him to write another detective story, gave him the idea for the book, gingered him along and kept pushing books into his hand to read! She bullied him into writing the book and he rightly dedicated it to her. He compares her to Jerome's St Paula: *The Vulgate* would never have been written but for St Paula saying, "Come on now".'

Let Dons Delight was a great success and Hilaire Belloc, who received a proof copy responded at once with enthusiasm, 'It is a masterpiece I was quite bowled over by it. It is astonishing ... It is one of the best things that have been done anywhere in my lifetime, and I remain gasping at it'. Evelyn Waugh comments on Belloc's review in more measured tones, but equally appreciative in *The Tablet*: 'It was, perhaps, the last new book he read with full comprehension; certainly the last he read with delight'.

Translating the Vulgate

Ronald had confided in Daphne quite early in their relationship that he wanted, not preferment in the Church, but a quiet retreat where he could write and most of all revise the Douai-Rheims-Challoner Bible, which had been unsatisfactory for more than a century. After much difficulty, he also persuaded the Archbishop, Cardinal Hinsley, who with great generosity and, one must say humility, wrote on June 30th 1938,

> I ought not to press my suit further in view of your reluctance to accept (ie the Presidency of St Edmund's) I understand perfectly. .. Your interests and wishes are decisive; I bow submissively ... I do agree completely with you that you should have time and opportunity to *write*.

The Cardinal offered to do anything he could to help. Then Ronald Knox told him of the desire closest to his heart to revise the Catholic Bible in English. He would of course do this from the Vulgate and use the original languages only as a guide in uncertain passages. The Cardinal did not have to find a place for him to do it. The Actons offered Aldenham and wanted him appointed chaplain to the household. Ronald Knox left Oxford at the end of the summer of 1939 as war came. He resigned his chaplaincy, was commissioned to translate the Vulgate and installed as private chaplain at Aldenham.

F F Bruce has supplied all the necessary information about his translation. He was fully obedient to the rules of his Church and translated from that version of The Vulgate which Clement VIII had authorised in 1592 and was so declared at the Council of Trent. He was not free to go behind this version to a better text even of the Latin Version. But he did pay regard to the Hebrew and Greek. Bruce gives ample examples of the effect of this poor text.

On 26th June, all his farewells were made in Oxford and he sold off his superfluous books before leaving for his dream life in Aldenham. The cottage was not yet ready for him, so he lived and worked in the house. Daphne was expecting a child in the September, but she gave him all the help she could, looking up his references and encouraging him. Lord Acton had moved his work from London to Birmingham and could return every night. The weekends saw the house full of guests. Ronald set aside definite times for working at his Hebrew. And for two months he led the life to which for the past two years he had looked forward. In September came the war.

The Second World War at Aldenham

Mobilisation for war meant that Lord Acton who held a commission in the county yeomanry, was called up and had to resign his work in Birmingham. This reduced the income of a family that was not rich and raised questions about the large house at Aldenham, which would probably be requisitioned in any case as a hostel for evacuees. Arrangements were made to anticipate requisitioning by inviting the nuns of Maria Assumpta in Kensington Square to take up residence at Aldenham. The first detachment arrived on 1st September 1939. Ronald was to act as their chaplain without pay! The Assumptionist nuns were teachers and they brought their girls with them. Ronald tried to hide his dismay. His Eden had been invaded.

Lady Acton was in the last stages of her pregnancy and went to stay with neighbours to have her baby; Lord Acton was with his regiment; Ronald got on with his Hebrew. But his fears turned to pleasure. He enjoyed the school. The girls had been told that he was engaged in a very important piece of work and they must not disturb him. He soon got to know the girls and the nuns. His services in chapel were quickly appreciated. Many of the courses he gave them appeared in published form as *The Mass in Slow Motion* (1948), *The Creed in Slow Motion* (1949) and *The Gospel in Slow Motion* (1950). Each of these very popular books is dedicated to an Aldenham girl.

The war years brought a change over his relationship with Daphne. From a pensive girl she grew into a robust woman and a mother of a growing family. She bore two sons in July 1941 and January 1943. At times dressed in Girl Guide uniform or in corduroy trousers, she let her intellectual interest lie fallow and devoted herself furiously to pig-farming! Ronald was not very good at practical things and, although he tried to help, he looked out of place in the robust farming world of wartime Aldenham. He was only in his middle fifties, but he looked old in the field.

In his study and conducting retreats he lost nothing of his mental vigour. Apart from his nine years hard labour on the Bible, he wrote sermons, radio talks, worked on his book *Enthusiasm*, contributed a monthly piece to *The Sunday Times*. In 1945, he wrote his penetrating essay on *God and the Atom*.

His work on the Bible was still unfinished when the Actons emigrated to Southern Rhodesia. He was without a home, but not for long. The Asquiths invited him to Mells and he became their private chaplain. Mells is about 15 miles south of Bath and there he worked for the next 10 years.

The Last Years at Mells Manor (1947-1957)

Ronald moved to a place and among people whom he had known for many years. He has an interesting comment on his first impressions: 'I don't know how I shall manage to work in a place where life goes on so dreamily!' He added, 'One curious effect of my present move is that for the first time in nearly forty years I am not living with people noticeably younger than myself. In fact, believe it or not, I am *under* the average age at the Manor House'. He was very comfortable at Mells and settled down to work on the Old Testament. Lady Acton did not go at once to Southern Rhodesia, because of the difficulty of finding a passage for her party of 17 and the pigs. She was able to visit Ronald twice at Mells before she left in March 1948. She found him very comfortable, a little heavier and recovering his equanimity. He complained of his idleness, but all things were relative. After handing in his provisional text of the Old Testament he had to contend with many suggestions for changing the text. The Psalms he had to do twice. Apart from the Bible, this last decade of his life saw many publications, chief of which was *Enthusiasm* (Clarendon Press, 1950).

Evelyn Waugh's judgement is that it enshrines some of his finest writing and he adds, 'There are many long-sustained passages that are fit to stand beside the most illustrious prose in the language'.

In 1954, Ronald Knox set out on a high adventure to visit the Oxfords in Zanzibar and the Actons in Salisbury. He left on 4th February and returned 29th March. Daphne with whom he stayed for almost a month found him more serene than when he was at Aldenham, less worried even by missing a plane and having his plans disturbed. He returned happily to Mells.

Despite this new-found serenity and the dreaminess of the West Country, he did not expect to retire into pleasant inactivity. He had seen his father, vigorous and active at eighty and he laid upon himself still the heavy burden of writing, translating *The Imitation of Christ*, a series of Meditations on the words of our Lord, an autobiography, and books of apologetics. He constantly revised his 1927 *Belief of Catholics*. His writing programme was not based upon any sense of the nearness of death.

His last public appearance was on 22nd June 1957 at a fete held in the gardens of Mells Manor House. He died on 24th August and was buried in the village churchyard at Mells. A Solemn Requiem Mass was offered by Bishop Craven and Father D'Arcy preached the sermon from his translation of Ecclesiasticus 38.39. How well his translation fitted him.

> But the wise man will be learning the love of former times, the prophets will be their study. Theirs it is to support this unchanging word of God's creation; craftsmanship is their title to live - lending themselves freely and making their study in the law of the most High.

The Jerusalem Bible

Catholics were becoming more aware that they needed a Bible translated directly from the original languages. Knox had given great attention to the Hebrew and Greek for the modification of certain details when The Vulgate was plainly wrong; but as Bruce points out, his version was an English translation of the Clementine version of the Latin Vulgate. Ironically what replaced him was an English version of a French translation.

Bruce rates the Jerusalem Bible very highly because of its excellent scholarship. But the scholars were French-speaking. The English Jerusalem Bible is not, of course a translation of the French, but it is heavily dependent upon it. The Jerusalem Bible is inconceivable without the work of the French Dominicans.

We must therefore include them in our discussions. This means looking at the history of the *Ecole Biblique* in Jerusalem. This remarkable school, although Dominican, and therefore Catholic is about as ecumenical as could possibly be. It is the ecumenism, not of the Councils, but of scholarship. All who work there are concerned with truth, whether they are studying the development of a Greek or Hebrew word, or excavating a biblical site, or studying the effect of landscape. They are not concerned with the logic of theology, but the accuracy of the Bible. Père Roland de Vaux, one of the principal architects of this French translation defined the goal of his school as 'to trace in its original tenor, the text inspired by God, and to grasp its every shade of meaning'.

The Jerusalem Bible School

At a conference held in Jerusalem in 1962, Père Roland de Vaux gave a brief account of the purpose of the Bible School, founded by Père Lagrange in 1890. He did not repeat the story, which may be apocryphal, that when in the midst of the Modernist crisis in the Roman Catholic Church, the Pope declared the Bible to be inerrant, Père Lagrange remarked that if it is so important we had better read it! He did, however, define Père Lagrange's intention:

> to create, in the land of the Bible, a centre for study, where those concerned could acquire a better understanding of the Scripture.

The two religious orders which have done most in France to render the Bible into the vernacular are the Dominicans and the Benedictines. They pioneered the way to the Second Vatican Council in their attitude to the Bible, treading a dangerous path, as many of them were disciplined for such almost Protestant attitudes. Dom Céleste Charlier, who edited a journal on Bible study was silenced. A Benedictine movement from Maredsous in Belgium, produced a popular translation in modern French.

Throughout all this 'biblical renewal' in the Catholic Church, the School of Jerusalem was the undoubted centre of biblical scholarship.

In 1882, Père Matthieu Lacomte, OP acquired a piece of land in Jerusalem which covered the ruins of the byzantine basilica of St Stephen. His intention was to found a Dominican convent, under the protection of the first Christian martyr, a place of prayer, meditation and study near to the Holy Sites. He already saw the possibility of a school for biblical studies. He died on 19th June 1887 and did not see his dream realised. With the blessing of Pope Leo XIII, the dream was realised by Père Marie-Joseph Lagrange, OP. The time was ripe. Pilgrimages, often badly controlled and with a western view of the Bible, had changed into a serious study of the origins of the Scriptures. Archaeology and the study of languages, scientific examination of texts and critical study of biblical history had made great advances in the second half of the nineteenth century.

Père Lagrange studied oriental languages at the University of Vienna and at the age of 34 was sent to Palestine by his Superior to do a feasibility study on the proposal to found a biblical school in the Holy Land. The difficulties were enormous, but Père Lagrange saw the possibilities. He was captivated by the charm of the Holy Land and felt the evocative power of its memories. He saw almost at once that the study of the Bible would be enriched and enlightened if undertaken in such privileged places of revelation. He reported to his Superior, Père Larroca, and had permission to go ahead. He opened the School officially on 15th November 1890 in the modest surroundings of an old Turkish abattoir! With very few men and little resources, he laid down the origin, purpose and programme of the enterprise: 'a *practical* school of biblical studies'. His key word was 'practical'. He did not want a theoretical study of the Bible, such as could be done anywhere. Such a practical study, he maintained, would enable us to understand the Word of God better, because it could be done in the actual locations where the Word had deigned to be incarnated. His programme was to include three principal activities: exploration of the country, courses in biblical studies, and publications. He was convinced that

> the systematic exploration of the soil, and one day the sub-soil, would discover and uncover those remains of the past which are susceptible to providing a better knowledge of the human *milieu* of the Revelation.

The courses were to instruct the students in this practical knowledge and renew an interest in the Bible. Lectures were to be given by French

Dominicans, but the students were to be drawn from all countries. The publications were to make known in the Church and in the Academic World the result of this research and the nature of the instruction given. These clearly defined intentions were rigorously adhered to and represent the main thrusts of the School to this day. His successors have seen the wisdom of the threefold approach and maintained it. The School was founded at the time when biblical studies had reached a crisis. The critical approach to the Bible was condemned together with 'Modernism' and men like George Tyrrel and Alfred Loisy were excommunicated for their views. Père Lagrange had to tread carefully. He accepted the predominance of divine revelation in the Scriptures, but was concerned to show the human element in their composition.

His main publication channel was the *Revue Biblique* and in that he and his colleagues wrote articles which appeared in 1895-6 and tried to solve the problem of divine authorship through human hands. They were not content to regard divine authorship as simply God dictating to man what he should write. The writers however were moved by the light of God, they were not entirely like other writers. They explained what they understood of the divine revelation. It was a complicated argument to retain the inerrancy of the theology of the biblical writings, as affirmed by the Church, but the need to study the exegesis of the writers. These articles were later developed at a conference to which Père Lagrange was invited in 1903 to explain his 'historical method'. In order to understand the revelation of God in the form and the accents in which he has given it through his servants, he argued, it is necessary to study the sacred writings with all the resources of modern science and technique. He outlined the need for textual, literary and historical criticism. He was able to show with delicacy the eternal and absolute message of God in the Bible transmitted by human and fallible instruments.

The *Revue Biblique* which Père Lagrange had founded just two years after the opening of the School became invaluable in disseminating and defending his ideas. It has remained to this day a most valuable means of communication for the School. Some dozen years later, in collaboration with his faithful friends, MM Lecoffre and Gabalda, he started to publish a series of biblical studies, which were effectively critical studies of all the books of the Bible. They were issued in paperback and any educated Catholic priest in France would have these little paperbacks on his shelves. The Gospel of Mark came first in 1911 and others followed slowly over the years. Not all were commentaries and translations.

His fertile pen produced related essays, in the same series - *Studies in Semitic Religions* (1903), *Messianism among the Jews* (1909), *Judaism before Jesus Christ* (1931), *History of the New Testament Canon* (1933), *Textual Criticism of the New Testament* 1935). There were more controversial booklets too, such as *Loisy and Modernism* (1928).

Opposition and Suspicion

This astonishing literary activity was all the more surprising because Père Lagrange was suspected of betraying the Catholic Faith. He had opposition also from the Jesuits who were at the same time reviving biblical studies in Rome. The old antagonism between Dominicans and Jesuits was thus revived and the Jesuits appeared as the defenders of the Faith! Père Lagrange was constantly having to justify his textual, biblical and historical criticism. On 15th April 1898, the Latin Patriarch of Jerusalem sent to Rome a copy of an article in *Revue Biblique* (January issue) which dealt with *The Sources of the Pentateuch*. He considered it to be alarming and dangerous. This was the first attack. The report of the Toulouse Conference in 1902 was also attacked.

The Superior General of the Jesuit Order hinted that Lagrange was supporting the attack upon religion made earlier by Strauss in his *Life of Jesus*. That was directly related to his historical criticism and Père Lagrange replied with alacrity, but he was soon criticised by several Jesuits, directing their attack against the 'new' method of study. The most virulent was from Père A J Delattre, SJ. When Père Lagrange replied to that with *A Clarification of the Historical Method*, he was not allowed to print more than 200 copies. His commentary on 'Genesis' had to wait until 1907 before the Pope gave permission for its publication.

In 1909, the Jesuits established in Rome the Pontifical Biblical Institute and confined its staff to Jesuits. This could have been thought of as an admission that more studies were needed and one order had simply learnt from another, but the dangers of rivalry were there. It threatened to rob Jerusalem of students who were already becoming too few. That the Jesuit Institute was in opposition to the Dominican School in Jerusalem became evident in 1912, when a Professor of the Institute wrote that it was the Pope's wish to see in this Institute 'an absolute guarantee of orthodoxy which is lacking in some other schools'. It was not difficult to guess what he meant by 'other schools'. The Rector of the Biblical Institute in Rome did not hide his intention of putting an end to the work of Père Lagrange, but he did not commit himself to writing!

A very severe setback came with a rebuke from the Sacred Congregation of Cardinals in Rome on 19th June 1912. The statement fell short of placing his writings on the Index, but it roused suspicions. After condemning certain German works as rationalist and hyper-critical of the Scriptures, it added, 'and other commentaries having the same relative attitude to the Holy Scriptures of the Old and New Testament, like several writings of Père Lagrange'.

Père Lagrange reacted with restraint and with humility. He saw the attack as upon himself and wished to maintain the Biblical School even if he had to sacrifice himself and his beloved work. He wrote to the Pope making his total submission, resigning his work on biblical studies and suggesting a change in the *Revue Biblique*, to become the *Revue palestinienne et orientale*, offering to leave Jerusalem for a year's sabbatical. The Superior of the Dominicans, Père Cornier, prevented the change in the *Revue*, which had been too hastily suggested; but Père Lagrange left Jerusalem to exercise an apostolate in France which had no more to do with the Bible.

At the end of a year or less, his humble submission had proved to the Pope that he was not the rebellious priest that he had been depicted as, and he was allowed to return to Jerusalem and take up his former duties. Père Lagrange had proved the purity of his intentions and had always been obedient. Within that context he did not compromise the integrity of his scholarship. None the less he remained under suspicion for many years. In 1920, the Papal Encyclical, *Spiritus Paraclitus* made very clear reference to the dangers of his type of literature without mentioning him by name. The School had to wait until 1943 in the Encyclical, *Divine Atlante* before it was mentioned with honour. By then Père Lagrange had been dead five years. After that the *Ecole Biblique de Jerusalem* gradually became the pride of the Catholic Church and the historical method accepted as essential. This happened in two stages: the approval of the Biblical Commission on the Historical Truth of the Gospels in 1964, and then the text of the Second Vatican Council on 'Revelation' which confirmed the necessity and the benefits of the historical method. Père Lagrange in his *Souvenirs personnels*, published in French as late as 1967 (he died in 1938) was able to say that the torments were passed and that better days lay ahead.

Père Roland de Vaux

While Père Lagrange still lived, the School developed its archaeological side intensively. This was partly due to the request of the British Mandatory Government of Palestine demanding a contact in the field of archaeology. The French Government asked the School to be the official contact. This put the School into a new league. Its status was greatly enhanced and it attracted many of the leading archaeologists of France and other countries. The threefold purpose was not abandoned. Several more Dominicans arrived in the 1920s and in 1932, came Père Roland de Vaux and Père Pierre Benoit - future directors of the School. The Second World War disturbed the School less than the First had. Père de Vaux had come with a special interest and qualifications in archaeology. While the war was still in progress Père de Vaux was able to direct the excavation of an old caravan inn and medieval church at *Abou Gosh*. There were few students during the war years, but they returned in 1945. It was soon caught up in the cross fire of the Arab-Jewish conflicts. In this situation Père de Vaux, the new director, put a special emphasis on the excavations. The official arrangement with the British Mandatory Government and later with Israel, as well as the official recognition of the French Government, enabled Père de Vaux to recruit help and undertake extensive excavations.

In 1946, he started the excavation of *Tel el Far'ah* and continued work there until 1962. It was a very profitable dig just north-east of Nablus, which identified the first capital of Israel, *Tirzah*, where Omri reigned before moving into Samaria (I Kings 16.23). After that, he co-operated with the Jordanian Department of Antiquities and the Rockefeller Museum to explore *Khirbat Qumran* and the surrounding caves which had been made famous by the discovery of the Dead Sea Scrolls. His main achievement there, was to trace the history of the Jewish sect which had taken refuge in those caves. He continued to excavate - collaborating also with the Government of Israel through its Department of Antiquities, and the last site that he opened up was at *Tel Qeisan*. In all of this, he was busily engaged with publications, describing his excavations, exploring the nature and history of early Hebrew and other religious rites and writing a history of Palestine. In a paper, given to the Conference arranged by the United Bible Societies in Jerusalem, May 14-17, 1962, Roland de Vaux described this work of the School and added a few details of personal importance to him. A few extracts from that paper will show the enthusiasm of this remarkable Dominican:

> The training of students is not the only task with which the teachers at the School are concerned. Faithful to the tradition established by Père Lagrange, they make it an additional duty to engage in personal research and study. The surface-explorations in which the School had become renowned at the very outset have been pursued, but during these last few years the actual archaeological work of excavation has been developed to an outstanding degree...
> At the same time, the discovery of the famous manuscripts of the

Dead Sea, in 1947, proved an inducement to the School to embark on yet a further field of work. The fact is that from the very beginning of the archaeological exploration in question, the School was associated with the work of the Jordanian Department of Antiquities and with that of the Archaeological Museum of Palestine, as regards all the research carried out around the Dead Sea: in 1949, 1952, and 1956, the exploration of the caves containing the manuscripts from 1951 to 1956, the excavation of *Khirbat Qumran*, uncovering the community buildings of the religious group which inhabited this austere region and left behind the precious manuscripts in question; in 1958, the excavation of *Feshka*, bringing to light an additional settlement of the same community, with its agricultural and industrial centre. The School also collaborated in the publication of the Dead Sea manuscripts. It is represented by two members on the international and interconfessional team responsible for the preparation of these manuscripts for publication, and three further learned men responsible for this work are accommodated at the School.

A further great achievement is the Jerusalem Bible... The School has assumed the task of supervising this work, from the scientific point of view, five of its members have translated some of the books of the Bible. Furthermore, they have already contributed or are now preparing some of the volumes forming the series of publications to accompany the Bible.

Père de Vaux assured us, as he finished, that the School had not abandoned its original tasks when it took on new ones. The *Revue Biblique*, he told us in 1962 was entering its 70th year. And to this day it is still being published.

La Bible de Jerusalem

Père Lagrange and Père de Vaux were directors and involved in the work that made the *Bible de Jerusalem*, Père Pierre Benoit was also closely associated with it. Essentially it was a group work, and there were other names - perhaps even more involved with the work.

Père Pierre Benoit, who succeeded Père de Vaux who died in 1971, describes the 'collective work' which with its wide distribution, he admits, has made the Biblical School known world-wide:

> It was realised in collaboration with the Dominican team of the *Editions du Cerf*, and particularly with the late lamented Père Thomas Chifflot, OP. He was the moving spirit, intrepid and

efficient, who wanted to put into the hands of Christian people a new translation, at once literary and scientific, with the sacred text accompanied by introductions and numerous marginal notes. He wanted people to be able to read the Bible with understanding and critically. At the time, that concept was new among Catholics. It was a great success. Of course, other teachers at the school played their part. It appeared first in 1946 in a series of small paperback booklets which were revised again and again. Books of the Bible were treated separately. Then, under the direction of Père de Vaux, it was brought into one volume in 1956.

The responsibility for this final volume was in fact divided between Père de Vaux for the Old Testament and Père Pierre Benoit for the New. It was revised in 1973 after Père de Vaux's death.

This *Bible de Jerusalem* became the guiding text for equivalent translations in English, Spanish, Italian, Brazilian, German.

Père Pierre Benoit died at the age of 81 in April 1987. All three are gone. They admit that the translation was a group work of the School, but the names of Lagrange, de Vaux and Benoit are the names of the makers of *La Bible de Jerusalem*, but they were not makers of an English Bible any more than Jerome was. They prepared the scholarship and in fact the notes to the English Jerusalem Bible were translations of their notes.

The Jerusalem Bible and the New Jerusalem Bible

There is first of all a publisher's story. In 1958, Frank Steed of Sheed and Ward, a Catholic publisher, saw the value of an English version of the *Bible de Jerusalem*. He was a businessman and a Catholic. He knew that his Church needed a more scholarly translation and one that was readable. The *Bible de Jerusalem* seemed to him to be what his English Catholics needed in English. He could not assume that it would be accepted. His own publishing firm was small and limited in resources. He therefore approached a larger firm - Longmans Green who at that time had a religious list. Michael Longman, a director and a devout Catholic, a younger member of the family which had long had major interests in the publishing firm, persuaded the Board of Longmans Green to pursue the matter. He could count on the support of John Todd as Editor. John Todd was the first key figure in this project and he continued with it throughout.

John Todd was born in 1918, educated in Wellington and Corpus Christi, Cambridge, where he graduated in history. He was at that time an agnostic until towards the end of the Second World War when he was converted to Catholicism. He took a keen interest in Catholic lay activity which took up most of his time after his conversion. In 1956, he became Editor of Catholic books for Longmans Green. There he worked with Michael Longman and after lengthy meetings with Père Chifflot of *Editions du Cerf*, secured a contract which was eventually signed. Père Roland de Vaux suggested that the best editor for the Jerusalem Bible in English would be Alexander Jones. The first task was to translate the study apparatus and this he proceeded to do. Then a misfortune occurred. Longmans Green decided to disband their Religious Publishing. Tim Darton, the Anglican Editor and John Todd the Catholic Editor, joined Michael Longman to form a new publishing firm to be called Darton, Longman and Todd. The three brought different qualities to the firm. Tim Darton was the oldest and most experienced; John Todd was not only an editor, but already a considerable author with a special interest in the ecumenical movement; Michael Longman brought his prestige and it was largely because of this that the *Editions du Cerf* were prepared to do business with the new firm. John Todd had already published a significant book on *Catholics and the Ecumenical Movement* (1956) and a highly praised biography of *John Wesley* (1958). He went on to become an important Catholic historian of the Reformation with his biography of Martin Luther (1964) and his first significant book with Darton, Longman and Todd, *Reformation* (1972).

The young publishing firm had taken with them from Longmans Green all the contracts that authors and proprietors were willing to give. There is no doubt that their biggest venture was the Jerusalem Bible. This would either break them or make them. In effect, it made them and is still an important part of their total output.

Alexander Jones was a translator and editor. The success of the Bible depended upon its scholarship and style. The scholarship came from the *Ecole Biblique de Jerusalem* and Alec Jones was content to translate and edit their notes. The style was another matter. The English was not to be a translation of the French but it had to consider the decisions taken in translating into French. Alec Jones needed help here and he assembled a formidable array of stylists and biblical scholars. The list of 'principal collaborators', printed at the opening of the Jerusalem Bible ran to 27 and it is headed by the comment, 'The list of those who have helped in the preparation of this Bible is too long to be given in its entirety'. The 27 listed are defined as, 'The principal collaborators in translation and literary revision'. They include Dominicans like Illtud Evans, Kenelm Foster, Edmund Hill; Benedictines, like Aldhelm Dean, Ernest Graf, Sylvester Houedard, all men who have distinguished themselves in the field of theological writing. It also included outstanding writers in a wide field: Anthony Kenny, Edward Sackville-West, Robert Speaigt, J R R Tolkien. The name of Alan Neame appears in the list and he was much used in providing a special edition of the Psalms because of his experience of the Near East and his knowledge of Semitic languages. Clearly such a group was not gathered to translate the French but to produce a new English translation from the original languages, noting the work of the French translators.

It was a co-operative effort and a publishing success when it appeared in 1966. A few years later, in 1972, the *Bible de Jerusalem* was thoroughly revised. That was too early to do anything about the English version. But in 1985, taking into account the developments in biblical scholarship and the more recent insights of the French Edition, The New Jerusalem Bible was published. This time it was put into the hands of a different General Editor.

Hans Wansbrough was born in London in 1934 and educated at Ampleforth College and Oxford, where he took a First in Greats (Classics and Philosophy). He became a monk of Ampleforth Abbey in 1953 and soon afterwards embarked upon a course of study at the Catholic University of Friburg in Switzerland. When the Abbot told him that he was to study theology at Friburg, an old family friend asked if there was anything she could give him. He asked her for a Hebrew Bible and the beauty of its calligraphy fascinated him and persuaded him to work hard at Hebrew until he could decipher that beautiful script. He had special tuition in Hebrew and never lost the love for it. At Friburg, he studied under Père Spicq and Père Barthelemy. He remembered the words of Père Barthelemy, 'you cannot understand the Bible unless you have smelt cameldung'.

At Friburg, it was decided that he should go on to biblical studies and with this in mind, he was sent to Israel to learn modern Hebrew. He discovered then that he had Jewish roots. His mother had been converted to Catholicism from a non-practising Jewish family. He had never heard her speaking Yiddish, but she could and when he returned from Israel she did! He became fluent in modern Hebrew and had a good grounding in classical Hebrew. The discovery of his Jewish roots and his mother's Yiddish brought out a new fascination with Judaism and Israel. He records the height of his achievement in modern Hebrew when he was hitchhiking and tried to justify monastic celibacy to a Jew! He did not claim success, but his knowledge of Hebrew was put to the test.

After this, it was obvious that he should do two things: explore the country further, and study at the *Ecole Biblique* in Jerusalem. The two objectives were easily combined. He was registered at the Ecole Biblique and started a 15,000 mile excursion on a Vespa through the Holy Land. He lists his adventures on that extended tour:

> Getting lost on Sinai, a breakdown in the desert between Amman and Baghdad, stoned by villagers at Naim, shot at in Negeb, rammed by a bus in Damascus.

He had smelt camel-dung before he was thirty! At that age, in 1964, he was ordained a priest and joined the teaching staff at Ampleforth two years later. He has been a tutor in Scripture and Hebrew there ever since and in 1969 he became a housemaster.

He has many writings to his credit and has taught as a visiting professor in the Catholic University of America in Washington DC.

It was important for him to keep up his contacts with the *Ecole Biblique* in Jerusalem and he seemed a natural choice to revise the Jerusalem Bible in English. It was Père Benoit, the director of the *Ecole Biblique* at that time who suggested he should do this. He used the same collaborators and added a few others. Alan Neame again played an important role in checking the translation. There were many other names. But the maker of the New Jerusalem Bible was undoubtedly Dom Hans Wansbrough, as Alec Jones had been of the Jerusalem Bible in 1966. Both were nominees and former students of the *Ecole Biblique de Jerusalem*: Alec Jones, nominated by Père Roland de Vaux and Hans Wansbrough by Père Pierre Benoit. The early work of Tim Darton as house editor of the *Jerusalem Bible* was also crucial and the publishing firm of Darton, Longman and Todd played a pastoral role in its birth. The first Jerusalem Bible was quickly accepted by the Catholics of Britain and corresponded with the advent of the vernacular Mass following the Second Vatican Council. Its text was printed in English translation of the Mass and when the *Anglican Alternative Service Book* was published in 1980 it was included as one of the four translations from which 'Readings' were taken.

It will be some time before these texts can be replaced by those from the New Jerusalem Bible, which has considerable variations.

11. C H Dodd and J B Phillips

As I come towards the end of this book, I realise even more than my critics, that I have missed out some of the great 'Makers of the English Bible'. Selection was always inevitable, but if that selection was difficult in the early centuries of this story it become well nigh impossible over the past fifty years. In that period, Bible translation has mushroomed and every religious publisher has had to adopt one translation to give a firm financial basis to the other religious books!

F F Bruce has listed and described most of the translations of the past half century, including Hugh Schofield, the distinguished Jewish scholar who produced *The Authentic New Testament.*, to which I devoted a chapter in my earlier book, *The New Translations of the Bible* (SCM Press, 1959.) There are so many Bible translations that it would be foolish to attempt to assess all the scholars, communicators, writers and preachers who have assisted in their making. It is also difficult sometimes to find the principal person behind a committee translation. F F Bruce has said all that needs to be said about The Good News Bible, which had such a popular success, and generally I must refer you to his book for details of very many of the translations that have appeared in the last fifty years.

In this chapter, I want to concentrate on two people. They represent two different kinds of translation. The one is part of a massive exercise of scholarship and organisation through several committees and translators, who produced eventually the New English Bible. The other acted alone and gave to us the first of those post-war translations which dared to speak the common tongue. They are C H Dodd and J B Phillips.

Charles Harold Dodd

A Welshman, born in Wrexham on 7th April 1884, brought up in a Welsh home, a Welsh chapel and a Welsh school. He was English-speaking and that was the language of the family, but from an early age he was fascinated by the Welsh language and learnt enough of it from maids and playfellows to communicate. He taught his brothers to count in Welsh. There were four boys in the family - no girls. His father was a school master and a deacon and his mother was one of the first women students to be trained as a teacher in London. She made good use of her skills in bringing up four boys, all of whom succeeded academically. Sir Goronwy Edwards makes a pertinent comment about those boys: 'I came from the neighbouring county of Flintshire and in my schooldays the four Dodd brothers were regarded by the rest of us as the most menacing competitors for university emoluments particularly in Oxford'. Charles Harold led the way. Two of his brothers followed him to Oxford also with scholarships, the third to the University of Wales.

C H Dodd went to Oxford and found it 'very heaven', but he had no difficulty as some students did to reconcile home and university. Home meant chapel too. During vacations, he was as much at home in Wrexham as he had ever been and was fully involved in the Independent Chapel of Pen-y-Bryn. Oxford never tempted him to the dominant form of worship there, which was, and is, Anglican. He went to University College, Oxford, but his spiritual home was Mansfield College, the stronghold of Dissenters and Puritans. He did brilliantly at Oxford - a double first in Greats. He seemed marked out for research and was encouraged to apply for a fellowship. Instead he took a teaching post in Leeds and distinguished himself. He did return to Oxford to do some teaching at his old College and study German. His special field of research was numismatics and for that he had to go to Berlin. The Welsh boy expanded under the influence of the great German theologians, particularly Adolf von Harnack, who was in his prime; and Berlin was the leading university for theology in Europe. The influence of Berlin on Dodd was immeasurable. Years afterwards he could remember sayings of Harnack:

> This I know: the theologians of every country only half discharge their duties if they think it enough to treat of the Gospels in the recondite language of learning and bury it in scholarly folios,

and also,

> The Christian religion is something simple and sublime: it means one thing and one thing only: Eternal life in the midst of time, by the strength and under the eyes of God.

The young Dodd responded to those deep convictions, as he did to Harnack's kind of Lutheranism - though scholarly and deeply devotional. He spoke of Christ, as Luther did, as 'the mirror of God's paternal heart'. He became Dodd's pattern: 'A supreme teacher-historian'.

Another influence, or perhaps counter-influence in Berlin was Albert Schweitzer. His book, *Von Reimarus zu Wrade* was later translated into English as *The Quest of the Historical Jesus*, (1910.) In the summer of

1907, however, when Dodd was in Berlin, it was talked of as the opposition to Harnack. The dialogue was of great importance to C H Dodd, who in later years made such an important contribution to our understanding of eschatology. He defended Schweitzer's claim that Jesus expected the 'end' to come shortly after his death. Some have said that Dodd fought against Schweitzer all his life. He returned to Wrexham and then to Oxford to find that he had been awarded a 'demyship' at University College. This was a fellowship on half pay! For two terms he lived the idyllic life in Oxford, returning in the vacation with pleasure, to be involved in the local Church and all its activities. These were times of research, but he also decided upon the ministry.

Mansfield College

For some time, both at Wrexham and in the challenge of Mansfield College, Oxford, he felt the insistent call to the Congregational Ministry. On 2nd June, 1908, he called on Souter and then had an interview with Dr Fairbairn about entering as a theological student with a view to the Ministry at Mansfield. On 10th October, he dined at Mansfield for the first time as a member of the College. For the next twenty two years he would be associated with it as student, graduate and staff. In reply to questions asked when he presented himself for ordination, he made clear how long he had considered this step, 'since first the definite idea of it took definite shape in my mind, during my second year at Oxford, the times when I felt myself nearest to God have been when I felt most constrained to seek this form of service'.

He was well equipped for his study of theology. Under Souter, he applied his classical skills to the New Testament and under Dr Bartlett, he continued what he had found so fascinating in Harnack. Hebrew was new to him and he applied himself to it. Dr Buchanan Gray not only encouraged him to work at his Hebrew, but also Syriac and inspired him to explore the rich inheritance of Semitic culture. He was very soon competent in Hebrew, Aramaic and Syriac.

In 1909, he travelled to Italy, with Rome as his objective, but stopping at Lucerne and Como on the way. He spent more than a month studying at the British School in Rome, went to High Mass in St Peter's and met John R Mott at the Student Christian Federation. He continued on to Naples and Pompeii. His 25th birthday was during this trip. He returned by way of Ravenna, Parma and Brescia, in all of which towns there are important inscriptions.

Shortly after his return, the Principal of Mansfield College resigned and Dr W B Selbie was appointed. A life-long friendship sprang up between the student and the Principal. Selbie advised him to get some pastoral experience. He tried at first a student pastorate at Benson which he thoroughly enjoyed. But Selbie encouraged him to get away from Oxford and then later invited him back to his staff.

On 21st January 1912 he preached at Brook Street Congregational Church, Warwick,'with a view' and was called to be their minister on 6th February. The day before Dodd met James Moffatt who was later called to the Chair of Early Church History at Mansfield College. Another important friendship was formed which has obvious consequences for translation work.

The Warwick Congregational Church

After a walking holiday with his father in North Wales, C H Dodd settled into the pastorate at Brook Street Congregational Church in Warwick. It was a church of some considerable size for a first pastorate, but the congregation knew that they had an unusual man. They had recently suffered from a series of rather short pastorates and they thought that this young man in his twenties, might be able to sustain a long and growing leadership for the Church. He entered with great gusto into his work, concentrating on the young people. He quickly established himself in Warwick and made close friends in many families. As he was not married, he was frequently invited out to tea and other meals, joining in the family life and encouraging many of his younger members to join him on his walks. Walking was a passion he indulged wherever he was! Monday was his day off and he explored the Warwickshire countryside. He visited a great deal. F W Dillistone says of him, 'To walk seemed almost as sacred an obligation as prayer!'. He saw his task as pastor and teacher. And he fulfilled this double role with conscientousness, ministering to all who worshipped at Brook Street Church. A reminiscence from one who was young in his congregation is interesting as portraying the young pastor in his early days:

> I remember Dodd as a small, spare figure of a man. Always spruce and immaculate in his dress and appearance. He had a good sense of humour and a ready laugh. A great and natural appearance of vitality always, and an easy and unconscious concentration in conversation on any subject under discussion. A wonderfully alert and logical brain.

And so he continued all his life. Warwick was a relatively untroubled pastorate and in 1912 it seemed a peaceful world. Both Britain and Germany were at the height of their prosperity, linked by family ties. He did not involve himself in political activities, but was content to concentrate upon his studies, applying them, in his preaching and counselling, to the daily problems of an apparently quiet people.

He kept a diary and there is much in it about the weather and his walks. Oddly there is no reference to the world shattering events of August 1914. We need perhaps to remember that total war had not been experienced before. War was the occupation of soldiers and excessive patriotism might produce volunteers. Britain had no conscription and at first it was assumed that the total population would not be involved. Then came conscription.

Dodd's first political activity was in 1916 as a member of the National Council against Conscription. He never became a crusading pacifist, although he did join the Fellowship of Reconciliation. When pressed he would say that there was no clear mandate for pacifism in the teaching of Jesus as recorded in the New Testament. Years later he could find no explicit teaching in the New Testament which would solve the concrete problems of war. Speaking to the Congregational Union Autumn Assembly in 1929, he put the matter clearly and calmly:

> it would be something gained if we could agree that war is in its nature a thing abhorrent to the spirit of the Gospel and lacking any sanction in the teaching of our Lord, even though we might still differ as to how far any individual, at any given moment, is free to dissociate himself from a war which his country may have undertaken.

His brother, Percy served in the army as an officer and, although he survived, his health was damaged to such an extent that he died at a comparatively early age.

C H Dodd did not make many changes in his Church. He wisely followed the tradition of the place, adding a Christmas morning and Good Friday service.

In May 1915, the General Assembly of the United Free Church of Scotland met and decided to invite James Moffatt to the Chair of Church History in their Glasgow College. That left a vacancy at Mansfield. There was no hesitation in the College Council. They were sure C H Dodd was the natural choice. On 18th June they offered him the Yates Lectureship in the New Testament for three years, after which, if all went well, he would become Yates Professor.

It was not easy for him to decide. He had been only three years in Warwick and had found great satisfaction in a preaching and pastoral Ministry. In the end he accepted. His denomination needed him and Oxford should have a Congregational voice at the highest level of scholarship. R I Hopwood, a close friend with whom he had first gone to Oxford from Wrexham in 1902, expressed the need and the suitability of the choice:

> No call could be clearer on the human side. Scotch professors are excellent in their way, so are some other erudite Englishmen, but for the purposes of Congregationalism in England and Wales I have felt they needed men at Mansfield (and elsewhere) with a different kind of 'touch'. You have just the blend of scholarship with the Welsh 'timbre' which will be so effective from my point of view - prejudiced no doubt!

In September 1915, Mr Dodd said goodbye to his friends in Warwick and took up his residence in the 'tower' of Mansfield College.

Oxford Again

It was a very difficult time to return to Oxford. The full impact of the war was being felt. The men were not available and those who were could not escape a sense of guilt that their contemporaries were fighting and dying in France. It was thought at one point that the College would have to close. It was not until the Michaelmas Term of 1919 that anything like normality began to return. Dodd soon found himself among congenial spirits in Oxford, with men who in their turn would contribute almost as much as he did to New Testament studies: B H Streeter, N P Williams, A E J Rawlinson. He was welcomed at Professor Sandy's Seminar on New Testament studies. He was at the heart of such study in England. While at Mansfield and before life stirred again after the war, he was approached to become President of Cheshunt College, Cambridge. It was an attractive offer and Cambridge was more congenial to Dissenters than Oxford! There was also a vigorous Church life at Emmanuel Congregational Church with a Mansfield man in the pastorate there. That had been Selbie's old Church. As President, Dodd would have a chance to put his own stamp upon a College which had never quite achieved its potential. He did not decide quickly, but consulted friends and advisers.. Eventually he disappointed Cheshunt and remained at Mansfield.

Dodd was happy at Oxford and every weekend he would be preaching somewhere in the country. But his home was itinerant and at the age of 30 he must have wondered if he would ever be the father of a family and build a warm home with someone he loved. His diary gives little clue to any growing affection until the entry for 6 December 1918. A diary which usually had comments on the weather, walks and a bare list of engagements suddenly came alive with capital letters, like a Latin Inscription from some Roman tomb: *Incipit Vita Nova*. He had visited London to see Lesley Griffiths, walked with her through the romantic Hampstead Heath, taken her out to tea and returned exultant to Oxford. He was in love. By Christmas they were engaged and in the early months of 1919 they visited together Wrexham, Oxford and her home in Bromley. They had many common interests and were both members of the Student Christian Movement as well as the Free Church Fellowship. He was happy at the thought of a life-long association and a more settled form of life. Then, for no reason that anyone has been able to discover, the engagement was broken off in March, on a day described in the diary as of 'wretched weather, cold and raw with sleet and snow continuously'. He was deeply hurt. He needed psychological help and found it with Dr J A Hadfield, an early practitioner in England of psycho-analysis or what was being called, 'The New Psychology'. Over a period of more than four years he paid periodic visits to Dr Hadfield. Apart from the personal help he gave him, Dodd learnt the importance of psychological insights and used what he learnt in later New Testament interpretations.

He found many colleagues who were recognising the importance of the New Psychology: Cyril Emmet, B H Streeter, W B Selbie, E R Micklem and later most important of them all - L W Grensted, a friend since 1903, who was assessing the relationship between psychology and theology. Grensted taught pastoral psychology later at Oxford and put the results of his studies on psychology and religion into his Bampton Lectures in 1930.

Dodd soon found that Dr Hadfield could not only help him sort out his personal problems, but also had things to say that should be heard by a wider audience than those who consulted him. A second figure also emerged, the Reverend W Fearon Halliday, whom Dodd also consulted. Halliday, even more than Hadfield, helped Dodd to use psychological insights in his interpretation of the Bible. Dodd arranged for both men to come to Oxford and lecture. In 1920, Hadfield delivered the Dale Lectures at Mansfield and they were published as *Psychology and Morals*.

This encounter with the New Psychology changed Dodd considerably. He was never content to 'treat of the Gospels in the recondite of learning and bury it in scholarly folios'. But the temptation of research is always to seek accuracy above all else and sometimes to sacrifice communication to it. He began to see the difference between accuracy and truth, not as exclusive choices, but as complimentary. The first fruits of this was *The Meaning of Paul for Today*, published in 1920. This was followed by an introduction to the New Testament especially designed for Sunday School teachers, *The Gospel in the New Testament*. Neither of these books would enhance his academic status and he did not find it easy to write them. His sights were on a more important book. James Moffatt had asked him to write a commentary on the Epistle to the Romans for the Moffatt Commentaries. This he did eventually with great success in 1932.

Marriage

The Reverend W Fearon Halliday was not beyond match-making! When he was minister at New Barnet, a young war widow with an infant son had come to seek his help. She was an Anglican by upbringing, but needed Halliday's help in her bereavement. She attended his Church. Halliday was also concerned with Dodd's problems. He eventually introduced the two and after much over-scrupulous agonising C H Dodd declared his love for Phyllis Terry. They were engaged in February and married in June 1925. After a honeymoon in North Devon they returned to Oxford to face the problems of house-hunting. Phyllis disposed of her flat in Harpenden and they looked for an appropriate house in Oxford. The problem was not fully resolved until 1927 when they bought No 3 Bevington Road. That was when their first child, Rachel, was born, and Dodd was invited to a Chair at Yale University. It was a very attractive offer but he remained at Mansfield. No 3 Bevington Road became a centre of hospitality and Phyllis entered into the strange world of university life. Dodd, although troubled by health problems at first, soon blossomed in marriage and was fulfilled. His first 'big' book had yet to be written and that came in 1928, *The Authority of the Bible*. It had an immediate success and his entry into the upper echelons of biblical scholars was marked by the conferring of an honorary doctorate by Aberdeen. It turned out to be the first of many. His old friends and students gathered increasingly in Oxford. He found himself involved in University affairs as well as Mansfield College. He was examining in the Honours School of Theology, serving on the Board of the Faculty of Theology and in 1927 appointed University Lecturer in New Testament Studies. He was probably better informed about German theological developments than anyone else in Oxford and in the Michaelmas Term, 1928 he offered a series of lecture on 'Form Criticism', explaining Rudolf Bultmann (ie before his demythologising period.)

Dodd was host to Professor Fick of Marburg when he came to give the Dale Lectures early in 1930 and it was about this time that he brought to the attention of Oxford the significance of Karl Barth. A tempting offer came from Manchester which he could not refuse. In August 1929, Professor A F Peake, the most distinguished Free Churchman then occupying a University Chair, died. He had been the first to occupy the Rylands Chair of Biblical Criticism and Exegis at Manchester and he brought distinction to it. The Chair was endowed by John Rylands a wealthy Manchester businessman, and, after his death his widow had endowed a Library in which theology was to be given pride of place. Peake had expressed his preference for Dodd to succeed him and the Vice Chancellor of Manchester University, Walter Moberly, persuaded Dodd to accept. The letter of invitation explained that the selection committee wished to make him their only nominee to the Senate and Council. They also explained that while Peake had held the Chair for Biblical Criticism and Exegesis, they wanted the new appointment to be for New Testament. He would be leader of the Faculty and a bridge between it and the Senate. The amount of actual teaching and administrative work would be small, leaving him considerable freedom for study and writing. After much discussion with Phyllis and a visit to Manchester to be entertained by the Moberlys, he accepted on 17th April 1930. He was 46.

Manchester

There is no doubt that one of the attractions of the Chair was access to the John Rylands Library which he used much during his time at Manchester. His whole pattern of life was also changed. After the closely knit community of Oxford and the generations of Mansfield men who clustered around him there, Manchester was cold and distant. Home and university were separated and he was driven in upon himself and his own resources much more. The stimulus from outside dried up. For him and for his family, there was personal loss, but he grew in stature as a writer and lecturer. F W Dillistone quotes a fellow Professor as describing a lecture by Dodd as like a ballet performance. He came into the room with a dancing, bird-like movement, took his place on the rostrum and then, in speech and gesture, even in the writing on the blackboard, played out a drama in which the whole man became intensely involved. He lectured at a rapid pace, but held the audience throughout, always finishing in time. He became a superb lecturer. His research and study went on at home. He was a devoted father and carefully reserved times when he could be with his children and tell them stories. They had two children, Rachel and

Mark, together with Phyllis' son John from the previous marriage. Ultimately, he published a book of these stories told to Rachel and Mark, with maps drawn by John and illustrations by his wife. It was called, *There and Back Again*, Phyllis knew the importance of her husband's work and protected him from disturbances. Again F W Dillistone has a perfect quote from a neighbour on this protection:

> My impression was that Phyllis was cushioning Harold from the outside world. His study was sacrosanct, and in spite of later intimacy, I never saw him inside it. Complete silence was the rule even outside the door and the nursery quarters were as far removed from it as possible.

This did not make him remote, he was a pastor still, and his books that issued from that cushioned study spoke to the hearts of many who had never studied theology.

The first fruit of this study was the completion of his Epistle to the Romans which he had started for the Moffatt Commentaries in Oxford. It was published in 1932. In that commentary he expressed his desire to get behind the text, dig down to the very foundations. Oddly enough he did not visit Palestine and he left his first visit to Greece until he was almost 80. Dillistone expresses this same wonder and adds,

> His concern after the initial study of sites and inscriptions, came to be with *language*, with translation, with style, with the semantic background lying behind overt expressions in written form. Continental scholars were tending to lay increasing emphasis on the *oral* background of the writings of the New Testament. He recognised the importance of this quest but still believed that it was possible to make new discoveries by excavating, as it were, the literature itself.

Dillistone is absolutely right in his assessment and that is clear from the first fruits of this work in *The Bible and the Greeks* published in 1935. Some of the material in the book is from his course of lectures on the Septuagint which he gave in Oxford, but what attracted scholars to the book was its originality. He explored the background of early Christianity by a highly original treatment of the Hellenistic influences. It covered two fields: studies in the New Testament and the literature of the Hellenistic age.

The Parables of the Kingdom

In 1935, he was invited to give the Shaffer Lectures at Yale in the Spring. It was an opportunity for him to systematise the extensive work he had already done on eschatology in the New Testament. Ever since he met the controversy over Albert Schweitzer's book in Berlin, he had worried about eschatology. What did the early Church believe about the return of the Lord and was it what Jesus had believed or did they misunderstand him? In the Shaffer Lectures he decided to tackle this through examining the most characteristic teaching of Jesus - his parables. As the parables were largely concerned with the Kingdom of God, they should yield some clue to what Jesus believed and taught. The first question was about their authenticity. How far were they in the form that Jesus taught and how far had they been edited in the intervening years before they were reduced to written form? This is where his excavating came in. He sought the original intention of Jesus as he unfolded each parable, layer by layer, within its original setting and the influence of subsequent teaching.

It was in this best known of all his books that he developed the concept of 'realised eschatology' to solve the dilemma of whether Jesus taught the coming of the kingdom here and now or in some distant time. Apart from this concept, the book gave an original reappraisal of the parables and outlined a fruitful method of interpretation. Joachim Jeremias, whose work on the parables is of the highest repute, read Dodd and assessed *The Parables of the Kingdom* with approval:

> In this extraordinarily important book the attempt has actually been made for the first time with success to relate the Parables to their situation in the life of Jesus, and thereby to open a new epoch in the interpretation of the parables.

It is rare for Göttingen to comment so approvingly on a British scholar. Dodd remained five years at Manchester and was succeeded by his friend T W Manson. He had made good use of his five years and grown in his task. But he missed Oxford and was ready to receive a call to Cambridge.

The Norris-Hulse Professor of Divinity

Since the Restoration, all divinity Professorships in Oxford or Cambridge have been confined to members of the Church of England. Dodd broke the mould when he was invited to become the Norris-Hulse Professor of Divinity at Cambridge in 1935. The only restriction was that unlike his predecessors he was not permitted to exercise the privilege of preaching University Sermons in Great St Mary's. Dodd had never held a teaching post in any specific college. He was without a settled home in the University but not without friends. Earlier he had taken part in British-German theological conferences organised by Dr Adolf Deissmann and

Bishop George Bell. These had brought him in contact with two Cambridge scholars: Edwyn Hoskyns and J M Creed. The latter proposed him as a Fellow at the College where he was Dean, Jesus College, and this was agreed. Jesus College was a good choice. F J Foakes-Jackson had done much of his work on early Christianity and the Hellenistic world while he was Dean of that College. Today, in their small portrait gallery, the two are given place of honour, almost side by side. More immediately, Bernard Manning was there, an 'Orthodox Dissenter', but like Dodd appreciative of other forms of worship. The two were often in Chapel together. Dodd was in Cambridge from his election in 1935 until 1951.

In all those years he was in and out of College and he was affectionately regarded by most students and staff. When he retired from the Professorship in 1949, he was made an Honorary Fellow. Here he found that closely knit fellowship which he had missed in Manchester. His Cambridge years were probably, as Dillistone says, 'the happiest period of his life'. His home and college life were once again co-ordinated.

He carefully divided his time to cover four tasks: His regular lectures, his own research, his supervision of advanced students, and his seminar.

He worked in lectures and research on *The Fourth Gospel*. The two volumes he eventually published did not appear until 1951 and 1963, but the body of his work was done in Cambridge days. His seminar was his greatest contribution to the academic life of Cambridge. His predecessor, Professor Burkitt had presided over a seminar for New Testament studies; but Dodd brought reconstruction and a new stimulus. Many senior members of the University set aside every Wednesday afternoon to give priority to this happening. Regular members included Stanley Cook, Regius Professor of Hebrew; F S Marsh, Lady Margaret's Professor of Divinity; C F D Moule; Wilfred Knox; R Newton Flew; Noel Davey. In addition were two very outstanding Jewish scholars of the time; Herbert Loewe and David Daube. The seminar met for two hours every week and Dodd in a remarkable way retained the confidence of this very varied membership.

The war years were difficult for Dodd and his health suffered. For a year he was confined to a hospital at Papworth with traces of TB. The absence in hospital clouded the home, but it remained a happy one despite the strains of war and father's illness. The children have the happiest memories of those years. They lived in No 3 Park Terrace.

On 30th September 1949, Dodd's tenure of the Norris-Hulse Chair came to an end. He was then at the height of his powers, fully recovered and a brilliant communicator. He broadcast frequently and one memorable series was in Advent, four sermons dealing with eschatology in a clear way that meant it could be broadcast on the Home Service and not limited to the somewhat elitist audience of the Third Programme. He could also give time to his major work on the Fourth Gospel. Many of us felt that it was a loss to scholarship when he was distracted from this and subsequent work by the proposal to produce a New English Bible.

A Wholly New Translation

F F Bruce has given us details of how this new translation was to be handled. The joint committee set up in 1947 appointed Dr C H Dodd as vice-chairman, but he soon became so involved that it absorbed all his work and time after retirement for the next twenty years. His great value in this enterprise was his scholarship and his style. Few knew the background to the Bible better and his scholarship was fully used. His role in determining that style was equally important. When a group of scholars work together they can find themselves talking a language rarely heard outside the Senior Common Rooms of Oxford and Cambridge. Dodd had an incomparable command of the English language and the New English Bible benefited greatly from that. When it was all over, it was he who explained it to the British public in print and on the radio. He never quite mastered the medium of TV.

During this period the only work he did outside the New English Bible was his Fourth Gospel. *The Interpretation of the Fourth Gospel* was published by the Cambridge University Press in 1953 and he was worried that it was priced as high as £5. In 1963, the same Press published *Historical Tradition in the Fourth Gospel.*

In 1971, Collins published his book, *The Founder of Christianity*, which had been published the previous year by Macmillan in the USA. Collins took the occasion of this publication to award him the Collins Religious Book Award. The presentation was made in the Jerusalem Chamber of Westminster Abbey. He was frail, but still quick in response and birdlike. All there saw one of the greatest New Testament scholars of our century.

He died peacefully on 22nd September 1973 at a nursing home in Goring-on-Thames, where for the last few months of his life he had gone, leaving Rachel and her family with whom he had lived in Oxford until April. His last months were very pleasant to him apart from his failing strength. He occupied a room with a lovely view over the river and the distant hills, a countryside which he had walked for many years. He retained almost to the end an interest in the different translations of the Bible that continued to flow from the presses.

John Bertram Phillips

Barnes is a suburb, in the south-west corner of London, and J B Phillips was born there in 1906. He retained a defensive attitude to suburbs and argued for their pleasant setting and decent way of life. 'I suppose it is their lack of flamboyance, their regularity of behaviour, their limited horizons, and their general respectability which irritates those of different and possibly more adventurous character'. He was proud to have been born and brought up in a London suburb. His parents were suburban and influenced him, both in different ways. His father thought of him as the bright one of the family, there were three children and he was in the middle. The father was ambitious for his son and pushed him. That left a scar which gave him a bad time throughout his life with a super-ego urge that he never completely dealt with. It may also have intensified his sensitivity which was a gain. He was deeply attached to his mother, but suffered from seeing her die of cancer. This deep attachment was strengthened when his father married again and he felt himself cruelly treated by the step-mother.

Cambridge

He did not win a county scholarship, probably because he had been put in for it too early, but his father felt the burden of having to pay. He was a promising classics student and enjoyed university life. He went up to Cambridge as an avowed atheist and took no interest in college chapel. Both Christian bodies descended upon him, the SCM and the CICCU. The latter won because of the transparent faith of some of its members: 'I had never met men before', he wrote, 'to whom Christ was a living reality, as real as any human friend. Their certainty about God, their utter personal devotion to Christ could hardly fail to impress a very young-for-his-age eighteen year-old.' He did not join the Union despite this attraction for several months. He was put off by their restrictive teaching and narrowness concerning such matters as smoking, cinema or theatre-going or apparently any worldly pleasures, but he could not accept them as evil. A significant event occurred in the spring of 1923 which led him back to the fold. His parents moved house, but vacation time found the new house at Woldingham not yet ready and Jack and his sister had nowhere to stay. His sister who was older than him was at that time a student at Westfield College, London. One of her friends was the daughter of a Rector in North Devon. He and his wife kindly allowed the three Phillips' children to stay with them as paying guests during the vacation. It was heavenly for Jack.

He got away from his step-mother and revelled in the beauty of North Devon. More important, he fell in love with his sister's friend. 'The sheer beauty of that spring', he wrote, 'added to my loneliness of spirit produced in me all the well-known symptoms of a very young man in love. It was gorgeous to be alive. This girl and I used to walk and talk a lot together, and before long I discovered that she had much the same spiritual outlook as the CICCU. She even asked me bluntly, "Are you a Christian?" And I was at a loss to know how to reply'.

When he returned to Cambridge, he looked again at the CICCU and thought that there must be something in it if it produced such attractive people. He attended daily prayer meetings and heard evangelical preachers. He had never heard such persuasive preaching and although he had been brought up to treat the Bible with respect, this was different. For these men, the Bible was the Word of God, the actual means through which the living God spoke to men. He was impressed and joined the Christian Union.

At the same time he was enjoying university life as best he could, working moderately and talking immoderately with friends and fellow students. It is neither lectures nor tutorials that constitute being up at Cambridge. It is the opportunity for endless talk and leisure to think, with the resources necessary. Not many students at university become scholars, but something of scholarship brushes off on them. In July, 1925, still feeling the effect of the wonderful girl, he was persuaded to go to Keswick. He could hardly fail to be impressed by the Big Tent, packed day after day, the hymn singing, the prayers uttered in deep sincerity and the powerful evangelical messages. He didn't take much of it in, but it was heavenly to be in this exciting place with the girl he loved among so many people who despite their funny taboos were plainly devoted to Jesus Christ. He was exhilarated and felt that he must throw in his lot with these lovable devoted people.

He had been doing rather badly in his exams and next term began to work harder at his classical studies. At school he had been thrilled by the classics, but he had never had a proper grammatical grounding in them. So it meant hard work to keep up with those who had been at such schools as St Paul's.

Father Trout

J B Phillips marks the summer of 1926 as the real change in his life and puts it down to the influence of Father Trout. The name is pseudo, but the person was real enough. He lived not far from their new home on the North

Downs at Woldingham, less than two miles away. He was a kindly clergyman, a little eccentric and about sixty. He had worked for many years with the Cambridge University Mission to the boys of Bermondsey. He genuinely loved these boys and adopted two of them and had them educated at his own expense. Jack's younger brother Ken introduced him. They were both a bit miserable at home and found Father Trout a hospitable person. Although the atmosphere was strictly evangelical there was much love, affection and friendship, laughter and gaiety. Jack felt instantly at home. Father Trout, at this time, was semi-retired, lived in a large house and had several young men staying with him. He was really running an informal course in Bible study for those men whom he thought might become missionaries or clergy. He wanted such men to be trained according to evangelical standards. He collected contributions from rich ladies who were rather afraid of modernism and High Church practices in the Church of England! He had great charm of personality. He invited all three, including Jack's sister, to stay with him during vacations. There was a real sense of welcome and the presence of seven or eight other young men was stimulating. There were no luxuries, but they were well fed and felt wanted. Every evening, Father Trout would lead them in an hour and a half of Bible study. He was no scholar but he knew how to make the Authorised Version come alive. Every Sunday he took them to a Church of his choice and of course his persuasion. His Churchmanship was of the lowest Protestant order. Apart from giving Jack a vacation home, Father Trout could from time to time help financially.

Academic Problems

Jack did not do well in classics, obtaining only a third. It was therefore decided that he should switch to English. His tutor was F R Leavis and he was greatly helped by him. His last year at Cambridge was thus much happier than it would have been if he had struggled on with classics. He read widely, liked his tutor, attended meetings of CICCU, sketched in watercolours, developed his skill in caricature and found the Keswick Convention disappointing. He managed to get a Second Class Honours degree in English, but was too young to graduate. He had thought of Missionary work in Africa or perhaps ordination, but he could not be ordained until he was 23 and he was not yet 21 in the summer of 1927. He decided to put in a year or two teaching at Prep school. He applied and was appointed at Sherborne Preparatory School.

Sherborne

He loved Sherborne. It seemed to be all that a small town should be with lovely country surrounding it. He took to teaching at once and explored the countryside with an ancient motor bike. He liked the boys and they liked him. He was able to bring an enthusiasm for Greek such as he had himself experienced at school. He was a conscientious and popular schoolmaster and could have made that his career. The passion for communicating ideas was at the heart of his success, but his mind was still on the Church and he did all he could to involve himself in Church work. He preached at several village Churches, addressed men's Bible classes on Sundays and tried to run a club for working boys of the town. It was at Sherborne also where his enthusiasm for scouting began. He was more or less expected to be assistant scout master.

J B Phillips stayed only a year at Sherborne, but it had been a valuable experience for him. He discovered his strengths and weaknesses. He was obviously good at communicating and related easily to young people. In the back of his mind was still the idea of teaching in Africa as a missionary. For this he felt sure that he should have experience in an English parish church at least as a curate.

He had no difficulty in being released after one year at Sherborne and put his name down for Ridley Hall. That meant back to Cambridge, but with a very different purpose now. He was prepared for the Anglican ministry and assumed to be an Evangelical.

The First Curacy

In the summer of 1929, he met Sidney Ford in Swanage and was offered a curacy in Penge. There, he continued with his scouting and one incident during a summer camp foreshadowed his future work. Around the camp fire he took out his Greek New Testament and fascinated the boys with the strange alphabet. They asked him if he could read it and he did. Then he put it into their language - they listened intently and he remembered.

He did not enjoy Penge. He found the suburb uninteresting, shockingly different from Sherborne or even his own East Sheen, the church ugly, and visiting a terrifying experience. He was soon heading for a nervous breakdown and after three years resigned his curacy. Like C H Dodd, he needed psychiatric help and he found it with Leonard Browne. The problem went deeper than Leonard Browne was able to uncover, and the unstable condition took the form of clinical depression and constantly returned. Meanwhile, he supported himself by writing and editorial work at The Pathfinder Press.

A Wartime Curacy

J B Phillips returned to the ministry of the Church in 1936 when Canon Gillingham invited him to become his curate at St Margaret's, Lee, which adjoins Blackheath in South East London. He was happy there with a good team of curates. It was there that he met Vera Jones, who had been brought up in Yorkshire, nominally Congregational. She lifted him out of himself and gave him a purpose in life. They were much in love and married on 19th April, 1939. They lived in a top flat in Blackheath and Jack had responsibility for a small church called Boone's Chapel until the outbreak of war when he became priest-in-charge of the Church of the Good Shepherd, about a mile from St Margaret's. This was his first real charge and in partnership with Vera he carried it through the worst of the war years. It was there that his translation work started. Some of their happiest times were with a flourishing group of young people called, the King's Own. By now the vicarage had become the centre of activities. At the close of meetings there, Jack used to read some verses from the New Testament, often from Paul's Letters. He chose the Letters because many of them were written by one Christian in difficulties to other Christians in difficulties. He was met by polite but complete lack of comprehension. Let me quote his own words from his autobiography:

> These youngsters, who were by no means unintelligent, simply did not understand Bible language. All my own passion for making truth comprehensible and all my desire to do a bit of real translation, urged me to put some relevant New Testament truths into language which these young people could understand. This I did and was rewarded beyond my expectations as they realised for the first time, not merely that the epistles of Paul really could make sense, but that the inspired words were extremely relevant to life as they knew it.

Letters to Young Churches

Out of these Sunday meetings, J B Phillips drafted a translation of Colossians and sent a copy to C S Lewis, whom he greatly admired. C S Lewis replied briefly on 3rd August 1943, encouraging him to translate all the Epistles. With this encouragement he proceeded. But towards the end of 1944 the Bishop of Southwark offered him a living at Redhill, the Church of St John. They arrived there in January 1945. It was a total change. For ten years he ministered there but not with the same joy that he had known at the Church of the Good Shepherd. That was inevitable. During the trials of total war the bonds between pastor and people are peculiarly intimate.

He celebrated victory in Redhill with his heart in Lee. He was a good vicar and the church grew under his care. He was conscientious and carefully allocated the time he felt able to spend on his translation and other writing. But eventually he felt the need for more time to write. This became urgent after the unexpected success of *Letters to Young Churches*, which was all the Epistles of the New Testament in the translation of J B Phillips, published in October 1947. The huge acceleration of sales began in 1948 when *The Living Church* (Protestant Episcopal, USA) gave it a powerful boost. His daughter, Jennifer was born in 1946. He was a good father and gave time to his daughter, never failing to read stories at bedtime. His translation made him famous and his publisher, Geoffrey Bles saw him as a possible successor to C S Lewis whom they also published. From 1948 he became a frequent broadcaster and was invited as chaplain to the BBC Religious Broadcasting Department summer conference. Billy Graham came to thank him for *Letters to Young Churches* in 1952. In that same year he published addresses he gave to a CMS Summer School at Bangor under the title of *Making Men Whole*. He was remarkably successful with a Mission at Dorking in 1956 and to an American Air Force Base in the following year.

He began to see that he had a gift for communicating the truths of the Gospel in understandable form, almost non-religious language. His publisher was hesitant and lost a very important book to the Epworth Press! *Your God is too Small* was published by the latter in 1952. This little book, was a huge success, selling more than 130,000 copies in Britain alone and translated into several European languages. He wrote more than 20 Lutterworth leaflets on popular themes, *The Comfort of the Atom Bomb*, *Are you a Man or a Mouse?*, *The Dumb Blonde* etc. That year, 1952 was incredibly productive. Working only on Tuesday mornings, lest he should neglect his parish work, he translated the Gospels and they were warmly received. Just in time, the blurb on the cover of one of his books was corrected. It had read, 'J B Phillips, *Author* of the Gospels!' After the Gospels came the Acts, which he called *The Young Church in Action*. Before that was published, he had prepared some imaginative broadcast scripts for the Third Programme. They were reconstructions of the summary sermons in the Acts.

Writing was becoming a major occupation and he left the daily grind of parish work to concentrate on this and to accept the many invitations that came to him to speak from all over the world. The family left Redhill in 1955 and settled in Swanage. He made his first lecture tour of America just before leaving Redhill in 1954. America was always to appreciate him more than England did and that is still true.

Swanage

He was happy and successful in Swanage. The halcyon period in which he achieved more than ten men, is best described as he looked back upon it after it was all over. It lasted until the early 1960s. Here are his words:

> I was in a state of some excitement... But it is very plain to me now why my one man kingdom of power and glory had to stop.
> (full text from *The Price of Success*, p 8)

His achievements were honoured by his church with Canonries in Chichester and Salisbury. He was awarded a doctorate by the Archbishop of Canterbury and later a D Litt from Exeter.

Depression

He was in full spate in 1961 and wonderfully successful as a communicator. Then in the summer of that year his speaking, writing and communicating powers suddenly stopped. He cancelled all the engagements for the rest of the year and rested, apart from the flow of letters asking for his help which he always felt bound to answer. He was fifty five, his physical health good, but all vision, drive and energy had apparently vanished overnight. The doctor thought he had been overdoing it for years. Vera took over the secretarial work and watched lovingly over him. The dynamo had stopped. It was not the end of his career, but there were times when he thought it was. The massive pastoral correspondence continued and he was sometimes helping people out of the depression he could not help himself out of. He consulted many physicians and went as a voluntary patient into a psychiatric clinic. He had something of a remission when he was persuaded to translate some part of the Old Testament. This he did extremely well. He chose the four eighth-century prophets: Isaiah, Amos, Hosea and Micah. It is impossible to find even now a more readable translation of Micah. *Four Prophets* was published in 1963 and it was during a signing session that another attack came on and he was plunged into the depths again. He described it as 'that fearful attack upon the central personality of a man, which indeed seems to threaten his very integrity and which in popular parlance is called a nervous breakdown or nervous collapse'. Much of his time now was spent with articulating what was happening to him in ways that helped many who could not articulate their own mental pain.

The Ring of Truth

The sixties were a time of great disturbance to the faith of many. *Honest to God* and *The Passover Plot*, broadcasts indicating that the Gospel story may not be true, angered J B Phillips. He set out to refute the doubters of the faith and published, *Ring of Truth* in 1967. It was enthusiastically received and reissued with samples of letters showing how damaging the critical works had been and how the book saved the faith of many. The correspondence brought letters from eminent churchmen who told of their depression and prayed for him. One which helped him greatly was from an eminent and popular preacher, who told of his loss of faith and deep despair and pointed out how much J B Phillips had done:

> Whatever happens in your mind you have wrought a mighty work for the kingdom of God. No one in your generation has done more. God bless you. You will find the way through and so shall I. May it be soon!

He needed such assurance at that time. His affliction, which lasted on and off for a long time, was rarely so bad that he could not work at all. As I had encouraged him to translate the *Four Prophets* and knew the agony of that work, I did not press for the rest of the Old Testament! But I did propose a plan of NT Commentaries similar to Moffatt's based upon his *New Testament in Modern English*. There were only four commentaries eventually published, but his total revision, a quite remarkable achievement for one in and out of depression was issued in 1972 and his own contribution to the series of commentaries, *Peter's Portrait of Jesus* in 1976.

He continued his battle against the darkness and died at home on 21 July 1982.

Epilogue

To use the language of the Epistle to the Hebrews, 'Time would fail me to tell of' William Barclay, who in the course of commenting upon every book of the New Testament felt compelled to do his own translation; of E V Rieu, who turned from a translation of Homer to include the New Testament among the Penguin Classics by translating the Gospels; of Peter Levi, at that time Professor of Poetry at Oxford University, who knew the importance of style in translation; and that great army of translators who carried through the revision of the American Standard Version and gave us the RSV or of equally dedicated biblical scholars who produced the New International Version, translators of The Good News Bible and the brave paraphrase of The Living Bible. All these, by faith and hard work, produced new and improved translations. One cannot say of these later translators that 'They were stoned, they were sawn in two, they were killed with the sword', except perhaps verbally in the reviews.

Every new translation meets resistance and there are even cases of burning, but in recent years only of the books. It is difficult to class them all alike, except again in the words of the Epistle to the Hebrews, to say: 'And all these, though well attested by their faith, did not receive what was promised'. None was satisfied with his own translation!

They had certain characteristics in common. They all believed in the value of the original, even if as in Wycliffe's case, it was the Latin that was used and Ronald Knox and the Douai translators were also confined to that translation. The great majority wanted to get back to the language in which the revelation had first been described. They all counted it of importance that these sacred texts should be understood in the language of the reader. This led some to emphasise clarity, others to assure that the style was contemporary. They wanted their readers to hear what God was saying through the text. They had no intention of using the translation to put across their ideas. Their task was to clear away the difficulties and let the Bible speak.

Several of them became popular writers of Christian apologetics; many had their own confidence in the Bible strengthened by daily contact with it in the intensity of translation. None, I think, regarded the task lightly and all were aware of handling sacred things when they put the witness of Prophet, Evangelist and Apostle into the common tongue. They knew it had to be done because the Bible belongs among the people, not in a museum of sacred books open only to the enlightened.

Bibliography

F F Bruce, *History of the English Bible*, Third Edition, Cambridge, The Lutterworth Press, 1979

J N D Kelly, *Jerome*, London, Duckworth, 1975

G M Trevelyan, *England in the Age of Wycliffe*, Cambridge, Cambridge University Press, 1899

Edwin Robertson, *Wycliffe: Morning Star of the Reformation*, Marshall, Morgan & Scott, 1984

J Z Mosley, *William Tyndale*, London, SPCK, 1937

Peter Levi, *The English Bible*, Worthing, Churchman Publishing, 1985

J Hay Colligan, *William Whittington of Chester*, London, Simpkin Marshall Ltd, 1938

V J K Brook, *Archbishop Parker*, Oxford, Clarendon Press, 1962

Paul A Welsby, *Lancelot Andrewes: 1555-1626*, London, SPCK, 1958

Florence Higham, *Lancelot Andrews*, London SCM Press, 1952

Ed Eamon Duffy, *Challoner and his Church*, London, D L & T, 1981

Standish Meacham, *Lord Bishop: The Life of Samuel Wilberforce*, Harvard University Press, 1970

Arthur Westcott, *Life and Letters of Brooke Foss Westcott*, Vols 1 & 2, London, Macmillan, 1903

Arthur Fenton Hort, *Life and Letters of Fenton John Anthony Hort*, Vols 1 & 2, London, Macmillan, 1896

Norman G Brett-James, *The History of Mill Hill School*, Reigate, The Surrey Fine Arts Press, undated

Index

Abbot, [Bishop] George 108
Aelfric, Abbot of Eynsham 31,32-3
Alaric 22,24, 25
Alcuin 31,32
Alexander, Bishop of Cappadocia 20
Alexandria 15,18,21
Alfred the Great 30, 32
Allen, [Cardinal] William 114-15, 116, 118
Anabaptists 89
Andrewes, Lancelot 96,97, early years 98-100, appointed chaplain 100-2, opposition to Puritanism 102-3, appointed Dean of Westminster 103-4, calls for new translation 104-5, preaching skills 105-8, death 108-9
Anglo-Norman version 33-4
Anglo-Saxon versions 30-3
Anne of Bohemia 29
Antioch 15,18,21
Apollinarius 15,21
Apology [More] 63
Articles of Faith 90-1, 94
Arundel, [Archbishop] Thomas 29
Augustine of Hippo 11-12, 21, 26-7, 28
Authorised Version 92,95-6,109-11, 119, 125, 135
The Authority of the Bible [Dodd] 200
Ave Maria [Wycliffe] 41

Bacon, [Sir] Francis 88,90,94,109
Ball, John 42
Barnes, Robert 49
Barrett, William 103
Bede [the Venerable] 30, 31-2, 33

Benoit, [Pere] Pierre 187, 188-9, 192
The Bible and the Greeks [Dodd] 202
Bible de Jerusalem 188-9
Bilney, Thomas 49, 88
Bilson, [Bishop] Thomas 95, 104, 110
Bishop's Bible 81,91,92,95
Blesilla 17-18,19
Bonner, [Bishop] Edmund 73-4, 78
Book of Common Prayer 125
Book of Martyrs [Foxe] 65, 113, 116
Brand, John 121
Bristow, Richard 115,118

Caedmon 30-1
Calvin, John 38, 46
Calvinism 98
Cambridge History of the Bible [N J Hunter] 33
Campion, Edmund 115, 117, 119
Cartwright, Thomas 93-4, 98
Casauban, Isaac 108
Cecil, William [Lord Burghley] 86, 88, 94
Challoner, [Bishop] Richard 113, 114, 118, 119-24
Charlemagne 32
Charles V 64, 65
Christian England [D Edwards] 112
Christian Union for Promoting International Concord 143
Codex Sinaiticus 131, 133
Cole, William 86

Colet, John 46, 47-8, 49
Collet, Anne 146
The Complete Bible [Goodspeed] 170
Confrontation of Tyndale [More] 62
Constantine the Great 12-13
Contra Celsus [Origen] 20
Convocation [1563] 90
Convocation [1571] 94
Courtenay, [Bishop, later Archbishop] William 36, 38-9, 42, 43
Coverdale, Miles 58-9, 65, 86, English Bible 67-8, danger from Henry VIII 68-71, *The Great Bible* 71-6, second exile 77-9, third exile and death 79-80
Cox, [Bishop] Richard 92
Cranmer, [Archbishop] Thomas 49, 70-1, 75, 76, 78, 84
Creed 31, 32
Cromwell, Thomas [Earl of Essex] 46, 60-1, 65-6, 69, 71-5, 97

Damasus, Pope 16
Darby, J N 131-2
Dead Sea Scrolls 187-8
Determinatio [Wycliffe] 34
Didymus 21
Dillistone, F W 196, 202, 204
Disciplina [W Travers] 99
Discoverie of the Manifold Corruptions of the Holy Scriptures [Martin] 118
disendowment 35-6
Dobneck, John [Cochlaeus] 53-4
Dodd, Charles Harold 167, early years 193-5, call to ministry 195-8, return to Oxford 198-200, first translations 200-2, later works 203-6
Donatus 13
Donne, John 107
Douai-Rheims Bible 119-20, 171, 178-9

Ecclesiastical History [Eusebius] 15
Ecole Biblique 182, 192
Ecumenical Council [first] 13
Edward III 34
Edward VI 70, 71, 76
Egbert of York 31
Elizabeth I 86-91, 93-4, 99, 105, 109, 112-13
Elliot, [Dr] 130
England in the Age of Wycliffe [Trevelyan] 36
The English Bible [Levi] 81
Enthusiasm [R Knox] 180, 181
Epiphanius of Salamis 16
Erasmus 46-51, 88
Essays and Reviews 129-30, 139
Eusebius 15, 20
Eustochium 17, 18-19, 20, 23, 25, 27
Evagrius 14

Fisher, [Bishop] John 46, 49, 55, 66
Fitzjames, [Bishop] Richard 48
Four Prophets [J B Phillips] 212-13
Foxe, John 30, 46, 47, 58-9, 65
Frith, John 49, 63, 64-5
Froude, Richard Hurrell 126

Gardiner, Stephen 49
Geneva Bible 80, 92, 95-7, 107, 111, 115
Gilby, Anthony 82, 86
Gladstone, William 128, 130, 141, 142, 161-2
Goodman, Christopher 83-4, 86
Goodspeed, Edgar 169-70
Gordon, [Lord] George 123-4
Gospel of the Resurrection [Westcott] 139
Grafton and Whitchurch 72
The Great Bible 70, 75, 76, 81, 91-2

Gregory XI, Pope 34, 36
Guildford, [Sir] Henry 51

Halliday, W F 199, 200
Hatton, [Sir] Christopher 105
Helwys, Thomas 102
Henry VIII 57-61, 64, 65-70
Herman, Richard 57
Higham, Florence 105-6
Hinsley, [Cardinal] Arthur 179
Historic Faith [Westcott] 140
History of Luther [Dobneck] 53-4
History of the Articles [Hardwick] 90
History of the English Church and People [Bede] 30
Hoare, H W 30
Hort, Fenton John Anthony 125, 132, 133, 135, 141, 142, schooling 145-7, at Cambridge 147-9, ordination and marriage 149-51, later years 151-4
Howard, Duke of Norfolk 115-16, 117
Hunter, N J 33
Hus, John 38
Huxley, T H 129

Innocent I, Pope 27
Innocent III, Pope 29
Institutes [Calvin] 46
Introduction to the Literature of the N.T. [Moffatt] 166
Irenaeus 153

James I 81, 95, 103-4, 108, 109
Jerome, [Saint] 11-12, early life 12-15, first translations 15-16, Gospel revisions 16-17, appeal to women 16-21, builds monastery 21-2, O.T. translation 22-3, commentaries 24-6, against Pelagius 26-8
Jerome [J N D Kelly] 17, 18
John, King of England 34
John of Gaunt 30, 35, 36, 40

Jones, Alexander 190, 192
Jovinium 22
Judgement of the Lambeth Articles [Andrewes] 103

Keble, John 126, 128
Knox, John 82-3, 86, 106
Knox, Ronald 167, early years 171-4, conversion to Catholicism 174-7, and Daphne Strutt 177-80, last years 180-182

Lacomte, [Père] Matthieu 183
Lagrange, [Père] Marie-Joseph 183-6, 188
Lambert, John 49
Latimer, [Dr] Hugh 49, 52, 71, 101
Laud, [Archbishop] William 96
Let Dons Delight [R Knox] 177, 178
Letter to the English [Bugenhagen] 53
Letters to Young Churches [Phillips] 211
Lever, Thomas 82
Levi, Peter 118-19
Lewis, C S 210-11
Life of St. Anthony [Athanasius] 17
Lightfoot, [Bishop] John Barber 139, 140-1, 142, 144, 148, 151-2
Lindisfarne Gospels 31
Lives of the Saints 32
Lollards 37-8, 41-2
Lord's Prayer 31, 32, 48
Luther, Martin 12, 38, 47-50, 52, 53, 56, 194
Lutterworth 34, 43-4

Magee, [Bishop] William Connor 140
Making of the English Bible [G Hammond] 86

Map, [Archdeacon] Walter 33
Marcella 17, 18, 25
Martin, Gregory 115-20
Martyr, Peter 84, 85
Mary Tudor 71, 79, 85, 112-13
Matthew's Bible 70, 71-2, 81
Maurice, F D 142-3, 147-8, 150
Melito, Bishop of Sardis 20
Memoirs of Missionary Priests [Challoner] 113, 114, 123
Milton, John 38
Mistery of Iniquity [T Helwys] 102
Moffatt, James 164-9, 196, 197, 200
Monmouth, Humphrey 51-3
More, [Sir] Thomas 46, 48, 51, 52, 55, 57-63, 66-7
Moulton 153
Mozley, J F 48, 54, 58, 66
Murray, [Sir] James 159, 161, 162-3

New English Bible 193
New Jerusalem Bible 189-92
Newman, [Cardinal] John Henry 126, 149, 152, 153
New Testament in Modern English [Moffatt] 213
New Testament in Modern Speech [Weymouth] 164
A New Translation of the Bible [Moffatt] 168
Norfolk, Duke of see Howard
Norman Conquest 33

Obedience of a Christian Man [Tyndale] 57, 62
Onomasticon [Eusebius] 20
Origen of Alexandria 15, 18, 20, 21, 26, 153
Origin of the Species [Darwin] 129
Orm, [Canon] 33
Orosius 26-7
Oxford Movement 126, 149

Pachomius, [Saint] 23
Parable of the Wicked Mammon [Tyndale] 56, 58, 62
The Parables of the Kingdom [Dodd] 203
Parker, [Archbishop] Matthew 88-95, 116
Paula 17, 18, 19, 20-1, 23, 178
Paula [granddaughter] 23, 27
Paulinus, Bishop of Antioch 15, 16
Peasants' Revolt 41-2
Pelagius 22, 26, 27, 28
Percy, [Lord] Henry [first Earl of Northumberland] 35, 36
Petre, [Bishop] Benjamin 122
Phillips, John Bertram 93, 167, 193, Cambridge 206-9, Curacies 209-10, first translations 210-12, last years 212-13
Pilkington, [Bishop] James 87
Pius V, Pope 113, 117
A Plain Introduction to the Criticism of the N.T. [Scrivener] 134, 135, 136
Politique Positive [Compe] 142
Pollanus 82
Pollard, [Dr] Alfred 68
poor priests 38, 41-2, 44
Porphyry 24
Porter, John 74
Practice of Prelates [Tyndale] 60
Prayer Book [Cranmer] 71, 78, 82-3
Psalter 31
Pusey, Edward Bouverie 126-7, 128

Reeves, John 121
Reformation 11, 38, 45, 55, 84-5, 101
The Resultant Greek Testament [Weymouth] 163
Revelation of the Risen Lord [Westcott] 140

Revised Version 125, 129, 130-1, 133, 143
Revue Biblique 184, 185, 186, 188
Reynolds, John 81, 109, 110
Rheims New Testament 116, 118
Ridley, Nicholas 84
Rinck, [Sir] Herman 54
Rogers, John 71, 112
Roman Empire 11, 12, 23-4
Roye, William 53, 54, 55, 56, 57
Rufinus 20, 22, 26

Sampson, Thomas 86
Savonarola 46
Schweitzer, Albert 195, 203
Scott Holland, [Canon] 140
Scrivener, Frederick Henry Ambrose 125, 132-6
Selbie, [Dr] W B 196, 198, 199
Smith, [Bishop] Miles 95, 110
The Social Gospel [Westcott] 142
Spalatin 54
Stilicho 24
Stokesley, [Bishop] John 65
Strutt, Daphne 177-81
Sudbury, [Archbishop] Simon 36, 38-9

Tischendorf, Lobegott Friedrich Konstantin von 131, 133, 138, 142
Todd, John 189-90
Tonstall, [Bishop] Cuthbert 50, 51, 52, 59, 61
Tractarians 126-7, 128
Tracy, Richard 73
Tregelles, Samuel Prideaux 132
Trevelyan, G W 36
Treves 14
Trialogos [Wycliffe] 44
Turner, William 74
Tyndale, William 30, 76, 81, Oxford influences 46-7, to Cambridge 47-9, first post 49-50, failure in London 50-2, N.T. translation 52-6, against the church 56-7, and Henry VIII 57-8, on the run 58-61, and More 61-4, friends martyred 64-5, imprisonment and death 65-7, influence on Coverdale 68, banned translations 75

Urban VI, Pope 43
Utopia [More] 51
Uvedale, John 73-4

Valence, Peter de 48-9, 68
Vaughan, Stephen 60-61
de Vaux, [Père] Roland 182, 186-9, 190
Vigilantius 22
Villiers, George [Duke of Buckingham] 109
Von Reimarus zu Wrade [Schweitzer] 195
Vulgate 11-12, 22, 29, 32, 47, 75, 115-17, 179

Walsh, [Sir] John 50-5
Walsingham, [Sir] Francis 110
Walsingham, Thomas 39
Wansbrough, Hans 191-2
Waugh, Evelyn 171-2, 177, 178, 181
The Way, the Truth, the Life [Hort] 152
Welsby, Paul 97
Westcott, Brooke Foss 125, 132, 133, 135, 136-45, 148-9, 151-2
Weston William 100
Weymouth, Richard Francis, early years 155-6, at Mill Hill 156-63, retirement 163-4
Whitby Conference 31
Whitgift, [Archbishop] John 99, 103, 104, 119
Whittingham, William 82, 83-8

Wilberforce, [Bishop] Samuel 125-31
Witham, Robert 121, 122
Wittenberg 52-3
Wolsey, [Cardinal] Thomas 46, 51, 52, 55, 56, 57-8
Wycliffe, John 12, 29-30, 57, 111, 115, 116, rights of church and state 34-6, training of Lollards 36-8, first translations 37, charges of heresy 38-9, against transubstantiation 39-41, 84, social injustice 41-3, translations at Lutterworth 43-4, *Trialogos* 44, death 44-5.

Zosimus, Pope 27